The Fog of War

MARK BOURRIE

THE FOG OF WAR

Censorship of Canada's Media in World War Two

Douglas & McIntyre
D&M PUBLISHERS INC.
Vancouver/Toronto/Berkeley

Douglas & McIntyre
An imprint of D&M Publishers Inc.
2323 Quebec Street, Suite 201
Vancouver BC Canada V5T 4S7
www.douglas-mcintyre.com

Cataloguing data available from Library and Archives Canada
ISBN 978-1-55365-949-5 (cloth)
ISBN 978-1-55365-950-1 (ebook)

Jacket design by Peter Cocking
Text design by Alison Carr
Printed and bound in Canada by Friesens
Text printed on acid-free paper
Distributed in the U.S. by Publishers Group West

We gratefully acknowledge the financial support of the Canada
Council for the Arts, the British Columbia Arts Council, the Province of British
Columbia through the Book Publishing Tax Credit, and the Government of
Canada through the Canada Book Fund for our publishing activities.

For Bob Vezina: soldier, journalist, and friend,
and to Paul Quilty, mentor.

CONTENTS

INTRODUCTION

IN TIMES OF TOTAL WAR, when the survival of the state and Canadian society is at stake, the media face political and social pressures to conform to the government's versions of reality. Journalists usually censor their own work to make sure it doesn't cause trouble for the government, the military, and the arms industries. Reporters and editors also know the information they gather can be very valuable to the enemy. In 1939, most of Canada's journalists—the ones who didn't rush to join the army, navy, and air force to fight—accepted the idea that German agents would paw through their articles looking for secrets. The thought of Nazis reading the *Globe and Mail* or the *Halifax Herald* might seem ludicrous now, but in World War Two, this country was an arsenal of democracy with access to many of the Allies' most potent secrets, including the workings of the atomic bomb. We sent hundreds of thousands of men overseas, built the fourth-largest navy in the world, supplied our allies with weapons, trained tens of thousands of pilots, and gave shelter to some of the refugees from Hitler's war.

Our soldiers, who were to die in Western Europe at rates higher than Germans and Russians on the Eastern Front, were often crowded by the thousands into the great liners of the day, the *Queen Mary* and the *Queen Elizabeth* to go overseas, offering targets that caused Pavlovian responses in German U-boat captains. Halifax and Sydney were the assembly points for the great convoys of soldiers, weapons, fuel, and food that kept Britain and Russia in the war. Every scrap of information, from convoy routes to routine weather forecasts, was useful to the men who were determined to sink the convoys.

We were attacked. The enemy assaults on Canada were minor, and, in the case of Japanese fire balloons, somewhat silly. Still, for at least a year, people along the British Columbia coast had a reasonable terror of bombardment and invasion by the Japanese, while, through the entire war, Canadians living on the Atlantic coast were in an active military theatre, much more than many of them knew. Hundreds died in U-boat attacks in Canadian and Newfoundland waters, submarines hunted all of Canada's Atlantic coastline, and Allied ships and planes hunted the subs.

For the sake of the war effort, the press had to keep military secrets. Most journalists also believed they had to show their patriotism, that they bore the same home-front responsibilities as the bureaucrat, the munitions worker, the farmer, the kid collecting scrap metal and bones for the war effort. Their children, close relatives, friends, and neighbours were in the armed forces, along with hundreds of thousands of their fellow citizens. Reporters and editors, who usually talk a good fight about censorship, were actually quite willing—sometimes even eager—to be guided by the strong hand of government. Often, with the dampening of competition caused by censorship, it was in their commercial interest to join with their colleagues in ignoring news. They turned a blind eye to many of the social issues on the home front—drunkenness, an explosion in incidences of venereal disease, juvenile delinquency, family breakdown—and ignored signs of bureaucratic incompetence and corruption. Canadian journalists were so pliant, in fact, that penalties for real resistance to censorship are difficult to determine because so few writers and editors on English-language papers tried to blatantly evade the rules.

The Canadian government censored the news for two main reasons: to keep military and economic secrets out of enemy hands, and to prevent civilian morale from breaking down. Ottawa was prepared to ignore most one-time breaches of the censorship rules, especially when they were honest mistakes. The French-language press realized quite quickly that Mackenzie King's Liberal government was not up to starting fights that could rip the facade of public solidarity in wartime Quebec. On paper, the Canadian censorship system, backed by the *War Measures Act*, was among the most draconian media-control mechanisms among the Allied countries. In reality, only the fringe Communist Party and ethnic presses suffered serious penalties.

There is a stereotype in the public consciousness of censors as being bureaucratic "news-killers" armed with blue pencils making arbitrary decisions that are invariably against the public interest. The Second World War censorship system in Canada as well as the censors themselves were far more complicated and much more nuanced. First, all of the front-line censors and most of the managers of the system were high-ranking journalists who still had respect for their craft and its ability to act for the public good. Through the war, they did not seek to increase their powers. Canada's press censors, like most citizens and people in the political class, believed a well-informed public was a bulwark of democracy. During wartime, politicians and military generals make mistakes. Factories make bad weaponry. People, including the country's military and political leaders, would do a better job if they knew their mistakes might be put in front of the public.

On the battlefield, the enemy is bound to make breakthroughs. From 1939 until the fall of 1942, the Axis was deciding where the war would be fought and how. They won almost every important battle, and few people realized that, in fact, the European war had been decided outside Moscow in the early winter of 1941, or that the Japanese lunge through the Pacific was 5,000 miles wide and an inch deep, without the industrial or manpower resources to take on the United States military. Most of the censors wanted to allow enough negative coverage in newsreels to keep people worried on the home front. The threat of military failure or even defeat made people more likely to accept rationing, overtime shifts, bond drives, family stresses, long separations from loved ones, even conscription. A public kept in a world of constant happy news would be overconfident, complacent, and less likely to accept the privations that come with war. But military intelligence officers and government officials thought the censors had a duty to help them manipulate morale by killing all types of bad-news stories. As chief English-language press censor Wilfrid Eggleston pointed out time and again in letters to government officials, the military, and some journalists, the suppression of bad news creates a fool's paradise, one in which people would eventually learn the truth—the way the French did in 1940, when, despite the make-believe world concocted by the heavily censored press, the Nazis showed up at the door. Suppressing stories about shoddy war equipment didn't make that material any better, Eggleston argued. Spiking stories about domestic dissent actually caused long-term political problems because society cannot develop lasting, solid consensus without free debate. Any decisions made with faulty information could hurt the war effort. Rather than adopt the customs of Ottawa and build a censorship empire, Eggleston and his colleagues fought back when cabinet ministers and top journalists wanted to entice them into taking complete control of the media. But the censorship system was politicized. Conservative newspapers were more likely to criticize and embarrass Mackenzie King's Liberal government, and the censors at first overreacted to political criticism of the King regime. As the years went by, the censors realized they needed to work at being non-partisan.

The prime minister and his cabinet played their own games, ignoring pro-Nazi and pro-Vichy forces in some of the Quebec press while sometimes strictly enforcing censorship upon the pro-Conservative Montreal *Gazette* and the *Globe and Mail*. The French-language press quickly realized it had a licence to publish anti-Semitic articles, stories tipping off the Germans that one of their spies in Canada had been "turned" as a double agent, and even bogus letters from Adolf Hitler telling readers in Quebec City the war was none of Quebec's business. Federal justice minister Louis St. Laurent and his deputy were quick to approve prosecutions and warnings for the press outside Quebec but usually ignored the sometimes outrageous behaviour of French-language newspapers and magazines within that province.

There were some bright moments when the censors did things that shone at a time when so much liberty was being sacrificed in

the name of the war effort. For instance, the censors often ran interference for the Japanese-Canadian newspaper, the *New Canadian*,
and fought off demands by the mainstream press in British Columbia and by cabinet ministers to have its brilliant young editor
thrown in jail. Here, in this book, and for the first time, I show that
when the media, governments, many of the churches, and most of
the public supported the mistreatment of Japanese Canadians, press
censors, backed by a few Ottawa mandarins, often acted with courage to protect some of the rights of these vulnerable people. Their
efforts paid off in an unexpected way: Tommy Shoyama, the editor
of the *New Canadian*, went on to have one of the most spectacular
public service careers of any modern Canadian.

It's difficult to understand how censorship worked during the
Second World War without having some knowledge of the media
and how they operate. First, journalists do not, and, despite the Hollywood image, did not, scrounge for news. There's always more than
enough to fill any newspaper, with a constant stream of press releases, news handouts, and event invitations to keep any newsroom
busy. It's the amount of advertising, not the volume of news, that
determines the thickness of a metropolitan daily paper. In fact, editors are challenged to find enough space for all the news that comes
in, either gathered by their own staff or sent by wire services. The
New York Times claims to carry "all the news that's fit to print," but
in reality it prints all the news that fits in the "news hole" that's left
over when the ads are laid out. Censorship does not create problems
for journalists in terms of reducing the *volume* of material that
comes into a newsroom. It simply changes the types of stories that
are assigned and gives reporters a mechanism that ensures they
don't waste time writing about banned subjects. And journalists, as
long as they are not beaten by their competition (in those few places
where it exists) are not usually distressed by the curbs put on their
writing. Many of them hate the pressure and alienation that comes
from writing negative stories about social and political elites and
about large organizations such as the military. Marxists might
dream that journalists, unleashed from their responsibilities to
their corporate owners and from libel laws that favour the powerful,

would react by leaping into investigative, insightful journalism. In fact, quite likely they would not. Journalists of the mid–twentieth century, like their counterparts today, tended to aspire to join the upper middle class. They also craved recognition as members of a profession, a status that continues to evade them simply because anyone can be a journalist if he can get his work published. (Now, with the ever-growing blogosphere, even that meagre bar is gone.) The public image of a pestering investigative reporter is of someone outside the social mainstream trying to force society to look at its failures, which is a thankless task in peacetime and a dangerous one when a country is at war. There may be a few of those people in the Canadian media, but there are far more press types hoping for the Order of Canada and/or a place in the management of their corporate masters.

In the six and a half years that the Canadian media were censored during the war, newspapers, magazines, and radio stations thrived. There was plenty of safe news—propaganda handouts from the Wartime Information Board, local stories that were inoffensive, national political reporting that was tame and incurious, and war news that crossed the Canadian border pre-censored by British and U.S. officials. And there was a lot of money to be made selling advertisements. Papers were able to maintain their political leanings. In English Canada, Conservative and Liberal papers supported the war. The papers were divided on party lines over the issue of a national draft, or conscription, of men to fight overseas. Otherwise, their real differences were minimal and only one paper, the *Globe and Mail*, consistently fought the censorship system. After the war, the censors believed the press had poorly served the Canadian people by sticking to very predictable formula news and refusing to apply political pressure for weaker censorship.

Maybe that was too harsh a judgment. Newsrooms were stripped to the bone: the kind of courageous, adventurous young man who would make a good reporter was also the type who was most likely to enlist, and many young journalists served with distinction in fighting units. Women replaced the men who went overseas. Many of these reporters, like the *Globe and Mail*'s June Callwood, could hold their own. This despite the added challenge, in Callwood's case and many others, of fending off lecherous bosses and dealing with officials, including censors, who saw them only as "lady reporters." Others, however, lacked the training, experience, and education to excel in their trade. By the time they found their footing, the war was over and most were forced out of newsrooms to make way for the men returning from battle.

It was reasonable that some people, even at the highest levels of government, panicked in those early years of the war. The Nazis' blitzkrieg of 1940 was a shock to the Canadian political system. The war, which had seemed far away and abstract, now became very real. People were forced to confront the thought of Britain losing the war and becoming, like France, a Nazi thrall. Ottawa quickly became an important place as French, British, and Dutch refugees and treasures found their way to the city. In the corridors of Parliament, people talked seriously of Ottawa becoming home to a British government-in-exile, with the Royal Navy steaming to a new home in Halifax. In the midst of the crisis, the minister of defence, Norman Rogers, was killed in a plane crash. Fear and excitement caused some people in the government and military to demand tough new secrecy laws, including a ruthless press censorship. "In the twilight war everyone had been reasonable and tolerant; as the bad news poured in and the foundations of life were shaken, reason gave way to passion and tolerance to blind fury," chief press censor Wilfrid Eggleston wrote in his memoirs. The top mandarins, used to life under pressure, hung tough. O.D. Skelton, the senior bureaucrat in the Department of External Affairs, Ernest Lapointe, the justice minister, and Mackenzie King backed the censors and rejected demands from junior ministers and military officers for tighter censorship of Canadian newspapers and of isolationist U.S. publications.

Canada could not escape the war. Much more of it arrived on our shores than we learn in the paltry bits of history taught in school. People burned or froze to death in submarine attacks within sight of the Canadian (and Newfoundland) shore. Japanese balloon bombs, which seem so ludicrous today, drifted over the West carrying God-knew-what. As hundreds of thousands of young Canadian men went off to war, thousands of German and Italian POWs were brought into the country and had to be guarded and put to work. The war affected everything from the length of women's skirts to the types of food that showed up on the table. For Japanese Canadians, internment camps and back-breaking farm work was their fate. In Quebec, the French-speaking majority suffered infighting over whether the war was Canada's business at all, and many people on both sides of the debate took to the streets to make their views clear to the government.

How could censors thwart German intelligence agents and build support for the war? How could they make rules that treated the press fairly? Some news, such as reports of convoy departures, obviously should have been banned outright, but what about radar reports, which the British military censors usually passed but were always killed by U.S. censors? Which political stories were so damning of the Canadian government's war management that they must be declared illegal because they hurt recruiting efforts and undermined morale in the military and its ancillary industries? Was there a point to banning stories about U-boat attacks in the St. Lawrence River when so many people on shore knew of them, including, of course, the German navy and civilians in the Reich who read about them in the Nazi press? Was it the censors' job to kill stories that were simply wrong, to correct media mistakes, should they let those errors run because most mistakes did not impair the war effort?

Canada was naturally conducive to censorship, as there was no constitutional protection for the press. Journalists in Canada worked under libel laws that presumed them guilty until proven innocent and contempt-of-court rules that gave sweeping powers to judges to jail journalists for criticizing anything about the justice system. The newspapers had already accepted a tough censorship in the First World War and were exhausted from a series of attacks on their independence and power through the Depression, especially from provincial governments.

If they had wanted to write thoughtful analyses of the war effort, few members of the press were skilled enough in history, geography, and military strategy to have done a credible job. In the main, journalists in Canada did not have a clearer grasp of the war than their readers. Like the rest of Canadians, reporters and editors got almost all their foreign news from U.S. and British wire services, so it came pre-censored and infused with foreign, albeit usually Allied, propaganda. Even after the invasion of Sicily, Canada's first major campaign, most Canadian war reporters stayed home. The correspondents who did go to the front lines were as much propagandists as they were observers, as coerced by the military's rules and indoctrination techniques as any twenty-first-century "embedded" reporter. Unlike modern war correspondents who take some of the training of combat soldiers and work alongside them, World War Two correspondents were given officers' ranks. They usually stayed in war theatres far longer than modern reporters and saw much more fighting. Their work was censored on the battlefield and by the Allied command in London. Now, reporters' work is sent back to Canada uncensored, but military public affairs officers have more subtle ways of influencing coverage. Access to real fighting is very limited, and Canadian reporters in Afghanistan, in search of something to write and film, settle for brief and relatively safe forays out of the fortified compound at Kandahar. Still, that type of coverage isn't completely safe: in 2009, *Edmonton Journal* reporter Michelle Lang was killed on one of these trips. And the nature of war has changed: unlike in the two world wars, there are no strongly defined front lines, the enemy does not wear a uniform and does not take prisoners.

And at home, the press is uncensored, allowing a vigorous debate on the nature of Canadian involvement, the reasons for the war, and the length of Canada's combat operations. Victory, and the road to it, seemed much more clearly defined in World War Two. Canadians don't need to worry about keeping secrets. They don't seriously worry about the government drafting people to fight al Qaeda and the Taliban. Quite simply, as the memories of September 11, 2001, recede, it has become fairly easy to ignore Canada's combat operations in Asia. War reporting has become an expensive frill for many of Canada's media companies, and the journalists in Canada who know enough about military affairs to be able to accurately analyze the military situation in Afghanistan could fit around a kitchen table. In World War Two, it was impossible for Canadians to ignore the war, although most people tried to. Everyone had relatives in the armed forces, most families had members in war jobs, rationing was a way of life, and the media were drenched with articles, films, and ads about the war.

In the winter of 1998, I visited the Ottawa home of a 100-year-old semi-retired political columnist, Fulgence Charpentier. He was the longest-serving member of Canada's Parliamentary Press Gallery, having joined it in 1920. In World War Two, Charpentier was the chief French-language newspaper and magazine censor and, during the closing months of the war, headed the entire Directorate of Censorship, which put him in charge of mail openings and phone taps too. Charpentier told me the records he had packed over fifty years earlier were a potential gold mine of news and feature articles. In fact, they turned out to be more than just a lode of suppressed stories from the Second World War. They are a very complete record of the way wartime news was manipulated by people like Charpentier, who believed managing the press was an important part of Canada's war efforts—but who also realized investigative journalism was vital to a democratic society.

Being a censor crippled Charpentier's writing career. Eggleston, the chief English press censor, left the service weighted down with questions and concerns about the media, so many, in fact, that he left journalism to become the chair of the country's first journalism school. Neither man was allowed to write much about what he had seen and done, but they left behind a record showing censorship was a quiet, complex type of warfare where some battles were won and some were lost. It could have been far more oppressive, if it had been in the hands of people who believed the press had no legitimate place in the democratic system. But on the home front, as on the battlefields of Europe, in the grey convoys of the Atlantic, and in Hong Kong, Canadians were usually well served by the people who took on the often thankless job of press censor.

PRELUDE

"You Can't Talk about That!"

AT THE BEGINNING OF 2009, people in many Western countries tossed the word *censorship* around, aiming their accusation at the Israeli Defense Force (IDF), which refused to allow war correspondents to tour areas along the Israeli–Gaza frontier attacked by the Israelis in response to rocket fire coming from Gaza. The tiny Palestinian territory, a mixture of crowded towns and some scraps of farmland, was ruled by Hamas, seen by the Israelis and most of the Western media as the more extremist of the mainstream Palestinian political parties. Hamas had allowed some sympathetic Western reporters and a few pro-Palestinian foreign VIPs to watch the fighting (mostly Israeli artillery bombardments and air strikes) from its side of the battle lines. The Israelis had refused to allow any media into its section of the war zone. However, they supplied TV networks with edited video of footage shot by its air force, and, in a hat tip to the sea changes in modern media, posted highlights on the Internet, along with commentary and analysis by the IDF. The Israeli military didn't cut the stories filed from Israel by the foreign press, but it has imposed military censorship in the past, including times when Israel was being bombarded with Scud missiles fired from Iraq during both the first Gulf War and when Israel made incursions into Lebanon.

Like Israel, Hamas did not allow journalists to range freely. Instead, they were taken to bombed areas of Gaza and spoon-fed the Hamas version of events.

What Israel and Hamas were engaging in, however, was not

censorship. It was manipulation of news coverage by controlling access to the battlefield, knowing journalists would, out of necessity, accept handouts and, if taken to the front, would show some gratitude for the favour. Except for the technologies involved, nothing in war reporting had changed since the time of Napoleon. Journalists have no absolute right to be on any battlefield, nor are soldiers obliged to allow reporters to tag along with them. Reporters who travel with armies and report on what they see always do it on sufferance. On the home front, journalists' freedom to write on war strategy, tactics, and the morality of the conflict without official or unofficial censure by the government or public pressure tends to exist in inverse proportion to the enemy's real threat to the survival of the state. The press in 1940 France was ruthlessly censored and the country fell into the hands of the Nazis. In England, heavy censorship killed most of the coverage of preparations for defence from a German invasion and kept Hitler's v1 and v2 weapons out of the media. Canada had a relatively benign censorship program. The United States, which was never seriously threatened, had the lightest censorship of the major Allies.

The Napoleonic Wars, which saw the first appearance of people we would recognize as war correspondents, also comprised the first "total" war. In those days, newspapers had very little freedom, but there were a few journalists who were willing to ask serious questions about the battles. Two generations later, during the American Civil War, the governments on both sides exerted strong controls on the press. In the South, the Confederates took advantage of paper shortages to decide which newspapers could live or die. In the North, Lincoln's government suspended many of the country's civil rights, jailed journalists, and intimidated publishers.

The British military began serious study of media manipulation during the First and Second Boer Wars. The Boers, portrayed in the foreign press as farmers fighting for their land (when, in fact, the land had fairly recently been taken from Africans), lost the military fight but won the propaganda war when the British resorted to rounding up civilians and starving them in concentration camps to deny Boer fighters the civilian support they needed. As a reaction to the Boer mess, the British developed concepts of propaganda and censorship that would impress both friend and foe during World War One.

Beginning in 1904, Canada was brought into the British plans for the control of news from naval bases at Halifax and Esquimalt, British Columbia. The British kept control over Canadian censorship until 1915. During the opening days of World War One, editors and reporters were caught in a conflict between the public's hunger for news and the military's demand for secrecy. The issue came to a head on August 12, 1914, at a meeting in Ottawa between senior military staff and the editors of most of Canada's major newspapers. The editors pledged their co-operation with a new censorship system as long as there was no interference with what they termed "safe and legitimate news" and no attempt to interfere with the debate of purely political issues. Journalists were expected to shy away from stories that would deter recruitment and publish articles that instilled confidence in the Allied effort. The government and newspaper executives settled on a voluntary press censorship system that placed the onus on publishers to ensure their papers did not cross the lines, wherever the government determined them to be.

The postmaster general, acting as deputy press censor for the British chief press censor, could ban any publication or writing and publishing of information respecting the war or its causes, contrary to the government's version of the facts. The maximum penalty for writing, publishing, circulating, or possessing anything banned by the postmaster general was a fine of $5,000 and/or five years in prison. The owner of the print shop where the material was published, along with the directors and officers of the corporation that controlled the premises, were each subject to the same fines and jail terms. The printer could be shut down indefinitely and the presses could be seized along with all copies of the offending publication.

The agreement was enshrined in the *War Measures Act*, passed on August 22, 1914, but made retroactive to August 4. Five days later, the secretary of state invited leading editors and publishers to a second conference in Ottawa to discuss the types of news and commentary that should be censored. A four-member committee was struck to help the under-secretary of state and a military officer appointed by the postmaster general write the main regulations of the new censorship service. The committee worked very quickly. The next day, delegates were presented with the draft of a schedule of rules and regulations for the press censorship system. These rules were printed in a pamphlet and mailed to newspaper offices, publishing firms, advertising and public-relations agencies, government departments, police departments, intelligence officers, and Allied governments.

The rules and regulations dealt mainly with two types of news: domestic stories from Canada and wire copy from the United States, which was still neutral. The government had no worries about coverage from the front. There wasn't any. The British and French controlled all access to the fighting zone. "War correspondence" from France came mostly from Britain's official "eyewitness" who was, through most of the war, Canadian Max Aitken (Lord Beaverbrook). Aitken was eyewitness to very little. He rarely went near the front, and simply wrote press releases based on memos from military intelligence agents.

Censorship was more concerned with public opinion, as the war could not be won unless the public gave its full support. As the battles dragged on, the Canadian censorship system became increasingly invasive and powerful. An order-in-council (a Canadian cabinet order) passed September 12, 1914, similar to one issued in Great Britain under the *Defence of the Realm Act*, was aimed at suppressing spies. Anyone who transmitted information "with respect to the movement or any disposition of the armed forces of His Majesty or His Majesty's Allies" was guilty under the *War Measures Act*. This law could also be used against the press. Less than two months later, cabinet passed a second order-in-council which outlawed publications "calculated to be, or that might be, directly or indirectly useful to the enemy, or containing articles bearing on the war and not in accordance with the facts."

These orders-in-council remained the legal underpinnings for the press-censorship system until the spring of 1915, when the government created the post of chief censor. Ernest J. Chambers (1862–1921), a former journalist and militia officer who served as Gentleman Usher of the Black Rod of the Canadian Senate (the upper house's head of security), was appointed chief censor. Month after month, Chambers tightened the screws. Films and plays fell under censorship. In the last months of the war, the censors began poking through record stores and demanded catalogues from the major U.S. record companies. Thirty-four records were banned, all of them foreign-language songs, including a version of "Deutschland Über Alles." Just a few weeks before the end of the war, the government banned all printed material in the languages of the enemy powers, a large swath of publications when one considers the ethnic mixture of the Austrian Empire.

No one could publicly criticize the army or navy. People were not allowed to advocate a negotiated peace and, eventually, could not even discuss the reasons for the war or suggest the Allies were partly to blame for it. The government, along with most newspaper and magazine owners, flooded propaganda into the marketplace of ideas. Censorship created the illusion that these official ideas were the only version of reality.

People might have expected the censorship to end when the Germans surrendered. But the Russian Revolution of 1917 had created a whole new set of villains to fear, and those villains had supporters in Canada. At their first postwar cabinet meeting, held on November 13, 1918, federal ministers passed an order-in-council to try to outlaw seditious talk. They banned the printing of anything advocating socialist revolution or criticizing capitalism. It was the only time in Canadian history that the media were officially prohibited from spreading political ideas in peacetime.

The postwar attack on Communists was no surprise to anyone who followed the work of Chambers. The censorship system had been, throughout the war, a mechanism for rooting out subversives and non-conformists. Its focus was on German and Slavic ethnic groups, pacifists, defeatists, or people who just doubted the sense of the war. It also worked hard to kill any mention of troop movements. The system survived, with a few tweaks, until December 20, 1919, when all of the orders-in-council dealing with press censorship were repealed.

Chambers didn't spend his workdays breaking up print shops. Instead, press censorship during World War One operated as a voluntary system, with editors and publishers often silencing themselves. Except for the *Victoria Week*, the *Sault Ste. Marie Express*, *Le Bulletin* of Montreal, and Quebec City's *La Croix*, all of which were banned, editors of commercial newspapers toed the line. They chose to discuss political issues from positions that did not reflect overly negatively on Canada's war effort and did not, like the *Sault Ste. Marie Express*, question the reasons for sending more Canadian soldiers to the front.

For an organization that wielded such power, the censorship program was remarkably small. Its Ottawa head office was staffed by the chief press censor; two press censors (one each for French- and English-language papers); an office manager; a German translator who was also an assistant censor; and a messenger. The department employed translators in thirty-one languages on a freelance basis. The department also had branch offices in Toronto, Winnipeg, and Vancouver, where the editors of the Canadian Press wire service were paid honoraria to advise their colleagues at newspapers and magazines. A very similar system of organization was established during World War Two but on a slightly larger scale and with a much gentler guiding hand.

During World War One, censorship authorities banned 253 publications, approximately 90 per cent of which were U.S.-based and almost 70 per cent written in a foreign language. Ninety-three of the publications were Marxist-oriented. During World War Two, the censors banned a similar number and similar types of publications but were more selective about the foreign-language press. The censors of that later era would agonize over whether small ethnic papers might be breaking the law, whereas Chambers shut them all down in the early days.

It was rare for English-Canadian journalists to be "unpatriotic," especially during the Great War. Most of them were first- or second-generation young male immigrants from Britain and Ireland, the same demographic groups that made up the bulk of the early enlistments. Ernest Chambers could win most arguments over media gag orders by appealing to the loyalty of the journalists. The same held true in World War Two: no mainstream journalist, even among those Quebec journalists who supported Vichy France, publicly beat the drum for Hitler, Mussolini, and Tojo. In English Canada, debate during both wars usually started from the premise that Canada was engaged in a righteous struggle but could do a better job of killing Germans.

Chambers was thwarted in his attempts to rein in the Québécois press. The World War Two censors would be thwarted too. Over the course of both world wars, the censors were vexed with *Le Devoir* and other Quebec-nationalist papers, which were largely isolationist, not pro-German. The situation did grow worse during World War Two, with a large block of the Quebec media opposing the war from the beginning and some publications evolving into Pétainist organs after the fall of France.

Media outlets in the United States posed problems for the Canadian censors during both wars. Stateside media reports, which flowed effortlessly across the border, could, until April 1917, carry whatever information editors saw fit to print, and many papers sided openly with Kaiser Wilhelm. (H.L. Mencken of the *Baltimore Sun* was one of the U.S. journalists who toured the fighting fronts from the German side and wrote approvingly of what they saw.) During World War One, some English-Canadian publications criticized the United States for not siding with the Allies (a theme that would be picked up by Canadian journalists after World War Two broke out), thus endangering diplomatic efforts to pull the Americans into the war. The chief press censor issued instructions to Canadian editors that asked them to refrain from publishing material "likely to cause irritation" in the States and other neutral countries, with the hope that they could be brought over to the Allied side. Chambers, though, was able to apply enough pressure on border-city newspapers that some U.S. editors and publishers asked the censors for guidance on the acceptability of literature for circulation in Canada.

When Chambers saw Canadian news stories he disagreed with, he issued press releases to set the record straight or demanded editors insert his version of the "facts" into news-wire copy. He also planted propaganda, handing out press releases and military photographs. The chief censor eventually allowed a press agency in Montreal to distribute authorized military and naval pictures, once they were received from the British Admiralty, its War Office, or the Canadian military. On November 9, 1917, the federal government appointed a director of public information, whose job was described as "furnishing to the Press and the public the fullest possible information concerning the progress of the war and measures adopted by the Government for the prosecution of the same." Still, the censorship bureau continued to be the official channel for communicating all information coming from cable and telegraph "through military and naval secret channels, such as news respecting purely naval and military matters, the movements of troops and shipping of all sorts, casualty lists, etc."

To Chambers, censorship was a recruiting tool, morale booster, and instrument for cleansing the news of inconvenient ideas. But the two world wars were very dissimilar conflicts. In 1914, despite twenty years of friction between Berlin and London, Germany (and Prussia) was a traditional ally of Britain and the two countries had never gone to war against each other. Kaiser Wilhelm, whatever his failings, was, at the outset, difficult to accept in the role of a war criminal and enemy of the West. In 1939, the memories of the agonies of the Great War were still visceral. This time, the Allies were fighting an ideology, fascism, which fomented a movement that really did seek to dominate the world. Hitler's regime was more militaristic than even the kaiser's, and much more aggressive. The Nazis had already seized two central European countries before the war began, and the Allies suffered one setback after another until the summer of 1942. Losing the war was a real possibility when the Germans were governing most of mainland Europe and U-boats were sinking ships within sight of the banks of the St. Lawrence River. There usually was no need to use a stick to keep the English-Canadian press in line during the fight against the Nazis. Everyone in the media was on the "team." When, however, the goal of censorship seemed to be to make the Canadian government look good, the newspapers rebelled, providing drama that the World War One censors never faced.

In the years after the 1918 Armistice, as Europe fell into one economic crisis after another, people in English-speaking countries realized how they had been manipulated over the course of the war years. During the months of the Paris Peace Conference, Americans started to soul-search about how they had been drawn—some critics said *tricked*—into World War One. In 1922, Walter Lippmann opened a debate on British news manipulation during the Great War with the publication of the book *Public Opinion*. In it, he argued Britain had used the most sophisticated media manipulation the world had yet seen to draw the United States into the war. German generals rushed their own analyses into print, with Field Marshal Erich Ludendorff's memoirs reaching the bookstores, in both German and English, before the end of 1919. Ludendorff argued the Wilhelmine regime's rough censorship and clumsy propaganda had hampered the German war effort. Sir Edward Cook's description of his career as Britain's chief press censor was printed in 1920. In it, and in other books by censors and journalists—including Sir Douglas Brownrigg's *The Indiscretions of a Naval Censor* (1919), Sir Philip Gibbs's *Realities of War* (1920), Neville Lytton's *The Press and the General Staff* (1920), and Major General Charles Callwell's *The Experiences of a Dug-Out 1914–1918* (1920)—were candid discussions of the new press-manipulation techniques used on U.S. newspapers. Often, the authors crossed the line into bragging about their propaganda coups. A decade later, Henry Hamilton Fyfe covered the wartime propaganda role of London *Times* owner Lord Northcliffe in *Northcliffe, an Intimate Biography* (1930), as had the extremely well-connected Lord Beaverbrook in *Politicians and the War, 1914–1916* (1928). Beaverbrook, who had worked as Canada's unofficial delegate at the British War Office, then as "eyewitness," was intrigued by the power of wartime news manipulation. In the interwar years, he studied the subject of media manipulation intensely and wrote glowingly of Britain's success in this domain, and during World War Two stepped into Northcliffe's shoes as one of Britain's most successful propagandists.

In the 1930s, U.S. isolationists, after analyzing British propaganda and censorship, concluded the United States had been tricked into declaring war on Germany in 1917. Their arguments convinced many people. Throughout the Great Depression, social scientists in the former Central Powers (Germany, Austria-Hungary and Turkey), the Allied countries, and the Soviet Union expanded this literature and drew from the World War One experience. New theories on propaganda and censorship were developed and even applied by totalitarian regimes, such as the Soviet Union and Nazi Germany. In these cases, the ruling party also directly controlled the newspapers.

The Canadian government's main war planner, Maurice Pope, had to take those attitudes into account during the Depression, when he developed what would be the Canadian press-censorship system for World War Two. Fortunately for Canada's next generation of censors, the Japanese and Germans were a far less scrupulous enemy than Wilhelmine Germany and the decrepit Austrian Empire. Still, the censors were never able to dominate the media the way Chambers had during the Great War.

CHAPTER I

A Good Fishing Trip Ruined:
The Genesis of the World War Two Censorship System

ON THE LABOUR DAY WEEKEND OF 1939, the Canadian National Railway's publicity director, Walter Thompson, was enjoying one of the best perks of his job, his antique private railway car. He had it parked on an isolated siding in northern Manitoba, just a few steps from a lake where the pickerel had never been exposed to the threat of a lure. On September 1, Hitler's armies ruptured the frontiers of Poland. The next day, Maurice Pope, the country's director of military operations and intelligence, put switchboard operators on Thompson's tail. He was summoned to a wayside railroad call box and told that Mackenzie King's government wanted him back in Ottawa as quickly as possible to run the press censorship system.

This was unwelcome news to Thompson. He had one of the country's best public-relations jobs. Barring a train wreck or some other disaster, his workday consisted of doling out free passes to reporters from big-city papers and entertaining them in his well-stocked private railway car. Thompson was reaping the rewards of a long career on Fleet Street, as well as in Australia, New Zealand, and Montreal. He arrived in Canada just before the outbreak of the Great War and worked as city editor of the troubled *Montreal Witness* and the *Montreal Herald* before making his soft landing on the national railway. Thompson expanded his already wide circle of journalistic friends when he handled the logistics of the media covering the hugely successful May 1939 Royal Tour, a boozy swing across the country with King George VI, Queen Elizabeth, Mackenzie King, senior federal leaders, and the cream of the country's press corps. The prime minister, a close student of public relations, had taken notice of Thompson's skills.

Censorship was hardly a line of work that would win him friends, but Thompson began his new job with the good wishes of the journalism fraternity. In an editorial, the *Globe and Mail* said Thompson was "the man for the job" and, a few weeks later, a "great and good friend of all newspapermen." Thompson's diplomatic skills were immediately put to good use. Before he unpacked the boxes in his temporary office at the Ottawa train station (now the Government Conference Centre, just kitty-corner to Parliament Hill), he met most of the editors of Canada's major newspapers and very quickly developed working and drinking relationships with parliamentary reporters in Ottawa. Thompson had no idea that all of these friendships would unravel so quickly. By Christmas, he would lose the trust of many of the reporters in the Parliamentary Press Gallery, the *Globe and Mail*, and editors of the powerful Canadian Press news co-operative, as well as the support of the prime minister.

Yet Thompson did not make most of the policy decisions of the new Press Censorship Branch. Real authority lay with chief English-language censor Wilfrid Eggleston, who signed almost all of the censorship orders and directives from the head office in Ottawa. Apart from being English immigrants, Eggleston and Thompson had very little in common. Thompson was a gregarious backslapper; Eggleston was a man who appreciated literature, was intensely shy and very bookish, a man who agonized over details. Thompson had often worked for newspapers that played fast and loose with facts. Eggleston worked hard through his reporting career to maintain his own integrity.

Eggleston had overcome his family's poverty—he was forced to quit school in grade 9 to work on the family farm—to get an education. He was mentored by a high-school English teacher, Ephraim Weber, who spotted the young dropout reading *Paradise Lost* in a Lajord, Saskatchewan, general store and coached him for his high-school matriculation exams. After studying at Queen's University, Eggleston worked for the Liberal papers owned by the Sifton family in the Prairies before moving east to join the *Toronto Star*, where he shared the progressive politics and stern morality of the paper's publisher, Joseph "Holy Joe" Atkinson. Eggleston was one of the hundreds of reporters at the big Toronto daily whose star burned brightly for a few years only to be extinguished by office politics. In 1933, just days after he was elected president of the Parliamentary Press Gallery, Eggleston was fired by the *Star*.

This was not a good time to be unemployed. Still, Eggleston was able to cobble together a network of small papers that would each pay him a bit of money for a weekly political column. Within a few months, Eggleston was making a better living, with far fewer headaches, than he had at the *Star*. The prime minister tracked the growth of Eggleston's freelance business with some interest. Eggleston was appointed researcher and writer on the Rowell–Sirois Commission, a panel that was expected to remake the relationship between the federal government and the provinces.

In the days after the invasion of Poland, 37-year-old Eggleston, a dedicated anti-fascist, seriously considered enlisting. Instead, he let Thompson trick him into becoming a press censor. At first, Eggleston despised the idea. He would take the job, he told a friend, only if he was convinced the country's survival was at stake. Thompson called Eggleston and made him a promise—soon to be broken—that Eggleston would quickly move on to a job writing propaganda. Censorship wasn't so bad, Thompson said. Forget the civil liberties problems: he would be a bridge between the media and the government. And, Thompson argued, Eggleston would be on the front lines of the war effort, keeping Canada's military and industrial secrets out of the hands of German spies.

To Eggleston, a free press was even more valuable in wartime than it was in times of peace. He came to believe France fell to the Germans in 1940 because the French public lived in a dream world created by their government's propaganda and censorship systems. The press must be allowed, even encouraged, to print bad news so people would be angry and upset. Frightened Canadians would work and fight harder if they believed there was a real chance they'd lose the war.

Few other people, including Thompson, had put that much thought into censorship. Major Maurice Pope, a well-connected military engineer (two close relatives were Fathers of Confederation and his grandfather was the principal secretary to, and a biographer of, Sir John A. Macdonald; his wife was a Belgian countess), had designed the system in the late 1930s, when appeasement, not war planning, was in style. Once Pope mapped it out, his meticulous plan was tossed into a drawer. When Hitler invaded Poland and Canada mobilized for war, Mackenzie King's cabinet rushed through Pope's censorship plan without even reading it.

The bureaucracy assembled by Thompson was tiny: one- or two-person bureaus were set up in Halifax, Montreal, Toronto, and Vancouver, with a small head office in Ottawa using borrowed space near Parliament Hill. Compared to the huge mail and telephone censorship systems that allowed officials to eavesdrop on Canadians, the resources given to the press censors were pathetic—a fact that probably was not lost on the country's journalists. The censors had no extra gas rations, worked in tiny borrowed offices, and they became testy when out-of-town reporters made collect calls to them. As the months went by, it became obvious to reporters and editors that the censors had no real power in their own right. Like almost all wartime power, it was firmly in the hands of Prime Minister King, his two justice ministers during the war, and a handful of trusted bureaucrats.

The censors spent their workdays in their small offices, breaking the monotony by visiting newsrooms. Typically, each newspaper—and there were far more of them in Canada in 1939, with most cities having at least two dailies—had a contact person who called a censor each day to vet stories that might be problematic. This was usually a mid-ranking newspaper staff member, someone who worked directly with reporters. The censors dealt with senior editors and publishers only in times of real crisis.

Thompson was good at holding meetings and courting people but he was an ineffective manager. Editors wanted a clear set of censorship rules and a simple system to help them quickly approve or kill stories. With the deadline pressures of the newspaper business, editors and reporters knew there was no time for hairsplitting and playing with nuances. Instead, editors found they were expected to decide, even guess, which of their stories might contravene the

Defence of Canada Regulations in the *War Measures Act*. Any delay left them open to being scooped by competitors.

Thompson tried to win the publishers and editors over by bringing them to Ottawa and providing the same boozy hospitality that worked so well during the Royal Tour. Most of the country's editors were in no mood to settle their differences with the director of censorship over drinks. They, along with members of the Parliamentary Press Gallery, knew that Thompson had threatened influential Hill reporter Floyd Chalmers of the *Financial Post* for refusing to stop his criticisms of the military. The cloak of secrecy had been thrown over the departure for England of the first Canadian army contingent in December 1939, and many editors felt the censors had overreacted to the few minor slips in security. The prime minister tried to salvage the situation by sending personal, or personalized, letters asking for co-operation with Thompson and his people. At the same time, he quietly decided to cut Thompson loose, making his decision known in little leaks to Liberal-friendly reporters.

Fortunately, King's timing was right. After Hitler's conquest of Poland in the fall of 1939, there was no major fighting until the Nazi invasion of Denmark and Norway on April 9, 1940. King still had a few months to tweak the system before the "Phony War" ended and fighting began in western Europe. Thompson's lethargy and disorganization were manageable while people waited to see if the war would somehow be called off, but the prime minister realized the censorship system would collapse in a real crisis.

Here, Mackenzie King was drawing on his own brilliant skills as a media strategist and his own good luck. This was a prime minister who understood how the media worked and how they could be used and manipulated in wartime. King was underestimated during his life and, if anything, his political skills are even more poorly understood now. It's easy to discount the man by focusing on King's perceived oddball spiritualism and his other eccentricities and ignoring the talents that kept him in power. King's biographers haven't taken a close look at the way King used the media. They should. It's a key to understanding why King holds the record as Canada's longest-serving prime minister. Few leaders in any democratic country had the longevity of King, and it's unlikely we'll see a challenge to King's record tenure as PM any time soon.

King was one of the first North American politicians to embrace polling and other modern forms of media manipulation. More than any Canadian prime minister before or since, King knew how to deal with journalists, especially those in the Parliamentary Press Gallery. This was one of the country's more exclusive men's clubs. Members were bound by rules set by members of an executive committee who knew the coveted label "insider" was earned by gathering and keeping secrets, and doling out just enough to prove their status. In King's time, reporters who joined or visited the press gallery were given a small booklet written by newspaper reporter Kennedy Crone explaining the expectations placed upon members and guests. A good reporter, Crone's booklet read, "is often torn between his zeal to publish news and his determination to 'play the game' with his sources of information. Aside from the ethics of the profession, a prudent reporter is aware that his future success depends on his present honor and discretion." (Eggleston was an insider, and he found it difficult and troubling to carry around so many secrets. Yet he took most of them to his grave.)

In the mid–twentieth century, Ottawa's press corps was dominated by men who, like King, wanted an independent Canada with a strong, centralized state that had its own voice in international affairs. The bulk of the reporters who covered Parliament were very similar to the people who held political power and ran the bureaucracy: university-educated, male, anglophone, and upper middle class. They could easily come to a meeting of minds with Ottawa's mandarinate and members of the Liberal caucus because they were, in general, the same kind of people. There were a few Tories—people like Grattan O'Leary, editor of the *Ottawa Journal*, and *Winnipeg Tribune* editor John Bird—but they were not major opinion makers.

The *Winnipeg Free Press*'s Grant Dexter kept his best secrets for his boss, not his readers. "The people who are responsible for our laws deserve respectful attention, and a spirit of levity and disrespect will not improve our government," Dexter wrote. "Once the public thinks all people in public life are crooked, hypocritical, and entirely lacking in any spirit of public service, a good man would not risk his character by becoming a member of parliament."

Ottawa's tiny social scene, centred on the men-only Rideau Club on Wellington Street directly across from Parliament Hill, gave journalists easy access to people in the highest levels of the government. At the annual stag, off-the-record press gallery dinner, journalists and politicians performed rowdy and often lewd skits. Trusted reporters were invited on canoe trips—a popular way of proving manliness among the Ottawa elite through most of the twentieth century—and to join the small, private fishing clubs in the Gatineau Hills. A journalist's acceptance by the capital's inner circles was governed by the partisan position of the person's newspaper or magazine, its circulation, and its location, but journalists' social skills, personal wealth, family and school connections, hospitality, and intelligence also counted, as did discretion and personal habits. King, for instance, could not abide the company of smokers and heavy drinkers.

Prime Minister King took office just as major Canadian newspapers shed their blatant party affiliations (and party financing). Still, he was able, over a span of thirty years, to draw media people—and their employers—into his political and, to a limited extent, personal life. *Toronto Star* publisher Joseph Atkinson, *Globe* publisher George McCullagh, and many other journalists were, or believed they were, ad hoc advisors to the prime minister and important members of the country's governing elite.

King was the only Canadian prime minister to make a living as a news reporter (though Mackenzie Bowell, Wilfrid Laurier, Pierre Trudeau, and Joe Clark were involved with journalism, to varying degrees). In 1895, he worked as a student reporter at the *Toronto News* and, after a few weeks, switched to the police beat of the *Globe*. After his return from graduate school at the University of Chicago, King wrote articles on economics for the *Mail and Empire*. Then he went to Ottawa and moved swiftly into the senior bureaucracy before being appointed Sir Wilfrid Laurier's minister of labour, the first person to hold this cabinet post.

In the spring of 1914, the Colorado National Guard was called in to crush a strike at a mine in Ludlow owned by the Rockefeller family. The troops attacked the strikers with appalling brutality, killing a man and a boy. Then they put the strikers' camp to the torch. Twelve children and two women suffocated in a hole under a burning tent. Once the camp was under National Guard control, three of the strike leaders were summarily clubbed and bludgeoned to death. What had been a violent but typical mine strike became a short, vicious war in the coal fields that ended with about 200 people dead, roughly half of them strikers and the other half strikebreakers. Peace came to the Colorado coal fields when federal troops were called in by President Woodrow Wilson.

Author and activist Upton Sinclair called Rockefeller a murderer. The industrialist could probably live with that, but disgust spread across the country and into the salons of the rich and to the halls of political power. Helen Keller, the blind-deaf activist, labelled Rockefeller a "monster of capitalism" and all sides in the dispute were hauled before a congressional committee. The heir to the world's biggest fortune decided he actually cared about his public profile. Rockefeller hired two men to salvage his reputation: Ivy Lee, the best public-relations man of his time, and Mackenzie King, who had lost his job as labour minister when the Laurier government was defeated in 1911.

It was King, not Lee, who pulled off one of the great PR coups in American industrial history. He realized Rockefeller had to change the way he dealt with the unions, but King also wanted to apply new theories of public relations and consensus building. He talked Rockefeller into making a campaign-style tour of the Colorado mine camps, where the Standard Oil heir danced with miners' wives and charmed their husbands. "I could never have made the trip without him," Rockefeller later said. "He knew exactly what to do. I learned more from him than anyone." King ingratiated himself with individual reporters covering the tour, fed them tidbits of news, and worked to ensure that the people they interviewed spoke fondly of Rockefeller.

Four years after the massacre, King organized a pivotal meeting between Rockefeller and Samuel Gompers, the president of the American Federation of Labor (AFL). The meeting was not a publicity stunt. King had prepared the groundwork so well that Rockefeller and Gompers, who had been bitter enemies in public, became fast friends. Both men feared Bolshevism, and Rockefeller gave Gompers money for his American Alliance for Labor and Democracy. King the stage manager then trumped himself: he brought Rockefeller and the great American leftist Mother Jones together. By the time King was finished, the Ludlow Massacre was a near-forgotten moment in labour-relations history.

King worked the same way in Canada by obliging the desire of journalists to be insiders. He did this very subtly and privately, leaving few tracks except in the memoirs of some Canadian journalists and in his own diaries. Each of King's relationships with journalists was a stand-alone affair, with every reporter thinking his relationship was special and unique. Journalists believed King was obsessed with secrecy, and, because most press gallery reporters were members of one- or two-man bureaus in friendly competition with the journalists representing other publications, each of them could be isolated by the prime minister and handled as a separate entity.

King's relationship with the editor of the *Ottawa Citizen* was typical. Although the *Citizen* leaned editorially toward the Conservatives, and, at times, Social Credit, King cultivated the paper's editor, Charles Bowman. On a trip back to Ottawa from Washington in 1922, King invited Bowman to dinner in his private railway car. He told Bowman about his troubles with Britain's Foreign Office and described some of the weaknesses in his own cabinet. As he left the prime minister's railway car, Bowman felt as though he now was a friend with special access to King. In fact, this magic moment was far from unique. But it worked: although King's government hauled Bowman and the *Citizen* into court twice to face charges for violating wartime censorship, and there's no sign that King listened to anything Bowman said, Bowman still bragged in his memoirs about his friendship with King.

As prime minister, King combined his public-relations work with his miserly personal habits. Unimaginable as it is today with the prime ministerial system that has evolved in Ottawa, wealthy newspaper owners sometimes found King alone on their doorstep with his valise and his toothbrush, planning to stay for an indeterminate time. Ruth Atkinson Hindmarsh, daughter of the *Toronto Star*'s publisher, would tell of the challenge of beating King to the washroom in the morning. In the capital, reporters were invited to King's East Block office; to Laurier House, King's Ottawa home; and to Kingsmere, his retreat in the Gatineau Hills, although they knew better than to expect to be offered a drink. Reporters who lived in Ottawa usually returned home the same day, but out-of-town media figures stayed as overnight and week-long guests of the prime minister. King had a phone beside his bed, along with a typed list that carried the numbers of a few friends, the vet that looked after his various Irish terriers named Pat, his housekeeper at Kingsmere, and the newsroom of Canadian Press, among others.

King was also a dedicated correspondent and an enthusiastic user of the telephone. In fact, his diaries show this man, who lived all of his life as a bachelor and who has the modern reputation of a recluse, spending most of his waking hours communicating in person, in writing, or on the telephone. He worked very hard to ensure that no potential supporter or friend became estranged because of lack of contact.

He kept in constant contact with J.W. Dafoe, legendary editor of the *Winnipeg Free Press*, until Dafoe's death in 1944, and with the paper's Ottawa correspondent, Grant Dexter, with whom King seems to have developed a very strong and genuine friendship (at least from King's side). Very often, Dexter sat on important "scoops" to maintain his good relations with King. For instance, in a conversation that has intrigued conspiracy buffs for years, King told Dexter on November 7, 1941, that Franklin Roosevelt expected the Japanese to attack U.S. military installations in the Pacific within the next thirty days. King kept him informed of the low morale within the British government during the Blitz of 1940, the progress of U.K.–Canadian–U.S. negotiations regarding the possible transfer of the Royal Navy to U.S. control if Britain fell, and the real extent of the U-boat problem in the Gulf of St. Lawrence. King often called Dexter to give his candid, and often very negative, views on ministers in his own cabinet.

Admission into King's inner circle was not automatic. King

hated the Montreal *Gazette* and its Tory publisher, John Bassett. The paper carried an editorial in 1948 saying King was as "informative as a gagged clam." Some untested Ottawa correspondents, such as Charles Lynch, were told to submit questions to King's staff in advance. These could be answered with a list of King's speeches, which were offered as the definitive policy statements of the government.

The relationship between the *Globe and Mail*'s publisher George McCullagh and King was remarkable for the speed at which it developed and collapsed, generating a vicious hatred in both men. McCullagh's competitor at the *Toronto Star*, Atkinson, was a fierce prohibitionist who, in the early years of the century, was willing to support any party that opposed the liquor trade. For more than fifty years, Atkinson was King's closest media confidant. He knew King's parents when the PM was a young man, and the two men shared a desk when they were cub reporters at the *Globe* in 1896. The day in 1935 when King was re-elected prime minister, Elmina Atkinson, the wife of the *Star* publisher, placed a wreath on the grave of King's mother and father in Toronto's Mount Pleasant cemetery. Joseph Atkinson had a hand in picking the cabinet, and, in return, put the pages of the *Toronto Star* at King's disposal. The influential newspaperman could be sure that the Liberal platform reflected his views, because, since 1919, he had been chairman of the committee that drafted it.

Patriotic Canadian journalists hoping to stay home and aid the war by lending their pen or blue pencil to the effort found a welcoming government in Ottawa. Bureaucrats and politicians encouraged newspaper managers to volunteer for the Publishers Committee for War Finances, which publicized Victory Bond drives. Executives like Clifford Sifton, who controlled the *Winnipeg Free Press*, were brought to Ottawa as "dollar-a-year" men to advise on wartime economic management.

During the war, some senior journalists were drawn into secret work for the government, especially in the years before the United States' entry into the conflict. Bruce Hutchison, then a *Winnipeg Free Press* reporter in the Parliamentary Press Gallery, eagerly accepted two invitations to become a government agent. In the summer of 1940, as France, the Low Countries, and most of Scandinavia

sized up their new Nazi conquerors, Hutchison's bureau chief, Grant
Dexter, ordered Hutchison to break off his vacation in British Columbia and return to Ottawa as quickly as possible. Hutchison
caught a flight to Toronto, where a telegram from Dexter awaited
him, instructing him to hurry north to Barrie on a secret assignment. He paid a cab driver the then-hefty sum of $50 to drive to
Barrie where he found, parked in a siding, a lavish government-
chartered train carrying distinguished U.S. reporters. The train,
with two dining cars, gourmet food, and ample liquor, took the
journalists through Ontario, Quebec, and the Maritimes, ostensibly
to visit arms factories and military bases. Mostly, the trip was a well-
lubricated ride meant to develop the near-unbreakable "drinking
buddy" bond between the U.S. reporters and their Canadian hosts.
The Americans were friends and quiet allies, but the trip still had
elements of cloak and dagger. In Halifax, Dexter and Hutchison
were told to watch one U.S. reporter with alleged Nazi leanings. He
managed to elude them, board a ship, and return to the States.

That fall, Hutchison was given what was, at the time, a huge
bankroll of $5,000 by "a group of five leading Canadian newspapers"
to travel with the Wendell Willkie Republican presidential campaign and attempt to sway journalists he met on the tour. The money, and the idea, belonged to the Canadian government, Hutchison
believed. Willkie was an isolationist but Hutchison did not attempt
to lobby the candidate, who, he rightly believed, had little chance of
beating Franklin Roosevelt. Instead, Hutchison visited newspaper
editors in cities where Willkie's campaign train stopped to try to
influence them to press for U.S. entry into the war, or at least to support Britain's war effort. He finished the tour believing it was a waste
of money.

Of course, not all journalists got to be clandestine government
agents, but the wartime censorship system gave even the lowliest
journalist a taste of the delicious secrecy of official Ottawa. Every
editor and reporter with access to the numbered confidential circulars of the Directorate of Censorship knew some of the country's
war secrets. Every subscribing paper received the entire set. There
was no attempt to create separate handbooks for different parts of

the country, so an editor in Regina received the same naval secrets as a counterpart in Halifax. Nor was the size of the municipality or publication a bar to accessing those secrets: the staff of the twice-weekly newspaper in Midland, Ontario, received the same hand-book as the reporters and editors at the *Globe and Mail*.

Most of the secrets contained in the circulars were of little real value to the Axis, but the material was sensitive enough to give its holder a feeling of importance. Of course, not every war secret was printed in the circulars. Reporters would inevitably come across sensi-tive facts through the course of their work, adding to their personal inventory of war secrets. The Wartime Information Board, the fed-eral government's propaganda and polling agency, also shared se-crets with reporters. Journalists who stayed in Canada could easily believe they were instrumental in counter-intelligence work and in building civilian morale in what was, as General Dwight Eisenhower was to call it, the Great Crusade. Those who had doubts usually kept quiet. The legal, social, and economic penalties for English Canadi-ans who were labelled disloyal were extreme, and even when papers like the *Globe and Mail* criticized the King government's war effort, the negative material was always framed as constructive criticism, the paper's contribution to a better war effort.

But what of the Canadian public? Citizens knew their press was censored, along with their mail and telegrams, and government snoops listened in on long-distance phone calls. Yet people believed they were getting a fairly accurate view of the war and the home front. In mid-1944, as Canadian troops pushed deeper into France, a poll taken for the Wartime Information Board showed 62 per cent of Canadians outside Quebec believed they received accurate cover-age of the war (about 28 per cent felt otherwise). In Quebec, where the press was, for political reasons that are explained elsewhere in this book, pretty much free to write what it wanted, the numbers were practically reversed (30 to 57 per cent).

Still, press censorship got off to a very bad start. Walter Thomp-son was replaced early in 1940 when Maurice Pope, now promoted to colonel, returned to manage it while also serving as vice-chief of the defence staff and military advisor to Prime Minister King. On paper, this placed a soldier in charge of news management. Eggleston, in fact, ran the press censorship system. He took over the post of chief English-language press censor just as the Germans lunged at Denmark and Norway, then at the Low Countries and France. The public and the press were, Eggleston later wrote, "bordering on panic and hysteria." Keeping up morale was part of the censor's job, but Eggleston believed his real task was to weed out Nazi propaganda from Canada's newspapers. Most of it came north from New York, Chicago, and Detroit. There has always been a strong current of isolationism in the United States. Until Pearl Harbor, the Republicans in Congress, backed by far-right radio commentators and celebrities like Charles Lindbergh, kept up a steady drumbeat of anti-British propaganda. There were some people who were German agents, especially in Detroit, where civilian spies were later caught helping a German flyer who escaped from a POW camp in Ontario. Communists, who supported the Nazi-Soviet Pact of 1939, also generated reams of printed material in opposition to the British. The Canadian government reacted to the extreme left and right in America by banning their newspapers from crossing the border and hunting the mails for their propaganda. The government also ordered the closing of the Toronto-based leftist daily *Clarion*.

Until Pearl Harbor, nothing could keep out of Canada news coming in from big media in the United States; before that time the United States was a neutral country where the Axis powers maintained ambassadors, consuls, and propaganda agents. At least half the Canadian public could pick up a U.S. radio station during the day, and everyone could get them at night when the signals of the big 50,000-watt AM stations "skipped" off the ionosphere. "Trying to insulate Canada from the propaganda circulating in the United States" was, as Walter Thompson said, "like trying to heat a Canadian house in winter if it had only three walls." The government reacted by making empty threats to ban the *Saturday Evening Post*, the Hearst papers, and the isolationist *Chicago Tribune*. In the end, they closed the border to just one mainstream U.S. publication, *Scribner's Magazine*, and made the order after it had gone out of business.

The *Tribune*'s publisher, Colonel Robert McCormick, called

Canada "a spot where freedom of the press does not exist," a remark that the *Globe and Mail*, usually no friend of the censors, denounced as "totally irrelevant and untrue." The press in Canada, the *Globe* editorialized in a piece that undermined more than eighteen months of its own criticism of the censors, "has all the freedom it could desire or ever had, apart from the limitations imposed by the war. It is not even prevented from reproducing the diatribes in Colonel McCormick's paper which Canadians deeply resent."

The entry of the United States into the war solved several of the problems faced by Canadian press censors. Mainstream isolationism quickly collapsed as a political force. The FBI and U.S. censors put an end to the Nazi propaganda circulating in the country and shut down pro-Nazi and pro-Communist publications. A continental press and cable censorship system was created by Canadians and Americans working together to keep information from the Germans, with the Americans adopting a censorship system almost identical to Canada's. In early January 1942, Eggleston and Charpentier travelled to Washington, D.C., to meet their U.S. counterparts to discuss ways of sharing information and policies, and, through the war, officials from the two countries were in touch daily by telephone and teletype.

The relationship was sometimes strained when Americans did not take Canadians seriously, even in Canada. The Far North was to be the battleground between Canadian censors and the U.S. military: the United States paid the bills for the construction of the Alaska Highway and the Canol Pipeline that ran alongside it. American planes were hopping through the secret Northwest Staging Route to the Soviet Union. Canada's North was an American war theatre, so U.S. officers called the shots. The Americans snubbed the Canadian censors time after time, giving U.S. media preferential treatment on stories about the war effort in the subarctic.

The shakeup of the censorship bureaucracy at the beginning of 1940 did not solve its problems. Eggleston's new boss, Brigadier Maurice Pope, was a great planner but a poor manager. He loaded his subordinates with work but was unwilling to delegate official responsibility over the system, even during the long periods when he was in London and Washington on military business. For more than two years, the censorship system drifted as Pope, a key planner at National Defence Headquarters and, after 1942, Ottawa's chief military liaison officer with the Americans, flitted from one war problem to another. Spurred on by the Americans after Pearl Harbor, Canada's intelligence leaders wanted tighter censorship, so, on May 4, 1942, King announced the reorganization of the press, radio, mail, phone, and telegraph censorship system.

Oliver Mowat Biggar was a logical replacement for Maurice Pope. Born in Toronto in 1876, he was the eldest grandson of Sir Oliver Mowat, one of the drafters of the 1864 Quebec Resolutions and later the Liberal premier of Ontario. The senior Mowat was a brilliant lawyer whose provincial-rights cases at the Judicial Committee of the Privy Council redefined the political balance between the national and provincial governments. His namesake was an Ottawa man with tremendous influence in Mackenzie King's capital.

Biggar trained as a lawyer at Toronto's Osgoode Hall, and then set up a practice in Edmonton, Alberta. At the outbreak of World War One, he joined the army, was commissioned, and soon afterwards became deputy judge advocate general in Calgary. By 1918, he was judge advocate general of Canada and a full colonel. He met King at this time, and, by 1919, King was an overnight visitor at Biggar's summer cottage.

Biggar was a member of the Canadian delegation at the Paris Peace Conference of 1918–19, and then became Canada's first chief electoral officer. In 1927, he left the public service to start the Ottawa intellectual property law firm Smart and Biggar (which still exists). In 1938, he argued the province's side in the *Alberta Press Act Reference* to the Supreme Court of Canada. He was also very socially active. During the late 1920s and the Depression years, Biggar grew his network of friends and contacts in the senior ranks of the bureaucracy. Norman Robertson, the mandarin in charge of King's external affairs ministry, was one of Biggar's best friends.

King announced the restructuring of the censorship administration and the creation of the Office of the Director of Censorship a week after the 1942 conscription plebiscite that saw the country split on French–English linguistic lines over the military draft. On

September 9, 1942, the government replaced its propaganda arm, the Bureau of Public Information, with the more effective Wartime Information Board (WIB). Control of press censorship passed from the secretary of state to the minister of war services. Soldiers, especially the leaders of Canada's small intelligence services, would have a greater say in censorship.

Biggar held the job of director of censorship until the summer of 1944, when he suffered a heart attack. Perhaps his health failed because of the pressure of his work: he kept several other wartime committee jobs while he ran the censorship system. Once Biggar's restructuring of the Directorate of Censorship was complete, power over censorship of the press was concentrated in the hands of Eggleston, and to a lesser extent Ottawa-based censor Warren Baldwin and chief French-language press censor Fulgence Charpentier.

Eggleston took over the position of director of censorship in August 1944. This was a huge job compared to his position of press censor. He was responsible for about 1,000 employees, mostly mail-openers in postal censorship. He was still chief English-language press censor and much of his daily routine focused on that aspect of the job. Eggleston stayed through the tumultuous weeks in the fall of 1944 when conscripts rioted in British Columbia and the censorship system was nearly taken over by the military. In the early winter of 1945, Eggleston resigned, leaving English-language press censorship in the hands of his assistant, Warren Baldwin. Charpentier, the new director of censorship, worked with Baldwin through 1945 to deal with reporters' postwar "now it can be told" stories, wind up the head office, and write the secret official final report given to the government and military at the end of the war.

The one-man Halifax office was responsible for censoring all the news from the Maritimes and sometimes the Gaspé Peninsula. The two full-time Montreal censors were given the daunting task of monitoring and advising the newspapers in Quebec, where much of the press, in both languages, was hostile to them. The Ottawa office was in charge of the copy from the Parliamentary Press Gallery, and vetted news printed in the three daily papers in Ottawa, the *Kingston Whig-Standard*, and the smaller papers in eastern Ontario. Toronto censors handled the city's three big dailies, the large Canadian Press newsroom, the magazines headquartered in Toronto, book publishers, and the print media in the rest of Ontario. The area covered by the Vancouver censors was huge: everything west of the Ontario–Manitoba boundary including the northern territories, although a part-time censorship office was later established in Edmonton to deal with news about the Alaska Highway projects.

Censorship orders and directives, sent by letter, or, in urgent cases, by telegram, were the reporters' and editors' primary guide. They were issued throughout the war and dealt with issues such as the British Commonwealth Air Training Plan; casualties in the armed forces; military and civil aviation; gold movements; escapes of Allied POWs and political refugees from enemy territory; shipping information and naval operations; war industries, shipbuilding, and secret war equipment; weather; and arrests of spies, internment, enemy aliens, and sabotage operations.

Canadian censors also had to deal with tricky issues of racism directed at African-American soldiers, some of whom were deployed on guard duty at U.S. installations in Canada. In March 1942, the *Sault Ste. Marie Star* submitted a story on "negro" soldiers in the United States Army defending the Canadian side of the St. Mary's River and its strategically important Soo Locks (St. Mary's Falls Ship Canal). Baldwin asked the paper to spike the story, believing, with some accuracy, the U.S. censors would oppose its publication. The following summer, Ontario premier Mitchell Hepburn, who, despite being a Liberal, hated King and hoped to embarrass him by showing Canada's forces were too weak to protect Ontario military installations from saboteurs, told a civic dinner in Fort William, Ontario, about the black troops. "We ought to hang our heads in shame," Hepburn told his audience. This time, Ottawa-based censor Jacques Girouard passed a story, saying it did not matter to the enemy what colour the soldiers were that guarded the canal. "The fact that Hepburn was using it as a political attack was taken into consideration in passing the item," Girouard wrote.

Most Canadian journalists reacted to censorship by playing dead. Canadian Press general manager Gil Purcell later wrote that many journalists simply abandoned inquisitive journalism. Censorship was easy to blame for the mediocrity of the news pages of major Canadian newspapers. The censors realized this was happening. "This was the danger point when freedom of speech hung in the balance," Purcell wrote after the war. "This was the time when the censors, knowing facts the press could not know, pressed hardest for the rights of the people against the conservative nature of bureaucracy." The censors found themselves in the odd position of fighting the military for the release of information to newspapers that didn't seem to care whether or not they got it. The mainstream press supported the government when it suppressed the ethnic, Communist, and extreme-right press at the outbreak of the war and then closed three Japanese-Canadian newspapers in the weeks after Pearl Harbor.

Prosecutions under the censorship laws were very rare. The *Ottawa Citizen* was acquitted of charges laid under the *Defence of Canada Regulations* in 1940 when its editor, Charles Bowman, proved the information in his paper's description of asdic submarine detection technology (a type of sonar) had been in the public domain long before the outbreak of the war. Bowman's piece was hardly subversive: the editor wrote it after a chat about technology with the governor general, Lord Tweedsmuir. Despite Eggleston's advice to ignore the *Citizen* editorial, naval intelligence pressed for a prosecution. It was, the censors believed, one of the low points of their wartime work.

In April 1941, the *Ottawa Citizen* was prosecuted for publication of an editorial attacking the King government over war profiteering. The government was pressured into laying charges by M.J. Coldwell, a vocal MP in the leftist Co-operative Commonwealth Federation (CCF), who claimed the RCMP was wasting its time shutting down small extremist newspapers and hunting Communists when there were powerful people in Canada who despised liberty more than they feared fascism. "When our mounted police turn their eyes to seek those who sympathize with the dictators, let them look above the gutter and the beer parlor, then perhaps they will find where the real danger to our democratic institutions lies," Coldwell said in the House of Commons. The *Citizen* was quickly acquitted by Ottawa provincial magistrate Glen Strike on the grounds that it merely intended in good faith to point out defects in the government.

In March 1942, the *Vancouver Sun* assigned Alan Morley to write a series of articles about the supposed weakness of the defences around Canada's Pacific Coast cities. The third article, "The Derelict Defences," was submitted to Vancouver censor Lew Gordon, who heavily edited it. The next day, after being told by Eggleston to take a hard line on Morley's series, Gordon stamped "Not for Publication" on the fourth story, an exposé on the lack of naval guns around Vancouver. The *Sun* ran the piece anyway. Eggleston tried to talk Minister of National Defence J.L. Ralston out of laying charges but the government went ahead with its prosecution. On April 21, 1942, the newspaper pleaded guilty to two of the five counts filed under Section 16 of the *Defence of Canada Regulations* and was fined the modest sum of $300. Later, when the government did spend some money fixing the defences of Vancouver, the paper printed an editorial asking for its money back.

At almost the same time, the Department of Justice launched a prosecution against the Ottawa French-language newspaper *Le Droit* for a March 4, 1942, article condemning the British bombing of the Renault plant at Billancourt, near Paris. The story, carried under a six-column headline, said "workers' children at the Renault plant used to come in the morning and play along the river. This morning they do not play anymore; they are at the morgue of Courbevoie . . . they are dead." The censors were angry that the story came from Vichy France's news service. *Le Droit* was fined $200.

In December 1944, Quebec City's *Le Soleil* broke a naval news blackout on the sinking by a U-boat of the Canadian National steamship *Cornwallis* off the coast of Maine. The paper eventually pleaded guilty to a charge of violating Section 16 of the *Regulations* and was fined $50.

Just one journalist faced charges under the censorship laws. Ed Rohrbough, a U.S. citizen working as a freelancer for *Time* magazine and the *Toronto Star*, was convicted for mailing a story to *Time* about the POW riot at Bowmanville, Ontario, on Thanksgiving weekend in 1942. He was given a one-year jail sentence, which was suspended.

More often, journalists received verbal and written reprimands. Among the more spectacular was Vancouver censor Lew Gordon's face-to-face vituperation of *Vancouver Sun* columnist Don Mason, who, while drunk, wrote a column about a burial at sea on a Canadian naval ship. Written rebukes were often sent to newspapers. For example, the *Globe and Mail* was reprimanded for a February 26, 1941, story that described medical research being done by Sir Frederick Banting on a device to prevent pilot blackout, which was accurately described in the article as one of Canada's main war secrets.

Often, personal diplomacy was an effective way of dealing with disputes, especially those involving some of the "characters" who ran small newspapers in rural Canada, people like J. Herbert Cranston, editor and publisher of the *Midland Free Press Herald*, who had been Eggleston's boss at the *Toronto Star*. Cranston, in his many fights with the censors, got away with blaming his women staffers for spilling secrets about his town's shipyards. This sympathy for small-town journalists was shared by Halifax censor H. Bruce "Jeff" Jefferson, who protected the *Sydney Steelworker and Miner*, a leftist newspaper run on a shoestring by an elderly labour activist. The Sydney paper ran a tagline across the top of the front page: "The Press Is as Free as a Caged Canary—And As Yellow. Workers of the world unite! You have nothing to lose but your chains; you have a world to gain—MARX."

Radio journalists also didn't put up much of a fight. Canada's broadcast landscape was far different from today and an empty vessel compared to the big American radio networks that had correspondents in every major wartime capital, and whose work could be picked up by most Canadians. Private broadcasters were scarce and their news broadcasts were simply rewrites of stories from local papers. The CBC, which was by far the most important radio network in the country, carried the BBC news every night at 6:45, even on its new French network. The rest of its news was clipped from the newspapers or came from Canadian Press. The CBC had no news reporters until it began hiring print journalists to go overseas with mobile broadcast units, where some of them performed spectacularly, even though they were at the tender mercies of Britain's tough military censorship, which examined recordings before they were shipped to Canada. Radio censorship was in the hands of R.P. Landry, the CBC's corporate secretary, who was officially seconded to the Directorate of Censorship. Each CBC station manager was made a local radio censor. All broadcasts in languages other than French and English were banned. The CBC carried about forty-five hours of "talks" each week, short lectures and homespun editorials by some of the country's leading print journalists, politicians, academics, and other people in the news. The talks had to be drafted well in advance and their scripts were given to CBC managers, and, in the case of the 1939 Quebec election, to specially appointed radio censors. No deviation from scripts was allowed. King's government did not need to worry about the CBC's talks, since the network showed a strong bias in its choice of speakers, excluding, whenever possible, Canadians who might criticize Ottawa's war policy. Still, the CBC was to hear criticism throughout the war for its inconsistent censorship on relatively unimportant issues, including, in 1944, accusations by Halifax press censor Bruce Jefferson that the popular radio program *The Happy Gang* engaged in loose talk by mentioning the names of Canadian military units deployed abroad.

Radio stations were sent a list of "don'ts"—specific information that was banned from broadcast. The list included ship movements, escapes of German POWs held in Canada or Canadians who had escaped from Axis detention, and most stories that mentioned the names of Canadian casualties. Radio reporters couldn't talk about political arrests or internments, or U.S. military activity in Canada, or give weather reports. They were also forbidden to broadcast listeners' musical requests or greetings requested by telephone in case the songs were codes for enemy secret agents.

Movies shown in Canada had always been under tight provincial censorship. Before Pearl Harbor, or U.S. newspapers, magazines, and radio commentators were divided between policies of isolationism and support for the Allies. Hollywood was not. The big studios, many of them managed by Jewish executives who abhorred Hitler, supported U.S. intervention. If Hollywood had come out with a pro-Nazi film, the provincial censors, who normally looked for smut, were empowered to screen it and pass their recommendations to the federal censors. Pre–Pearl Harbor, newsreels from the States were slightly more vexing to the censors, as they sometimes contained material shot by German military film units. On May 10, 1940, as the German army sliced into France, the provincial smut cops were deputized as news censors.

The censors were more concerned with the newsreels that were shown in theatres—often along with Hollywood-produced propaganda cartoons—before the feature attraction. These were mixed in with short propaganda films, many of them made by the Canadian government's National Film Board (NFB). The NFB's producers sometimes ignored Canadian and U.S. censorship rules. In late 1942, the NFB's film *Battle for Oil* was criticized by U.S. censors for showing scenes of oil-covered sailors from tankers sunk by U-boats being pulled into lifeboats and rescue ships.

On paper, the censorship system had enormous power. In reality, it acted as shepherd to Canadian media that were usually all too willing to play the role of sheep. It was impossible for a small group of people to protect every military secret and police the newsrooms for stories that might convince young men not to enlist or undermine our relations with Britain and the United States.

CHAPTER 2

Censorship and Military Intelligence

PRESS CENSORSHIP IS A WAY of manipulating public information, but it's also a type of counter-intelligence. Enemy agents did monitor the media to mine it for "open-source" material: military stories; the latest on scientific research; statistics on war production; news about public attitudes. On a second front, the enemy tried to seed the media with propaganda that undermined military and civilian morale.

All three branches of the military intelligence took a professional interest in censorship, but the Royal Canadian Navy was obsessed with it. The intelligence agents in the navy believed the Germans pored over Canadian newspapers and monitored Canadian radio stations looking for news about U-boat attacks on the Atlantic and in the Gulf of St. Lawrence. If Canada's admirals had their way, no news of the Battle of the Atlantic, the St. Lawrence U-boat attacks, or the accounts of the capture of Werner von Janowski, the Nazi spy picked up in 1942 in the Gaspé, would have been published.

The army also put pressure on the censors. The generals worried about the reporting of troop movements across Canada. The Germans could use that information to sink one of the big Cunard liners after it left Halifax and use news of troop buildups to piece together Allied plans for the invasion of Europe. To hide the fact that soldiers were leaving the country in the fall of 1939, the censors ordered photographers to literally remove tears from the cheeks of wives, girlfriends, and mothers of Canadian soldiers at send-off events. When they submitted photos of a send-off event in Toronto, censors told the papers to airbrush the tears.

The Royal Canadian Air Force, which operated bases across the country to train Allied fliers, hunted subs along the East Coast, and chased Japanese balloon bombs in British Columbia and the Prairies, demanded the censors keep a lid on stories about the hundreds of plane crashes, badly aimed practice bombs, and reckless flying incidents across the country.

Domestic intelligence agents working for the military and the RCMP wanted to know if there were ties between the Quebec nationalist press and France's post-conquest Vichy regime, which was rightly seen as a puppet of the Nazis. The censors were able to prove that there were links. They also kept track of journalists visiting Canada from neutral countries and advised military intelligence agents and the Department of External Affairs on the background and credibility of some Canadian reporters and editors.

Censors worked hard to develop good relations with intelligence officers. Most of the time, they failed in this regard. The military had its own ideas about press control and had strong influence in the committees that set press censorship policies. When the military tried to interfere with their work, the censors negotiated with intelligence officers to determine if security risks were the real reason that the military wanted a story killed. If there was no serious threat to the war effort, the censors officially advised the media against publication but at the same time unofficially admitted that charges were very unlikely. Most media took the hint and published the disputed material.

Military intelligence officers, believing the press was sloppy with secrets, decided to visit press conventions and newsrooms and seemed surprised to find Canadian newspaper owners and their staffs were "imbued with a spirit of lofty patriotism." Still, by publishing rumour and by getting local angles on speculative stories from the United States, Canadian newspapers and magazines had printed material "that ought never to have been divulged," facts of "great importance to the enemy." This included, during the mid-Atlantic wolf-pack convoy slaughters of 1942, publishing and broadcasting news of fake distress calls from ships in the Atlantic, a ploy used by the Germans to gather information on Allied shipping (and, presumably, to attract rescue ships to waiting U-boats). Canadian reporters had already helped the U-boat captains by publishing details of the departures of ocean liners and mentioning that some of these ships carried both troops and civilian passengers. This gave the enemy, according to a senior naval intelligence agent, "a priceless argument why German submarines should attack ALL liners." He said the September 1940 sinking of the *City of Benares*, with the loss of dozens of child evacuees from Britain, was a typical result of that kind of story.

Still, more than fifty years after the end of World War Two, Fulgence Charpentier, the last chief of the Directorate of Censorship, said the military needed to clean up its own house before attacking censors and the media. He said in 1997, "The biggest problem was with people in the army. They just talked all the time. I remember having to pull people away at a party and tell army officers 'don't say that.'"

While Maurice Pope had pre-war ties to military intelligence from his years as a war planner, strong official links were not established between the censorship system and the country's top spies until May 21, 1942, when O.M. Biggar called the first meeting of the Censorship Committee on Intelligence and Security. It was a cumbersome group, probably too large to keep secrets or deal effectively with policy, with about thirty members drawn from the various censorship departments; External Affairs; the Wartime Information Board; the NFB; the directorates of intelligence of the navy, army, and air force; the Department of Munitions and Supply; the RCMP; and liaison officers with British and U.S. censorship. The group met in the Supreme Court of Canada building. Its size was not the committee's only structural problem. Membership was extremely fluid, with the armed forces, the U.S. legation, and the British often changing the people sent to fill their chairs. Meetings were sporadic, sometimes once a week but usually about twice a month.

The committee dealt with issues that arose in press, broadcast, cable, and mail censorship, along with control of foreign travel, secret government documents, and the word-of-mouth spreading of news, especially by merchant sailors in Halifax and members of the armed forces everywhere.

Other government departments shared information important to the domestic front on issues such as food production, rationing, and price controls, but the military rarely gave the censors any advance warning of plans or events that were bound to cause a flurry of press inquiries. The censors had at their fingertips figures on the production of parsnips in Canada that they received from the Department of Agriculture, but the army was so secretive that the censors learned of the invasion of Sicily from U.S. radio stations while their office phones rang with calls from journalists wanting to know what they could report.

Eggleston made his case for more openness in an August 13, 1941, memorandum to Captain T.A. Stone, head of External Affairs' intelligence section. Eggleston explained the censors were placed in an often awkward situation where they had to balance issues of morale and national security. The latter was something in which the censors had more than a "detached academic interest." In fact, wrote Eggleston, the censors' main duty was to interpret the clauses of the *Defence of Canada Regulations* that spoke of somewhat vague concepts such as "information of use to the enemy." What was information of use to the enemy? Eggleston often asked himself. By some definitions, virtually no newspapers should have circulated. Nor, in fact, should *Hansard*, the record of the debates of the House of Commons, have been read widely. The Bank of Canada should have stopped giving out its economic analysis, and censors would have had to block some governmental units, such as the Department of Munitions and Supply, from publishing contract-tendering information.

Eggleston could see the military justification for the blackout of news of convoy sailings from Halifax, but could not support the government's attempt to suppress stories of the four-day strike at the aluminum smelters in Arvida, Quebec, in July 1941. A public airing of the dispute might have opened a communication channel between management and the workers, exposed real grievances, and led to a quicker settlement, he argued. In the end, all bad news had to be weighed to determine whether publishing the stories or suppressing them would be the more beneficial to the war effort. It was an interesting stand for a press censor.

The censors also faced off against military intelligence officers at the Advisory Committee on Publication of Military Information, which met fourteen times between April 16, 1943, and August 9, 1944. The meetings were chaired by Biggar or A.D. (Davidson) Dunton, general manager of the Wartime Information Board, the government's propaganda and polling agency. (A former editor of the *Montreal Standard*, Dunton would later become chair of the CBC and co-chair of the Royal Commission on Bilingualism and Biculturalism.) This committee was in charge of maintaining news blackouts about Canadian and Allied military bases in Canada, including the top-secret Camp X, the British spy-and-commando training base near Oshawa, Ontario. It dealt with the sensitive issue of reporting about U.S. bases in Canada and New-foundland. It was also the battleground between Lieutenant Commander C.H. Little, head of naval intelligence, and Eggleston over censorship of news of submarine attacks in the St. Lawrence River in October 1943.

At this committee, Colonel W.W. Murray and Lieutenant Colonel Eric Acland of army intelligence pressed for a tightening of a loophole in the censorship rules that war correspondent Ross Munro had used to report the names of the Canadian units that fought at Dieppe. (Because Munro had already been allowed to name them while covering training exercises in England, their presence could no longer be considered a secret.) External Affairs had its own objective: the suppression of photos of air raid damage to German cities, which the department's intelligence chief, T.A. Stone, worried would turn Canadians against the carpet bombing of civilian targets. He wanted the *Winnipeg Free Press* punished for running two photos on April 15, 1944—one showing the devastated Potsdamerplatz section of Berlin and another the ruined Charlottenburg Opera House. The censors would not ban the pictures or recommend charges against the paper.

It is difficult to know how much of a real role any type of

censorship played in counter-intelligence. Direct German intelligence gathering in Canada seems to have been, at best, weak, possibly a reflection of the disorganization within Germany's foreign intelligence agencies. Before December 1941, German consuls in the United States clipped Canadian papers, and it is possible that fascist Spain and Portugal's envoys in Canada did the same through the entire war, but the Canadian counter-espionage community could never prove there were Nazi spy rings in the country.

Vichy France, the puppet regime set up by the Nazis, was a real intelligence problem. Canada was put in an awkward diplomatic situation by Winston Churchill, who used Canada's chargé d'affaires in Vichy, lawyer Pierre Dupuy, as both a window into occupied France and an errand boy. (A quarter century later, Dupuy would be commissioner general of Expo 67 after serving as Canada's ambassador to France.) There's serious doubt that Dupuy's three visits to Vichy were of any real use to Churchill, and his work was undoubtedly worthless to Canada. Although it had no pressing need for contact with Vichy, Canada continued to honour Churchill's request to recognize the collaborationist regime of Marshal Pétain, headquartered in the old resort city of Vichy, until November 1942, when the Germans occupied the southern part of France. Britain had broken off relations with Vichy in July 1940, seizing French ships and other assets wherever possible and attacking the main French fleet at Mers el-Kébir, near Oran in Algeria, killing about 1,200 French sailors. The British raid touched off an undeclared war between the British and Vichy and between Gaullist and Pétainist forces that eventually spread to Gibraltar, Syria, Iraq, West Africa, and Madagascar, and, in several ways, to Canada. In return for providing Churchill with a courier to Vichy, Canadians had to tolerate Vichy's diplomats on their home soil. These operatives set out to sabotage Canada's war effort.

France's ambassador to Canada, Réné Ristelhueber, stayed in Ottawa after Pétain established his collaborationist regime. Ristelhueber was a man of dubious politics and questionable loyalties who managed to charm Mackenzie King. Under Pétain, he followed the Vichy government's anti-Semitic policies and ordered a purge of

Jews employed in French diplomatic missions in Canada. On October 22, 1940, Undersecretary of State for External Affairs O.D. Skelton asked Ristelhueber to promise that Vichy's diplomats in Canada would not send any information to France on Canadian shipping. Despite Skelton's request, Ristelhueber decided to leave Consul Auguste Tambon in Halifax, a place that should have been of little interest to a country that had, at the time, no maritime trade with Canada, but might have been of some importance to the Vichy diplomats in New York who were transmitting Allied shipping information to the Nazis.

Canada's military intelligence agents knew Vichy's diplomats were working hard to turn Quebec public opinion against the war by distributing collaborationist propaganda to the French-language press. Vichy's diplomats' telephones were bugged and their mail was steamed open, but they still had use of diplomatic pouches and couriers to carry their most secret mail to New York, then by Pan American Clipper to Axis-friendly Spain and on to France. Ristelhueber's cipher privileges were withdrawn by the federal government in 1941 after he was caught sending a cable boasting about his success promoting the work of pro-Vichy Canadian authors. Henri Coursier, Vichy's consul in Montreal, was also busy, making "sizeable" contributions to anti-conscription groups in Quebec. And, as explained later in the chapter on censorship and the press in Quebec, Vichy encouraged the nationalist press to publish pro-Axis articles, including material sent directly from Vichy's propaganda department.

Despite the activities of Vichy's agents in Quebec, Ristelhueber was given asylum in Canada when Ottawa ended diplomatic relations with Vichy. Prime Minister King made the offer to Ristelhueber in a tearful scene in King's office in November 1942, when the Vichy diplomat bawled to King that he hadn't really wanted to pit English and French Canadians against each other, he was just following orders. Ristelhueber joined the faculty of the Université de Montréal, where he had a distinguished career as a sociologist studying postwar population movements.

The French-owned islands of St. Pierre and Miquelon off the

west coast of Newfoundland came under Vichy control after the fall of France. The islands posed both an intelligence and a political problem until Christmas 1941, when they were seized by Charles de Gaulle's Free French forces. Although far from mainland France, the people of these islands had a strong attachment to their motherland. Despite their patriotism, the people of the two islands had always lived on the edge of legality. For much of their history, smuggling has been almost as important as—and during Prohibition, much more so than—its fishery, which was usually its largest employer. About 400 men from the colony served in the French military in World War One, with an appalling 25 per cent fatal casualty rate. In World War Two, 500 men served and 27 died. These enlistments were drawn, without conscription, from a population of fewer than 5,000.

After the British attack on the French fleet at Oran (Mers el-Kébir), Algeria, on July 3, 1940, public opinion in St. Pierre split into pro-Vichy and pro–Free French camps. Most of the war veterans and sailors from metropolitan France who lived in the colony when Paris fell opposed the 1940 armistice with the Nazis and supported de Gaulle. The administrator of the colony, Count Gilbert de Bournat (and his Alsatian-German wife Suzanne), most of the civil servants, and the more prosperous merchants in the town of St. Pierre sided with Vichy.

Local war veterans pushed for a referendum on maintaining links to Vichy or going over to the Free French. In 1941, men from St. Pierre brawled with sailors on a Vichy warship because the vessel trained its guns on a low-flying Canadian airplane, sparking an open split between the two French factions. In an attempt to quell the anger in the colony, de Bournat held public meetings and tried to create a split in the veterans' group. Many of the young men of the colony voted with their feet, quietly leaving the islands to join the Free French. Some who stayed behind began a leaflet war with the Vichyite colonial elite. The Free French faction in the town of St. Pierre demanded that Canada, which handled the islands' mail, censor all of the French newspapers that came into the colony to remove pro-Vichy propaganda.

Canadian signals intelligence officers were worried because

they knew it was very likely that French authorities in St. Pierre and Miquelon transmitted shipping information obtained locally and from the regime's diplomats in Canada to France, which forwarded it to the Germans. The Allies were also worried about fascist taps on a major transatlantic telephone and telegraph cable that ran through the islands. From May 26 to June 11, RCMP inspector Oscar LaRivière visited St. Pierre and Miquelon with permission from Ristelhueber and the local administration, ostensibly to check on liquor smuggling. Instead, he found a powerful shortwave transmitter.

The RCMP commissioner, T.S. Wood, wanted the islands seized and the transmitter shut down. The King government's more cautious reaction, on August 19, 1941, was to open a consular office on the islands. Christopher Eberts, the Canadian diplomat sent to St. Pierre, could not find out what was happening at the transmission station. On December 1, 1941, Norman Robertson of External Affairs proposed to the War Committee of cabinet that Canada dispatch the ubiquitous External Affairs intelligence chief T.A. Stone, an expert in signals intelligence, along with military censors, to the island in a corvette (a small patrol and convoy escort ship) to analyze the equipment to determine what it was being used for.

Prime Minister King, who had not been briefed on the plan to send Stone, reacted in horror when he found out and killed it out of fear of angering the United States—which had a deal with Vichy that allowed the regime to keep its colonies in the western hemisphere—and generating a backlash from Vichyists in Quebec. Instead, he wanted to press Vichy to "invite" Stone to take control of the transmitter. Through the fall, King and Robertson argued over whether to use force if de Bournat rejected Stone and his censors. Robertson favoured backing Stone's mission with naval power, while King believed the Canadian seizure of the Vichy colony could give Pétain an excuse to turn the remnants of the French navy, now headquartered at Toulon in the south of France, over to the Germans.

In the third week of December, in what Halifax press censor Bruce Jefferson called a "Gilbertian expedition," a Free French force left Halifax on the giant monitor submarine the *Surcouf*, bound for the islands. Jefferson knew the submarine was leaving, and he snapped several pictures of it for his collection. On Christmas Eve, Free French Vice-Admiral E.H. Muselier seized the town of St. Pierre and fired de Bournat, along with the rest of the Vichy administration. The United States—with the Pearl Harbor attacks still raw—suspected Canadian complicity and, on December 26, Secretary of State Cordell Hull issued a press release saying Canada should restore the status quo in the colony. Canada did nothing, although de Gaulle was taken off the External Affairs Christmas card list.

Upon his arrival in St. Pierre, Muselier seized the records of the transmitter and found, he said, evidence that the authorities in the colony were sending "very secret" information to France in codes that could be read by the Germans and Italians. Strangely, Vichy diplomats in Canada continued to transmit ciphered messages from Ottawa to St. Pierre. Canadian code breakers were unable to read them, but Sir Desmond Morton, Churchill's personal assistant, later said the transmitter was "one of the chief means whereby the Vichy and German Governments were able rapidly to communicate instructions in cipher to their agents and supporters in the Western Hemisphere, and to receive secret information in return."

With Muselier's attack, the obscure islands suddenly became news. The *Toronto Star* tried to hire Etienne Daguerre, the manager of the St. Pierre branch of Toronto-based Tip Top Tailors clothing stores, to file a 1,000-word story but Daguerre did not deliver. The *Toronto Telegram* was luckier, finding a freelancer on the island who sent daily stories to Toronto for about a week. The Canadian Press office in Halifax was tipped off by the Free French to the timing of the raid and carried bulletins of the takeover while it was happening. On Christmas Day, Andy Merkel, Canadian Press's manager in Halifax, called Ottawa-based censor Warren Baldwin to ask him to clear news stories submitted from St. Pierre. Charpentier, listening to Montreal AM radio, learned of the takeover and was shocked to hear commentary that the occupation "would throw the Vichy Government into the hands of the Nazis," which, as the day progressed, turned out to be Washington's official line. The following day, the British United Press (BUP) submitted a story to Baldwin suggesting the Canadian government "was really chuckling up its sleeves" (i.e., secretly happy with the way events unfolded), which Baldwin believed "is probably the case" but Baldwin told BUP to take those inferences out of its story.

A packet of photos of the takeover arrived in Halifax on December 27. The new Free French regime in St. Pierre asked the Canadian censors to clear the photos before giving them to Canadian Press, which, in turn, was supposed to put them on the Associated Press wire. Someone in St. Pierre had packed them poorly, causing the emulsion to smear on some of the pictures. Jefferson, who had his own darkroom, cleaned them up as well as he could and took them to the Canadian Press news service office, where he gave the staff advice on how to use their new photo wire machine. Through the rest of the evening, Jefferson followed the progress of the wire photos by reading cable censor intercepts.

While the Canadian Press wire service knew of de Gaulle's plans, the capture of the French colony in the Gulf of St. Lawrence took Jefferson, Charpentier, and the rest of the press censors by surprise. If the Canadian military or intelligence experts in External Affairs knew of the Free French plan, they did not let the press censors in on it. This was standard practice during the war. The intelligence chiefs in the military treated the censors with contempt. The chief press censor's day often began with at least one nasty phone call from an intelligence officer complaining about what he'd read in that morning's paper, and the irate calls kept coming through the day. On May 6, 1942, the day's hostilities began with a call from Eric Brand, the navy's liaison with the censors, complaining about a story in the British press based on an interview with Canadian Lieutenant Commander T.P. (Two-Gun) Ryan that Canadians were operating a captured Nazi submarine in the western Atlantic Ocean. Brand threatened to write "another letter" to the Canadian secretary of state asking for "a complete overhaul of Press Censorship so far as naval information is concerned." Moments later, Brand admitted he knew very little about the story. Ottawa censor Jacques Girouard tracked the story down to the *Victoria Daily Times*, which had published the piece without vetting it with the censors. The *Daily Times* had been given the story by a senior Canadian naval officer who,

Girouard told Brand, could reasonably be expected to be a credible source.

Brand went into another rage and demanded the censors go after the Victoria newspaper. The censors turned him down, telling Brand to take his anger out on his own men rather than the censors and the press. Girouard told Brand the *Daily Times* was a responsible paper that was not careless with secrets. Brand was not satisfied. He demanded prepublication censorship of all naval news items, but Girouard told Brand the newspapers should be able to trust information given to them by senior officers in the navy. That round went to the censors.

At the army's request, the censors banned almost all reporting on Axis POWs held in the prison camps scattered across Canada. They also tried to block any reporting of news from voice broadcasts of Canadians held as POWs in Japanese-controlled areas. The censors believed the Japanese faked some of the POW broadcasts, using Canadian or U.S. collaborators, or recorded the voices of prisoners and broadcast them months later, even if the prisoners were dead. Journalists were also warned not to report the contents of Japanese propaganda broadcasts, which provided intriguing listening for many people along the Pacific coast. The censors also prevented reporting of Allied forces' killing of Japanese prisoners. For instance, on October 5, 1944, the *Toronto Star* submitted a story based on an interview with Signalman R.A. Duthie, a Torontonian serving with U.S. forces in the Pacific. The censors cut the following: "'Prisoners,' he said. 'Yes, we take some but the Aussies don't. We have a good many prisoner of war camps but the Aussies don't need camps because they don't bother with prisoners—and the Japs know it.'"

In June 1942, when the British government hunted the newsrooms of *La Presse* and other Montreal newspapers—outside of *Le Devoir*—looking for French-speaking spies to work in the French colonies in Africa, the censors stopped news stories on the recruitment drive. The censors lost one of their own to Britain's MI6: Willie Chevalier, a *Le Canada* reporter who worked part-time for Eggleston. Newspapers in Quebec printed stories saying the journalists were going to work for the Free French, an error the censors did nothing to correct. Charpentier recommended four other young men for the spy work, including his 18-year-old son Georges, who had just completed his bachelor's degree.

Censors also snuffed out stories of British spies working in occupied Europe. In January 1945, Bert Perry, the Toronto censor, suppressed what he called a "perfectly delightful" CBC story about British actor David Niven, who turned his acting talents to espionage. Journalist Nancy Anderson, who interviewed Niven in Toronto, learned he had travelled to the German-occupied Channel Islands and, disguised as a local, chatted up German officers and civilians about the strength of the local garrison. Anderson planned a story that would have left out Niven's name but Perry spiked the piece out of concern for the residents of the islands, which stayed under German control until VE day. Anderson agreed to hold the script for the duration of the war.

When the Germans attacked the Soviet Union on June 22, 1941, the censors faced a new challenge: dealing with Russian reporters posted to Canada. Quite rightly, the Canadian government believed they were spies and tried to screen their copy. In September 1942, Nicholai Zhivaynov, the Ottawa correspondent of the official Soviet news agency Tass (and almost certainly a Soviet spy), complained his copy was being cut by U.S. telegraph censors in New York. The Canadian press censors agreed to help Zhivaynov by pre-screening his stories and stamping them "passed by Canadian censors."

In the end, the Soviet spy rings in Canada and the United States would pull off one of the great coups of espionage: stealing the secrets of the atomic bomb. The Nazis, far less adept at cultivating spies, probably pulled very little useful information out of North America. Their only recourse was to drop agents along the North American coast, a move that would draw the press censors further into the clandestine war.

CHAPTER 3

Spy Games in the Maritimes

CENSORS FACED ONE OF THEIR GREATEST CHALLENGES in the fall of 1942, when a 14-year-old boy caught a genuine spy in the Gaspé Peninsula. Along with the military and the police, censors failed to keep this intelligence coup under wraps and probably blew the chance to turn the captured spy into a double agent. Or they may have fallen for a mind-twisting German spy game that pitted a captured agent against the RCMP and Britain's "Double Cross" team.

The government saw the Gaspé as a front-line position, a place that had easy access to roads and railways and a thinly inhabited coastline. Military intelligence officers wanted publicity for defence efforts in the region as long as the news stories played up the presence of Québécois coast watchers and were vague on details. The articles, Canadian intelligence officers believed, might deter foraging parties of German submariners, prevent the landing of spies on the Gaspé coast, and bolster martial spirit in Quebec.

The arrest of eight German spies dropped from U-boats along the coast of the United States in 1942 caused a sensation throughout Canada, especially in the Maritimes. That spring and summer, newspapers in the region often carried articles about the landing and capture of Nazis, who were part of the Germans' Operation Pastorius, a sabotage campaign similar to the one launched against American East Coast industries during World War One. All of the Canadian spy reports were wrong. The *Halifax Herald* ran a story on April 1, 1942, entitled, "Sub Reported Landing German, on Coast:

Spies Come Ashore, Report Back to Boats." Three days earlier, the *Toronto Star Weekly* published a full-page colour map revealing "North American Towns and Cities Now Shadowed by Axis Bombers" and warned its readers a Pearl Harbor–style attack "can happen here." Spy landings, the paper said, would be the opening gambit of such an operation. Quebec's French-language press also predicted the arrival of spies.

On August 13, 1942, a reporter for the *Halifax Star*, in one of his paper's few scoops of the war, picked up a rumour that police were hunting German agents who had been dropped by a submarine on the Nova Scotia coast, somewhere near Yarmouth. The *Star* checked with Halifax censor Bruce Jefferson, who traced the story to an RCMP circular sent across the country. For the next week, police in Nova Scotia stopped cars and searched farms in southwestern Nova Scotia. The *Star* was allowed to use the original story but Jefferson put a lid on follow-up stories until the police could determine whether the spies existed. This time, it was a false alarm.

The *Halifax Herald* asked on July 29, 1942, "Can spies and saboteurs land on Canada's East Coast?" The answer, it insisted, was "yes they can." However, the paper also predicted that any spies would find their way to the nearest jail. In one case, this turned out to be an accurate prediction.

When a spy finally arrived on Canada's shores, the censors were not surprised. In the pre-dawn hours of Monday, November 9, 1942, *U-518* surfaced, cut its engines, and drifted toward the rocky south shore of the Gaspé about 6.5 kilometres west of New Carlisle, Quebec, touching bottom at the base of a 15-metre bluff. The sub was caught for a moment in the headlights of a car moving along the coast road, but the driver didn't notice. A dinghy launched from the U-boat carried 38-year-old Werner von Janowski, wearing a tailor-made German naval sub-lieutenant's uniform sporting an Iron Cross, 1st Class. Von Janowski, a former *Toronto Star* freelancer who had returned to Germany, struggled with a wooden box containing a wireless radio and lugged a duffle bag that held his civilian clothes and various espionage tools.

Von Janowski, on his second major assignment for the German

military intelligence agency Abwehr, was given a shave and a haircut by one of the crew of U-518 but he must have reeked of sweat and diesel oil, since no one on the sub had bathed in the six weeks they had been at sea. It had been an eventful mission. On its way to the Gaspé, U-518 had stopped at Bell Island, Newfoundland, raided the iron ore docks at nearby Wabana, and sunk two ships in a daring night attack.

Once ashore, von Janowski changed into civilian clothes, buried his uniform with a shovel he carried with him for precisely that purpose, chucked the shovel into the sea, hitchhiked to New Carlisle, and checked into the village hotel. He told the 14-year-old desk clerk he was not planning to stay, he just needed a bath. Von Janowski smoked strange-smelling German cigarettes. He lit them with matches from a box that clearly said on it, in English, "Made in Belgium." He paid for his room with Canadian currency from 1917, oversized dollar bills that had been taken out of circulation in 1935. The suspicious boy asked his father, the hotel's owner, to call the Quebec Provincial Police (Sûreté du Québec). By lunchtime, von Janowski was in jail, waiting for the RCMP and angling for a new life as a double agent. One of von Janowski's first acts after his capture was to lie to his interrogators, telling them he had landed on the St. Lawrence side of the peninsula at Metis Beach three weeks before, had wandered more than 100 kilometres through the wilderness, and had waited at New Carlisle for three days for the submarine that was scheduled to pick him up. He misled Canadians long enough for U-518 to escape. The night of his capture, he put on a great show from his jail cell, seemingly hearing noises coming from the coast and pretending to wake up with a start, saying, "This is my submarine, which has come to get me."

Police found an assortment of spy hardware, but they should have seen, by the size of von Janowski's bankroll, that he was arriving, not leaving. He carried a mixture of Canadian and U.S. cash in high-denomination bills, plus fifty U.S. $20 gold pieces (all minted in 1924) that were worth $5,995.11 in aggregate. The Nazis may have given him old, suspicious currency, but they weren't stingy.

The "turning" of von Janowski could succeed only if news of his capture was kept out of the newspapers. At the Directorate of Censorship, O.M. Biggar received one of censorship's few important tips of the war, a call from the director of naval intelligence on the evening of November 9, telling him a German agent had been caught in the Gaspé. By then, despite a plea by Quebec premier Adélard Godbout for recognition of the provincial police's role in the spy's capture, the King government had decided to impose a blackout on the story. Biggar told the wire and telegraph censors to look for anything about it. He then called Jefferson in Halifax and asked him to warn off papers in the Maritimes and call the radio station at New Carlisle to put a lid on local coverage. Biggar called censor Ed McMahon in Montreal and told him to stifle coverage in the Montreal and Quebec City media. Canadian Press was also informed of the spy's capture and told not to move anything on that subject.

Shortly before noon on November 10, Warren Baldwin got a call from RCMP headquarters saying reporters were calling the police for information "and to ask if we could shut these up." Baldwin wondered how reporters knew about the arrests, but the RCMP call was soon followed by one from Jack Marshall of the *Windsor Daily Star*, who said the *Detroit Times* was carrying a story that several German agents had been landed on the Gaspé Peninsula and that one of these men had been caught. Biggar asked Marshall to "hold everything" and called the RCMP back. By then, the RCMP had phoned the FBI to ask for help to kill the story.

Meanwhile, staff of the *Detroit Times* phoned friendly reporters in Windsor and censor Bert Perry in Toronto. Officials of the U.S. press censorship system told Baldwin the *Times* got the story from Detroit city police officers, who had been tipped off about the arrest by the chatty RCMP constables working at the local border crossings. This information was relayed to the RCMP headquarters.

In fact, police gossip had spread the story through the U.S. northeast. At 3:00 p.m., Baldwin received a call from U.S. press censors in Washington saying news of von Janowski's capture had been carried on the New York State Police teletype system. Soon afterwards, the RCMP contacted the NYSP and asked the force to send a message telling all of its officers to stop talking about the spy. In light of the leaks, pressure built in Washington for an official press release on the capture of the German officer. At the same time, regional offices of the Directorate of Censorship fielded calls from more reporters who had learned of the arrest. By the end of the workday, reporters and editors at the *Windsor Star, Toronto Star, Toronto Telegram, Le Soleil, Montreal Star,* and *Montreal Standard* knew the story.

The censors' decision to suppress the spy story was taken particularly hard by the editors at Quebec City's *Le Soleil*. When Fulgence Charpentier applied for a job at the paper after the war, he was rudely turned away by its angry editors, who accused him of suppressing the best story the paper ever had. In fact, it was Biggar, Baldwin, McMahon, and the RCMP who had killed it. Eric Dennis of the *Halifax Herald* not only had been tipped off but was also calling around trying to make travel arrangements to New Carlisle. Dennis was not planning to make the trip himself but was inquiring in his role as a freelancer, planning the trip for *Toronto Star* reporters who arrived in New Carlisle by train on the afternoon of November 11. By November 13, Montreal's *La Presse* had the story. Under pressure from Biggar, the *Toronto Star* called off its reporters from New Carlisle and their story was spiked for the duration of the war, as was copy filed by a *Montreal Standard* reporter who was in New Carlisle by November 18.

On November 19, the U.S. magazine *Newsweek* came out with a one-sentence story on von Janowski's arrest in its weekly "Periscope Notes" feature: "Watch for an announcement revealing the capture of a German submarine commander near New Carlisle, Quebec." This was enough to convince Baldwin and Perry that the blackout should be lifted and Perry told the *Toronto Star* it could prepare to publish the stories and pictures gathered earlier in the week by its team. The *Toronto Telegram* was also tipped off, and editors from both papers arrived in Perry's office with long articles and bundles of photographs. The New Carlisle residents who had been involved in the case had been very friendly to reporters, giving them information about von Janowski's arrest and posing for pictures at the various places the spy had been before and after he was caught. The

Star also had pictures of his German cigarettes and old-fashioned money. However, at 4:10 p.m. Baldwin called Perry to say the stories and pictures could not run.

Lieutenant Commander C. Herbert Little was the navy's representative on the Censorship Committee on Intelligence and Security. He was in on the plan to offer von Janowski his life in return for betraying Germany. After the *Newsweek* story ran, Little believed the Germans must have known von Janowski had been arrested, so he was willing to let the Toronto stories go to press. The RCMP, which by then had von Janowski in custody, was working on its own plan with Britain's MI5 to make an offer to von Janowski. The Mounties asked Baldwin to hold the stories for at least two more weeks. Censors in Washington promised to try to prevent the export of that edition of *Newsweek*, and the chief U.S. press censor wrote a letter of warning to the publishers of the magazine.

Von Janowski was ensconced in a suburban Montreal house, sending messages to Germany at the behest of the RCMP and MI5. Very quickly, the British Secret Service decided von Janowski was a fraud, that he had somehow made the Germans aware of his "turning" and may have even been sending them data in code. He was given a code name that fit into the alphabetical listing of "turned" German agents, but this name does not appear on the official list of "Double Cross" spies captured in England. (The Double Cross agents were invaluable to the British. Their greatest work was done leading up to D-Day, when they helped convince Hitler that the invasion would happen near Calais. Months later, agents sent messages saying that the V1 bombs that tended to fall short of London were actually destroying the centre of the city.)

Over a number of months, the von Janowski story kept leaking: Quebec MLA Onésime Gagnon rose in the provincial legislature on March 4, 1943, and announced von Janowski's arrest. British United Press put the story on its radio wire twice on March 13. Baldwin told BUP's management the story had important security implications and the news agency, which had acted within its rights to quote the proceedings of the Quebec legislature, promised to use discretion. Stories on Gagnon's comment were also printed in *La Presse* and *La*

Patrie (Montreal), *L'Action catholique*, *L'Événement-Journal*, the *Quebec City Telegraph*, the *Chronicle* (Quebec City), *Le Droit* (Ottawa), and *Le Petit Journal* (Montreal).

Still, the RCMP believed they were fooling the Germans, even as the leaks kept coming. On March 17, J.F. Pouliot, a Quebec MP, told the House of Commons about the spy. Louis St. Laurent, the justice minister, interrupted debate and moved that the comment be expunged from *Hansard*. The motion passed and the censors warned newspapers not to print anything about Pouliot's remarks.

That spring, rumours of new arrests of spies circulated through the Maritimes. It is difficult to say whether these stories helped cloak the fact that von Janowski had been picked up. The stories circulated by word of mouth and through the mails. Baldwin and Eggleston checked with Canadian naval intelligence to see if the stories were true. When they learned the spy tales were just gossip, the Ottawa censors called their regional offices in Eastern Canada to warn them to watch for any coverage of them.

The censors and military intelligence officers were shocked when the June 14, 1943, edition of the *Fredericton Daily Gleaner* carried the full story of von Janowski's arrest. It was based on the reportage of the *Toronto Star* team sent to New Carlisle the previous November. The story was somehow released to the *Gleaner* by the *Star*'s feature syndication service. The RCMP believed the story may have been read by German POWs being treated at Victoria Public Hospital in Fredericton. By then, senior RCMP finally began believing it was likely von Janowski's Double Cross status was known by Germany. The *Montreal Star* reported on July 29, 1943, yet another public leak of the secret, this time by Lieutenant Colonel Léon Lambert, assistant director of the Sûreté du Québec, who was speaking to a Montreal convention of police and fire chiefs.

Lambert's was the last breach of the news blackout on von Janowski until the end of the war. When the ban was lifted, a remarkably large number of newspaper reporters knew the main elements of the story of von Janowski's arrest, although the fact he supposedly had become a double agent was still secret. On May 9, 1945, Baldwin asked reporters to hold the story for three months, but they refused, so on May 14, 1945, he lifted the embargo. Montreal *Gazette* reporter Larry Conroy broke the story of von Janowski's "turn" on May 15. The RCMP and the military were horrified by the leak and confronted Conroy. It turned out Conroy had pieced the story together from threads of facts he had picked up while working the police beat. Refusals by police to confirm or deny in 1943 whether von Janowski's case was closed led Conroy to suspect von Janowski was still in Canada. Starting there, he was able to weave together the story from strands of information picked up while working his beat. The RCMP and the censors managed to convince the Canadian Press and the country's newspapers to ignore Conroy's scoop. On August 9, 1945, the Canadian Press moved a story on von Janowski, written by one of its reporters, Jack Brayley, saying the German was a double agent and had sent radio messages to Germany from Montreal. The story, which was carried in most of the country's newspapers, contained several major and minor errors, including the inaccurate claim that von Janowski was back in Europe working as an investigator and translator for Allied war crimes investigators.

Von Janowski's arrest was one story that could justify a censorship blackout. The German government would certainly want to know if von Janowski had been arrested. The sheer number of reporters, police officers, parliamentarians, and public servants who knew this secret, and the volume of censorship breaks both in the widely read *Newsweek* magazine and in local papers, strongly suggests that the Germans would have encountered little trouble tracking von Janowski if they'd had a reasonably effective intelligence-gathering network in Eastern Canada or the United States. While the censors continued to suppress the story, it may well have made its way back to Germany within days of von Janowski's arrest and compromised his value as a turncoat. The fact that the German military stopped issuing his pay the week he was caught casts a strong hint that this was the case.

Either way, landing in Canada saved von Janowski's life. Whether he was part of the German campaign of 1942 to land spies and saboteurs along the U.S. Eastern Seaboard, a one-off agent sent to

Canada to gather information, or a deliberate triple-agent plant, his capture left him open to very serious punishment. The Operation Pastorius agents caught in the U.S. in the summer of 1942 had, like von Janowski, committed no acts of terror. In fact, they had gone their separate ways and used the money issued to them to try to settle quietly in the U.S. for the duration of the war. The Germans were caught when two of them turned informant, thereby saving their own skins while dooming six of their colleagues to the Washington City Jail's electric chair. The spies were convicted by a military tribunal, the first since the U.S. Civil War trials of the alleged co-conspirators of John Wilkes Booth, and the last until the hearings for Guantanamo Bay internees in this century. As well, fourteen U.S. residents who helped the spies were rounded up, prosecuted, and jailed.

Rather than parade von Janowski in front of reporters, as the FBI did with the Operation Pastorius spies, the RCMP decided to forgo the propaganda benefits of von Janowski's capture and get as much use as possible from the agent. As for von Janowski, he was released from his English prison without charges in 1947 and sent back to Germany. There, he pressed the new postwar government for military back pay covering his time in captivity. Years after the war ended, he did get one little bonus: the $5,995.11 seized by the Canadian police in New Carlisle, Quebec. The money was held in escrow accounts for enemy aliens and was transferred, in his name, to Germany in December 1955. He bounced from one low-paying job to the next before landing a position in 1963 with the German navy. He died in 1978.

In the von Janowski case, the censorship system failed Canada's intelligence community, although the RCMP continued to act as though von Janowski's "turn" had not been compromised. Media outlets, eager to go public with something as exotic as a spy story, sidestepped the boundaries of the censorship system, one that fundamentally needed to conceal any fact of military value to the enemy. Reporters did not know until 1952 that a second spy, Martin Langbein, surrendered himself to naval intelligence officers in the fall of 1944. To this day, the details of his mission are vague.

Langbein claimed to have been sent to Halifax or Montreal to watch for convoys and report ship departures so U-boats could position themselves. Supposedly, he decided not to spy, to simply lie low in Canada for the duration. Yet, of all the places in Canada he could go on the thick bankroll he had been given by the Abwehr, Langbein chose the Grand Hotel, on the west side of Ottawa's Byward Market just a block from Parliament Hill.

Langbein's adventure began on April 25, 1942, when Amelung von Varendorff, the captain of *u-213*, had the secret agent come aboard his U-boat in a submarine pen at Lorient, France. Off the coast of Portugal, *u-213* stalked a British convoy but, before von Varendorff could get his torpedoes off, his vessel was attacked by a British destroyer. The sub's crew raced forward to weigh down the U-boat's nose as it crash-dove to 200 metres. Ten depth charges went off, close enough to make the lights flicker and the hull shake. Several of the sailors, most of them fishermen from the Baltic Sea, began to cry and sob. The sub's tough first officer tried to talk them back to their senses while the captain lay silently on his bunk, his automatic pistol at his side. (Von Varendorff would get to make that choice on his next mission, when *u-213* was sunk with depth charges by British destroyers.)

The rest of the mission was tedious. The sub fought the Bay of Fundy's tides and emerged May 12 near St. Martin's, New Brunswick. Just after midnight, the sub surfaced. Langbein left the sub with a Lieutenant Kueltz and two sailors who helped haul Langbein and his gear across the boulder-strewn beach and scale the eighty-metre bluff along the shore. By 7:30 a.m., the dinghy arrived back at the sub and *u-213* disappeared.

The man they left behind was born on April 6, 1903, in Graefenthal, Thuringia, Germany, where Langbein's father, Willy, worked as an insurance broker. With a penchant for travel, the younger Langbein went to Shanghai and found a job as a special constable on the police force. He returned home in 1926, but jobs were hard to find. His father's firm was failing. In 1928, Langbein sailed for Halifax. He took a train across Canada to find a family in Pearce, Alberta, that he had met on the ship. In Alberta, he found a job as a surveyor, then went to northern Manitoba to work as a railway labourer. Langbein had been caught in a cathouse in Flin Flon, but never got into serious trouble.

He wandered to Ontario, where he worked briefly as a free-lance writer. Langbein arrived home just as Hitler took power. Through the rest of the Depression, Langbein ran a small factory in Germany, then supervised construction of four kilometres of an autobahn—both jobs that had a whiff of party patronage. By the beginning of the war, he was married with a daughter (a son had died soon after birth) and he was waiting for his army call-up papers to arrive in the mail.

Instead, Langbein got a phone call from an old school friend, Oscar Homann, who invited him to Hannover to talk business with a mysterious stranger, Dr. Nicolaus Bensmann, a former patent agent for a U.S. oil company operating in Romania. After a few formalities, Langbein was packed off to "The Nest," the spy training school in Bremen that also taught sabotage to Abwehr agents. Langbein turned down one assignment, parachuting into England to scout airfields and anti-aircraft gun emplacements, saying his German-Canadian accent would betray him. Then his spymasters planned to set him up in a fishing boat operated by Belgian collaborators that would scout the English coast. This plan was foiled when British planes sank the fishing boat in Flushing, Holland. A spying expedition with Bensmann in Romania was also a failure. Instead of spying, Bensmann spent most of the time trying to collect money owed to his U.S. employers.

The Abwehr had a new plan: Langbein would do a U-boat drop in Canada, bury his equipment, get to Halifax or Montreal where British convoys assembled, find a job and blend in for about three months, then return to the landing place to get his radio. After three months, the Germans would listen for his signal every night at 11:00 pm during German summertime. If Langbein did not retrieve his radio, he could write letters in invisible ink and send them to mail drops in neutral Switzerland and Portugal. Langbein christened the mission "Operation Gretl" after his wife.

The U-213's crew was led to believe he was a reporter in

Germany's elite Propaganda Kompany. Langbein was given his fake ID and $7,500 in U.S. $50 bills. The spy realized with some horror that the wartime registration card, vital for employment, was made out to "A.B. Haskins, Young Street, Toronto." Langbein knew Toronto's main street had been spelled incorrectly, and he was sure someone would catch him because of it. After the sub left, Langbein slept for a few hours. Then he traipsed through bogs to St. Martin's, New Brunswick, where be bought a razor and some soap. The spy managed to hitch a ride to Saint John in a lumber truck. He told the driver he had a cold, and spoke in hoarse whispers to disguise his strong German accent.

His biggest challenge was cashing those U.S. $50 bills. He spent much of the next two years shopping, looking for stores that would accept large-denomination bills. Usually, he let them keep the 10 per cent exchange.

Arriving in Montreal by train, the spy checked into a rooming house where he had stayed a decade before. On June 18, while the eight Operation Pastorius spies were still free in the States, Langbein went to a store to buy a couple of pipes. The owner couldn't make change for the $50 bill Langbein offered, but a furtive little man grabbed him by the shirt sleeves and pulled him down St. Catherine Street and into a house on a side street. It was a bordello. The madam said she could get change. Langbein later said he stayed long enough to collect his change and have a beer, but he didn't drink it fast enough to avoid a police raid. He was booked as a "found-in" under the name A.B. Haskins—his lack of real identification and strong German accent obviously of little concern to the vice squad—and eventually let go on $50 bail, the Canadian change from his U.S. $50.

When he got back to his rooming house, he packed his belongings and caught the first train to Ottawa. The spy claimed he flagged a cab at the Ottawa train station (now the Government Conference Centre, right across from the Château Laurier) and asked the driver to take him to a good hotel. If Langbein told the truth, the cabbie drove him roughly a block, to the Grand Hotel on Sussex, about where the Rideau Street Chapters store now has its parking lot. There, Langbein made himself at home.

The hotel was a watering hole for politicians, civil servants, and the hundreds of soldiers rolling through the city at any given time. It was exactly the place you'd *expect* a spy to set up shop.

Yet, for more than a year, in a city that was the headquarters of the RCMP and Canada's military intelligence, the 40-year-old stranger with a heavy German accent and a seemingly never-ending supply of U.S. $50 bills held court within shouting distance of Parliament and a five-minute walk from the military's headquarters on Cartier Square (now the site of Ottawa's city hall).

"The night after I arrived in Ottawa, I seriously considered surrendering myself to the RCMP or any other suitable authority and spent considerable time consulting the phone book to decide the most suitable authority to approach," Langbein later told Canadian intelligence agents. Instead, he adapted to life in Ottawa and made an interesting group of friends.

Langbein bought a Ping-Pong table from a store on Rideau Street because one of his air force friends liked the game. So did Langbein: he had learned Ping-Pong from a friend in the Abwehr. He made friends with some of the hotel staff. Two of them had girlfriends who worked as secretaries for naval intelligence. During his first six months in Ottawa, the spy left the hotel at 9:00 every morning and returned about 5:00 in the afternoon. "I would put in the day as best I could, taking long walks, going to picture shows and taking in any sporting events that might be in progress."

Eddie Sabourin, a cook in the hotel, was his best friend. Through him, the spy became part of a group of young people who liked to party at the Grand Hotel. On summer weekends, they took short drives along the Ottawa River to Constance Bay and Buckingham to picnic and drink beer. Langbein usually picked up most of the tab.

At least once, a friend had taken him into the naval intelligence offices in Temporary Building 8 at the Ottawa Experimental Farm. Still, month after month went by without Langbein raising suspicion among the dozens of army, navy, and air force officers, the politicians and political staffers, and the war bureaucrats who drank with him at the Grand Hotel. His biggest problem was homesickness.

There was just one close call. In the early summer of 1943, while riding home from a Hull bar in a cab with "Bea," the sister-in-law of the owner of the Grand Hotel, and her soldier boyfriend, the soldier looked at Langbein and said, "I think you're a spy." When the drunken soldier left the cab in Hull to look for a cop, Langbein talked Bea and the cabbie into heading for Ottawa. Presumably, the Hull police paid no attention to the soldier's accurate suspicions.

Once he got back to the Grand Hotel, Langbein avoided Bea and started looking for a new place to live. With some help from a waiter in the Grand's beer parlour, he found a place to live in Lowertown. He took a room with the family of Oscar Renaud, at 303 St. Andrew Street. The Renauds, who spoke poor English, thought Langbein was Dutch and was in Ottawa on secret business paid for by the Americans. The spy bought their loyalty with $50 bills. By the fall of 1944, his $40-a-month room and board was paid in advance for an entire year, and Langbein bought the family luxuries they could not afford.

Langbein and his friends enjoyed those rural trips in the warm months of 1943 and 1944. In the spring of 1944, tired of lugging his cash in a money belt, he stuffed forty of his bills into a pop bottle and buried it beside a large boulder at a picnic area in Buckingham, Quebec. During the summer, Langbein read of the arrest of Abwehr chief Admiral Wilhelm Canaris in the wake of the failed July 20 bomb attack on Hitler and about the show trials of hundreds of military officers supposedly involved in the plot. Somehow, Langbein also heard the pro-Soviet propaganda broadcasts from Moscow of Field Marshal Friedrich Paulus, who had surrendered his Sixth Army at Stalingrad.

Langbein, while following the carnage in his old spy agency and the collapse of the Nazi regime, had begun an affair with a woman named Eva Rose. She seems to have been an expensive date: within a few months, he had blown $1,500 entertaining her. By the late summer, he was back in Buckingham looking for that pop bottle. After an all-day bus and walking trip, he couldn't find the picnic area or the boulder. He went home, tried again a few weeks later, and still had no luck. Presumably, the cash is still there.

On Monday, October 30, 1944, Langbein walked to the naval

intelligence office in the Ottawa Experimental Farm to give himself up. Langbein stood around the front door for a few hours, lost his nerve, and walked back to his apartment. The next day, he made the trip again. Again, after a day worrying that he would be executed or imprisoned for the rest of his life, he walked back home. On his third try, he managed to summon the courage to surrender, dropping a note on the receptionist's desk. A surprised lieutenant took him upstairs and called the RCMP.

"While accepting the mission to Canada, crossing the Atlantic and during my stay in Canada, I had no intention to follow orders. I intended to stay undercover to the time that normalcy and peace would come to Europe. For several months I tried to make up my mind to give myself up to the authorities," Langbein said in a statement on November 4, 1944.

The military intelligence officers who were members of the oversight committees of the censorship system knew about Langbein's defection. Captain Herbert Little, the navy's intelligence liaison with censorship, read Langbein's detailed technical statement about his submarine trip (in which the spy conspicuously feigned ignorance of anything regarding the Enigma code machine) and attached a note calling the statement "a valuable document to support our censorship and security stand." Actually, there was no reason to suppress the Langbein story. He was not offered the role of double agent and, if his defection had been made public, people in Ottawa would have been given the opportunity to fill in some of the gaps in his story.

In the end, military intelligence preferred secrecy to openness. Its agents could not draw the type of information from press censorship that it received from mail censorship, cable monitoring, and signals interception. Its interest in press censorship lay primarily in preventing the publication of material that it believed should be kept from the Axis, and in keeping German propaganda out of the Canadian media. The challenges were daunting. Intelligence officers in the three armed services as well as at External Affairs dealt with a relatively decentralized press-censorship system whose managers wanted to limit secrecy.

It appears the censors and the intelligence agents simply could not communicate. The military should have taken the senior censors into its confidence to allow them to be ready when there was a surge of requests for vetting of important news stories. Instead, the censors must have often come across to the reporters who knew the von Janowski story as inconsistent, ineffective, and out of the information loop.

CHAPTER 4

The Silent Service:
Naval War Censorship

HALIFAX WAS CANADA'S FRONT-LINE CITY, the one town in the country where no one could forget the war. If they needed a reminder, they could just glance at the harbour, which was usually crowded with Allied warships and freighters engaged in the dangerous task of keeping Britain supplied with food, oil, and weapons. Thousands of recruits to Canada's navy were crammed into the city, along with merchant sailors, crews from Allied fleets, and war workers. It was one place in Canada where a spy could do serious damage to the Allied war effort.

The federal government, at the urging of the navy, slapped special secrecy and censorship rules on Halifax to prevent leaks of information. The navy's attitude was summed up well by one of its officers: "Upon sealed lips depend not only our ships, not only the lives of fighting seamen in our warships, and merchant seamen engaged in holding the lifeline firm, but the success or failure of our arms. Should we lose command of the sea, we cannot hope to win the war." Word hadn't filtered down to the often chatty sailors and soldiers who had nowhere to stay but in crowded rooming houses and barracks. Most of these young people spent their time on the streets and in beer parlours, easy prey for Axis spies and inquisitive local reporters.

Maintaining a blackout on ship movements in Halifax was a daunting task: anyone could climb a hill in the city or look out from a high building and watch the convoys, warships, and troop transports, including Cunard's *Queen Mary* and *Queen Elizabeth*, which were used as troop ships.

The strict press, mail, and wire censorship became the butt of jokes across the country. At the end of the war, the Montreal *Gazette* told its readers that the cancelling of censorship rules at Halifax made life in the port more bearable. "Some people," the paper's editors wrote, "are no doubt pleased, including the proud father who is said to have got much annoyed in Halifax when, hurrying frantically from a maternity hospital to the telegraph office to inform his parents in Toronto that 'Little Mary arrived today. Old Mary fine.' He was promptly taken aside and questioned for two hours by three or four detectives on suspicion of reporting troop movements!"

Relations between the navy and the censors were usually strained at best. Very quickly, the censors learned to ignore some of the navy's more extreme demands, including senior officers' insistence that they kill wire service stories on the fight between British warships and the *Graf Spee*, which were already running in the world's newspapers and broadcast by hundreds of radio stations. Certainly, the German navy knew the *Graf Spee* had been cornered in Montevideo's harbour, but the navy wanted the Canadian people to be kept in the dark.

Captain Eric Brand, a British intelligence officer seconded to the Canadian navy, was the link between the Canadian navy and the censors. He usually kept Halifax censor Bruce Jefferson ignorant of major losses, and censors were often blindsided by reporters' questions. "If Captain Brand had not been quite so mysterious in his recent disclosures we easily could have prevented even the vague and uncertain publicity that appeared this morning," the Halifax censor wrote in 1942 after being surprised with questions about a major sinking.

Through the war, censors kept a lid on details of U-boat attacks off Canada's coasts, chopping out the most interesting details, suppressing them completely, or delaying them until they had become old news. This was a daunting challenge in a town with so many mobile, chatty people. Attacks by German U-boats along the Canadian and Newfoundland coasts did happen, and some of them—like the daylight raids on iron ore docks at Bell Island, near St. John's, Newfoundland, killing sixty-eight people—were common knowledge in the Maritimes and Quebec, where some people actually watched the action from shore. Enemy submarines penetrated the St. Lawrence River within 300 kilometres of Quebec City, making it upstream almost to Rimouski to sink ships within easy sight and sound of people on the south shore of the river. Everyone in Halifax knew German submarines lay in wait just outside the city's harbour to pick off stragglers from convoys: the hulks of damaged ships were often towed into Halifax harbour, where people could see the holes blasted into them by the U-boats. Rescue ships landed sub-attack survivors at communities in the Gaspé, Charlottetown, Halifax, and Sydney. The sailors who had lost their ships usually were talkative with friendly reporters, especially journalists like Eric Dennis of the *Halifax Herald*, who trolled the waterfront bars.

The government and the navy were not eager to spread the news of U-boat losses off Canada for several reasons. Real-time media reports of submarine attacks allowed the Germans to know if the U-boats had found a convoy. Successful U-boat raids made valuable propaganda for the Germans, while Allied media reports of losses could undermine morale. Canada tried to balance itself between the British Admiralty, which wanted every U-boat story killed, and Washington, which was open about losses. Canadian censors were willing to pass human-interest stories on survivors of U-boat attacks as long as they did not give explicit details of shipping losses. People needed to know the war had come to Canada's shores, Eggleston, the most analytical of the censors, believed. They might become angry enough to do something about it: enlist, buy a war bond, or volunteer for an overtime shift.

The censors tightened the screws on the press after a naval intelligence briefing about sub-chasing strategies. The navy brass explained that they used High Frequency Direction Finding ("huff duff") submarine-radio-location technology to triangulate the position of U-boats. German submarines usually surfaced soon after their attacks to send a report to Germany. The navy's intelligence analysts believed the sub captains would not take the risk if their headquarters could pick up details of attacks from the Canadian media. After the 1942 attacks in the St. Lawrence River, the censors accepted that argument and told journalists there had to be a substantial delay between submarine attacks and stories about them.

Halifax censor Bruce Jefferson was a crotchety, round, bald, and very smart middle-aged man who could not qualify for military duty in World War One because his left eye wandered. He was a natural reporter with a keen eye for detail and a remarkable ability to cultivate sources, including Angus Macdonald, who left his job as premier of Nova Scotia to be naval minister in the federal government and still ruled as the region's political boss. Jefferson bounced around the East Coast newspaper business for nearly three decades before landing his war job, which gave him the money to fend off the bill collectors who had been chasing him for years because of a bad investment in a small-town newspaper.

If any enemy spies were serious about prying out the secrets of wartime Halifax, they should have snatched Jefferson. He was insatiably curious, and he recorded everything on paper and film. Jefferson took pictures of the ships entering and leaving Halifax harbour, but, to maintain secrecy, he developed the pictures himself, and Jefferson's collection makes up an important part of the Nova Scotia public archives. He kept a detailed diary of events in the city and managed to find time to write thousands of words to Ottawa giving his opinion on everything that happened in Halifax.

The city's most important paper, the *Halifax Herald*, was owned by the Dennis family, and the reporting of one of its members, Eric Dennis, would dominate Jefferson's censorship workload. Dennis worked the bars and flophouses of Halifax's dockside, talked his way onto some of the blasted freighters, and wrote dozens of stories based on interviews with sailors and passengers who recounted their survivals of U-boat attacks, harrowing escapes from wrecks, long voyages in lifeboats and successful counterattacks against the subs. There was a strong local demand for this news. The Halifax dailies went into the war locked in a nasty fight for circulation. The *Herald* combined an aggressive home-distribution sales campaign with a ferocious approach to newsgathering. After the war, Eric Dennis believed his dominance of the coverage of wartime Halifax shattered the spirit of his competitors at the *Chronicle*. Certainly, it hurt their business: the *Herald*'s circulation rose by 55 per cent during the war, while the *Chronicle*'s stayed flat. (After the war, the *Chronicle* was absorbed by the *Herald*.)

Jefferson believed Eric Dennis and Dave King, a *Herald* photographer, deliberately provoked military authorities. The *Herald* men refused to show passes to guards at the harbour and sneaked aboard ocean liners to interview soldiers and officers. The Halifax censor believed the *Herald* won the news battle because its reporters and photographers were simply more aggressive than their competition, and he admitted he gave in to its persistent demands for access to the docks and clearance of stories simply to get the *Herald* off his back. Midway through the war, Jefferson, angry with the attempts by Halifax reporters to push censorship to the limit, advocated levying small fines against newspapers that went too far. He thought $5 fines would be enough, since the papers and their reporters "operate on comparative shoe-strings."

The *Herald* had little political clout: it tended to support the Conservatives, who were rarely in power in Ottawa. Robert J. Rankin, the managing editor, had a distinguished career covering federal and provincial politics but knew that he and his employers were on the political outs. He blamed interference from the federal Liberals for many of Jefferson's decisions. Jefferson, for his part, thought Rankin was short-fused and unreasonable. In the written explanations for his rulings, Jefferson often mentioned Rankin's fits of rage and his charges the censors were engaged in a campaign to cover up government stupidity and waste. In one memo to Ottawa, Jefferson explained that the CBC defied a news blackout and beat the *Herald* on a U-boat attack story: "Mr. Rankin went through the usual *Herald* 'frightfullness' [sic] routine, enlarging upon the various degrees of Hell they expect to raise at Ottawa over this ... scoop," Jefferson warned his colleagues. In September 1941, when Australian airmen earmarked for Britain stomped off the *Empress of Asia*, saying the ship was filthy, Rankin called Jefferson "in great glee to announce that at last they had something with which they could 'go to town' on us." Censorship, Rankin said, was covering up official inefficiency. "Mr. Rankin said he was going to play this story to the limit, appeal to the Prime Minister, rouse the country, and generally show up everybody, including the embarkation people and press censorship," Jefferson told censorship headquarters in Ottawa. The airmen later sailed on another ship. The story was held for several days because it violated directives against describing troop movements until they were completed. Through the censors, the Royal Canadian Air Force asked the *Herald* and Canadian Press to tone the story down, "not only for its effect against recruiting in Canada, but because of its possible use in the United States and on German radio."

One of the worst failures of maritime wartime security happened far from the sea, in Ottawa. At the end of 1940, the British liner *Western Prince* was torpedoed off the Irish coast. Many of the country's smartest industrial planners and economists, including C.D. Howe, the minister of munitions and supply, were aboard. There were also a couple of millionaires who would have made fine catches for the Nazis: financier E.P. Taylor, the richest man in Canada; and W.C. Woodward, head of the Vancouver-based department store chain that carried the family name. Liberal MP Gordon Scotts was killed when he fell between one of the lifeboats and the *Western Prince*'s hull; and the captain, second officer, and captain's steward went down with the ship.

The passengers and crew, adrift in lifeboats, struggled to survive in the cold grey swells until help arrived. Some of them were killed when one of the lifeboats rolled in the heavy seas. For eight grim hours, Howe and the rest of the 152 survivors waited for rescue. They were finally picked up by a coal freighter and arrived in London on December 18.

New York–based MacKay Radio, an agency that sold tips to the U.S. press, intercepted the *Western Prince*'s distress call and passed the news to a New York newspaper. The *Ottawa Citizen* picked up the story, confirmed with Howe's wife that the minister was on the ship, and published it under the banner front-page headline "C.D. Howe and Party on Torpedoed Steamship?" while Howe and his assistants were still in the lifeboat. The censors recommended the laying of charges against the *Citizen*, but the Department of Justice let the paper off with a warning.

Despite Eggleston's belief that Canadians needed to be toughened by bad-news stories, articles that might drag down civilian and military morale were usually eviscerated of any interesting facts or killed outright. In April 1941, Eggleston, in Ottawa, cut a line in an article picked up by the *Ottawa Citizen* from the New York *Mirror* that said, "[A]nd no matter how you look at it, the Royal Navy is losing the battle of the Atlantic today." In Halifax, the censor watched for stories that might frighten or depress merchant crews and navy sailors, especially details of drownings and the even more horrible stories about sailors who burned to death in U-boat attacks on oil and gasoline tankers. At the same time, material that put a happy face on the offshore carnage was passed. Photos of the survivors of the sunken Canadian destroyer *Margaree* were cleared for publication because, Jefferson wrote, they showed "happy, laughing groups of sailors bicycling or walking along Bermuda roads." (HMCS *Margaree*, formerly HMS *Diana*, was a River-class destroyer built for the British navy in 1931 and transferred to the Canadian navy on September 6, 1940. She sank, taking with her 142 crew members, on October 22, 1940, after colliding with the freighter *Port Fairy* in the North Atlantic while escorting convoy OL-8.)

The censors also passed a few stories that showed U-boat captains in a positive light. Following the daring raids by Otto Kretschmer in *U-99* off the English coast and Gunther Prien's *U-47* at Scapa Flow, some sub captains had developed a dark glamour in Canada in the early months of the war. On December 16, 1940, Eric Dennis submitted a story based on an interview with a local survivor of the cargo ship *St. Malo*, sunk by *U-101* on October 12 while it was straggling from convoy HX-77, describing how the U-boat came alongside a lifeboat. The U-boat commander expressed regret for sinking the *St. Malo*, but added "war is war." He then asked *St. Malo*'s crew if they needed anything. This being the 1940s, the answer was, of course, "smokes." The captain tossed a large package of English cigarettes to the sailors before saying goodbye and leaving the scene. Censors also passed stories about friendly encounters between U-boats and Canadian fishing schooners, which frequently occurred in the early years of the war. The stories were of interest to the navy's intelligence officers, who asked Jefferson to track down the sources of the articles to determine if they were true. In the summer of 1942, the unofficial truce between the offshore fishing fleet and the U-boats ended. In late July, *Lucille M*, a 26-metre Lockeport, Nova Scotia–based schooner, was sunk by shell fire from a U-boat 160 kilometres north of Seal Island on Georges Bank. Three of its ten survivors were wounded when the Germans machine-gunned one of the schooner's dories. The navy quickly gave Jefferson permission to clear the story for the Halifax newspapers.

Despite his dust-ups with the local censor and the navy, Eric Dennis was more likely to have his stories passed by the censor than were out-of-town reporters, unless they were old friends of Jefferson. Indeed, *New York Post* freelancer Eve Fayne, who arrived in Halifax in February 1942 and set up headquarters in the Lord Nelson Hotel (where Jefferson lived), was targeted by Jefferson, who quickly ran her out of the city. Fayne's presence was detected by cable censors who intercepted a telegram between the *Post* and the London-based reporter after she arrived in Halifax. The paper assigned Fayne to confirm rumours the submarine war had shifted from the eastern Atlantic to the Canadian and U.S. coasts, and that there had been more attacks in the Halifax area than in British coastal waters (a claim that was, in fact, fairly accurate at the time). Working with the cable censors, Jefferson held up the telegrams to force Fayne to come into his office to discuss her assignment, then made it so difficult for her to operate in Halifax that she gave up on the *Post*'s assignment and left for Capetown, South Africa. She had lasted just two days in Jefferson's city.

(Jefferson had little use for female reporters. When June Callwood of the *Globe and Mail*, whom Jefferson referred to in his memoranda as "June Callwell, *Globe and Mail* sob sister," was given an interview with Lieutenant Alex Joy of the navy, Jefferson praised Joy as "a true member of the silent service and Miss Callwell, a very charming person, could not get him to say much.")

Still, Jefferson actually acted as a buffer between naval authorities who wanted a complete blackout on all action off Canada and the reporters who wanted to mine the deep vein of wartime news in Halifax. Jefferson often tangled with naval intelligence (whose complaints were sometimes called "bleats" in the censors' correspondence) and navy public-relations officers (PROS) who, Jefferson and his bosses in Ottawa believed, tried to prevent, for political reasons, legitimate press investigations of incompetence, bungling, and waste. Jefferson quietly wished reporters would challenge the navy's PR machine. Instead, they happily accepted the pictures and scraps of news that were handed out by the navy.

Partly to get around Jefferson's hawk eye over Battle of the Atlantic news, the three Toronto dailies hired local "stringers," reporters on the Halifax papers who made money on the side as freelancers. The *Toronto Star* had deals with Eric Dennis and with Nathan Dreskin of the *Saint John Times-Globe* to file stories to the *Star* before they ran in their own newspapers. It is unlikely the *Herald*'s management knew the extent of Dennis's work, which ran in the *Star* without bylines. Jefferson exposed Dreskin's deal to the management of the *Times-Globe* when Dreskin tried to do an end run around him by sending an uncensored story to the *Star*. The telegraph censors intercepted the article and passed it to Jefferson.

Jefferson decided to try to muffle the *Toronto Star*'s coverage. After talking by telephone with Tommy Lytle, the *Star*'s news editor and stringer den mother, the Halifax censor wrote that he had found Lytle surprisingly personable as "from some of our experiences with *Star* enterprises down this way, I had been inclined to visualize Lytle as a gent with horns and tail." Still, the *Toronto Star* remained Jefferson's biggest nuisance outside of Halifax, breaking a string of stories on sub attacks that rankled the navy and the sensors.

Jefferson had to deal with a major hole in the censorship system: stories coming from St. John's, capital of the British colony of Newfoundland. On June 16, 1941, the Halifax censor reached the limit of his patience when the Canadian Press moved a dispatch from St. John's that went into great detail about the torpedoing of two British steamers and the rescue of sixty-four sailors. It was time, the censors said, to shut down the St. John's leak, so Ottawa started tapping all the telephone and telegraph lines that came out of St. John's, which passed through Canadian territory. Ignoring Newfoundland's status as a British colony, not a Canadian province, Jefferson tried to impose Canadian censorship rules on St. John's journalists. He was supported by his British counterparts in Newfoundland.

In January 1942, Jefferson erased Halifax and the rest of the towns and cities of the Maritimes from the journalistic map. Ottawa issued a circular with new, standardized place names to obscure the locations of naval action. Halifax and the other harbours were now "an East Coast port." The "western Atlantic" was to include any place between Halifax and a point 160 kilometres east of Newfoundland, "mid-Atlantic" anywhere between 160 kilometres east of Newfoundland and Iceland, and "eastern Atlantic" the part of the ocean between Iceland and the mainland of Europe.

Ships became invisible because their names were routinely chopped from stories. So were the names of the sailors quoted by Dennis and his colleagues. Hundreds of merchant sailors from Poland, Norway, Denmark, the Netherlands, and France who had escaped the Nazi occupation of their countries passed through Halifax, and some of them turned up among the crews rescued from U-boat attacks. They hated Germany and most were eager to talk to reporters. The censors wanted the sailors' names out of U-boat attack stories to prevent Gestapo reprisals against their families.

In January 1942, German admirals Karl Doenitz and Erich Raeder pushed the U-boat fleet inshore to attack shipping in Canadian and U.S. coastal waters. The Americans, now officially enemies of Germany, practically offered up their coastal steamers to the U-boat captains. Cities along the Eastern Seaboard were not blacked out, so their lights carried for miles offshore and served as lit screens to silhouette U.S. coast vessels, which usually travelled without escorts because the U.S. navy insisted they weren't needed. Hundreds of ships went to the bottom within sight of the mainland. Most nights, people living on Long Island and Cape Cod could see the glow of burning gasoline tankers lighting the eastern sky.

Raeder's coastal campaign did not stop at the Maine–New

Brunswick border. In the first months of the year, the U-boats prowled the Grand Banks and the southeast coast of Nova Scotia, picking off fishing boats, stragglers from convoys, and the ships that left smaller harbours bound for the Halifax and Sydney, Nova Scotia, convoy assembly points. That summer, some of the German submarines moved into the Gulf of St. Lawrence. News of these attacks was more difficult to suppress than stories of wolf-pack attacks in the mid-Atlantic. People on shore could see some of the raids, and Canadian fishermen came ashore in dories, furious that their unofficial truce with the sub captains had ended in massacre. On May 11 and 12, 1942, *u-553*, which had moved from a position off Halifax to quieter waters between Anticosti Island and the Quebec mainland to make repairs, sank the British freighter *Nicoya* and the Dutch ship *Leto*, killing seventeen sailors. It was the beginning of the Battle of the St. Lawrence.

The attacks in the St. Lawrence began just six days into Ottawa lawyer O.M. Biggar's term as director of censorship and just a few days after the plebiscite on conscription that split English and French Canada. News of *u-553*'s attacks reached Prime Minister Mackenzie King on the morning of May 12 as he was about to enter a meeting of Liberal MPs to discuss the political fallout from the plebiscite. King was depressed about the vote results. The news revived his spirits. He saw the sinkings as a political windfall that would show Quebecers the dangers of the war and still justify to English Canada his policy of hoarding Canadian military resources in Canada. King gave the MPs a dramatic and detailed account of *u-553*'s attack. Through the day, he mulled over his good fortune. Such a political windfall could not be a coincidence or an accident, King believed. He went back to Laurier House, his mansion just east of Parliament Hill in Ottawa's old Sandy Hill neighbourhood, and wrote in his diary that *u-553*'s exploits were "evidence of guidance" from the spirit world.

Naval Service Headquarters immediately issued a press release on the submarine attack, saying a freighter was lost and forty-one survivors had been landed. The press release said no more news on sub attacks would be given out because it would be of use to the enemy. This strange, politically motivated press release was the first and last time the media would receive prompt news of an attack in Canadian inland waters. It can be interpreted as a political act against the politicians and press in Quebec who opposed Canadian involvement in the war, and who argued the fighting could simply be ignored because Quebec was too remote to be a battleground. Here, King's government tried to show, was a real threat to their province.

The British reined King in. A senior member of the British navy's intelligence staff was visiting Ottawa. He went to see naval minister Angus Macdonald on the morning of May 14, shortly before the minister announced in the House of Commons that there would be no new information about the St. Lawrence attacks.

People working in the censorship system were already demanding the politicians stop talking. The first call for a news blackout on the St. Lawrence sinkings came from Montreal's chief cable censor, who phoned Montreal press censor Ed McMahon during the lunch hour on May 12 to tell him a ship had been sunk in the St. Lawrence by a U-boat and that McMahon had to stop all stories on the attack. From Ottawa, Warren Baldwin tried to dampen the enthusiasm of reporters, telling them the press release hadn't changed the rules: "the usual survivor stories could be allowed and . . . the usual regulations would prevail." This meant that the names of the vessels, the place of the attacks, the identities and nationalities of the people aboard, the places where survivors were brought ashore or were interviewed, and the ships' cargos could not be published. McMahon phoned the editors of the wire services and executives at the bigger Quebec papers, then sent telegrams to the smaller newspapers to make sure they understood the rules.

When a British United Press reporter submitted a story from Mont Louis saying survivors had landed there, the Montreal censor told him to change the place to "a St. Lawrence shore village." McMahon did pass a story written by H. Higgins of the *Montreal Star* for the *Boston Sunday Advertiser* that said angry French-speaking Quebecers were crowding into recruiting offices, particularly those of the navy. When the cable censors reported a Canadian Press journalist was phoning Gaspé towns and asking to speak to survivors, the cable censors asked McMahon to warn the news agency that censors were listening in on the calls and would cut the telephone connection if reporters asked for the names of attack locations or ships.

The Canadian Press managed to pull together a complete description of the May 11–12 attack, but censors in Ottawa killed the article. A *Montreal Gazette* story, which was a combination of the information supplied by CP and details obtained independently by the *Gazette*, was approved because it was vague about the location of the attacks. Censors also passed an attack story in Quebec's *Le Soleil* filed from Rimouski because the details about the ship and its sailors were obscured and the community was called "a town on the shores of the St. Lawrence." At noon on May 13, a journalist at the *Quebec Chronicle-Telegraph* telephoned McMahon to say he had received instructions from a Lieutenant Barrow of the navy to use "East Coast Port" instead of "town" or "village on the shores of the St. Lawrence." McMahon told the journalist not to bother. Because of the loose talk of politicians in Ottawa, "this change would be silly," the censor said.

Federal Conservative leader R.B. Hanson wanted even more openness about the attacks. He demanded Macdonald "review" his news blackout policy "in view of the fact that the enemy must have information of these sinkings and that the government of the United States are announcing their losses from time to time, and that periodically Britain has announced similar losses." The navy's silence caused rumours to take the place of fact, Hanson argued, "and the stories grow in repeating them." The once-talkative Macdonald, now muzzled by British and Canadian naval intelligence officers, replied he could see no reason for changing the censorship policy.

The German press picked up on the stories of the St. Lawrence sub campaign in a rare instance when the Nazis claimed to have monitored Canadian media coverage. At 9:15 a.m. on May 12, Berlin radio broadcast a report on the previous day's attack, telling listeners a U-boat sank a 6,000-ton U.S. freighter carrying a cargo of jute from India to Montreal. "The ship had made the long voyage from India safely, only to be sunk in the St. Lawrence," the Nazi radio

station announced. "This is the first time that U-boats have operated so far from the sea." The Nazis reported the news of the sub
attacks "broke like a bombshell in Canada and the United States."

Ottawa's news blackout did not stop reporters from trying to
get accurate accounts of the St. Lawrence attacks. In Toronto, censor
Bert Perry approved three pictures from Rimouski, including a
photo of the survivors, but would not authorize a picture of officers
and sailors gazing into the open coffin of a crew member who had
frozen to death in their lifeboat. The politicians' loose talk and the
blizzard of news stories were bound to cause another hostile salvo
from the "silent service." On May 15, Captain Eric Brand of naval
intelligence called Eggleston "to complain that the press was running wild on the St. Lawrence sinking." Brand objected to the dateline "a St. Lawrence port," rather than "an Eastern Canadian port,"
and was angry the censors had allowed the press to publish the
number of survivors in the most recent attack. Eggleston happily
explained to Brand that the minister in charge of the navy, not the
censors, released the fact that attacks were in the St. Lawrence River.
The words "St. Lawrence port," Eggleston said, added no new information. Eggleston asked Brand what information was given to the
enemy by telling the number of survivors. The change in numbers
quoted in recent stories, Brand argued, from forty survivors to eighty,
clearly showed that there was at least one more ship involved. He
said the press "had now gouged this information out [of the navy]."

Eggleston didn't know there had been two sinkings. He told
Brand he was surprised to hear of the second ship. Perhaps if the
navy had told the censors the truth, he said, they could have done a
better job of keeping a lid on the stories.

The stories kept coming through the spring of 1942. Independent MP J.P. Roy used his parliamentary immunity to ask questions
in the House of Commons about the sinkings in May and June.
L'Action catholique reported Roy's speeches, spreading a fairly detailed report of the first St. Lawrence U-boat battle to all of the parishes of Quebec. The Canadian Press asked Eggleston on June 9 if it
should quote Roy's information. Eggleston told the news agency it
could use anything printed in *Hansard*.

At the beginning of July, naval intelligence officers warned Eggleston of another U-boat foray. Eggleston passed the vague report to McMahon, who was ready on July 8 when he received an early-morning call from the newsroom of *L'Action catholique*, which knew that another ship had been sunk in the St. Lawrence. The paper was tipped off by a sailor of an inbound vessel who reported cargo ships had been blocked by naval patrols in the Gulf and that survivors of a sub attack had come ashore at Cap Chat. On July 6, 1942, *U-132* launched its first torpedoes in the St. Lawrence River, striking at a fourteen-ship convoy near Cap Chat and sinking three freighters, the Greek *Anastassios Pateras*, the Belgian *Hainaut*, and the British *Dinarik*. Two weeks later, *U-132* torpedoed the British *Frederika Lensen*, killing four men but leaving the ship salvageable.

McMahon told *L'Action catholique* to hold its story on these attacks until Ottawa issued an official statement. The navy wanted the story banned for at least a couple of days while it hunted the U-boat in the confines of the river. Within an hour, Quebec City's *Le Soleil* called McMahon about the same story and was given the same advice. By the end of the day, the *Toronto Star* knew about the new attacks and sent a reporter to Montreal to interview survivors and get photos.

Meanwhile, a Canadian National Railways official in Moncton told Jefferson a U-boat fired torpedoes at the ferry *Prince Edward Island*, narrowly missing it but hitting a munitions ship nearby. The navy warned the censors that the submarine had not signalled its kills to Germany so it was still vulnerable to "huff-duff" direction-finding, but attempts to silence the media reports of the submarine attack were thwarted by Roy, who rose in the House of Commons on July 10 to announce details of the entire raid and to demand better protection for shipping. The censors received calls from frantic Canadian Press editors who said the story on Roy's revelations was known in newsrooms across the country because Parliament Hill reporters had phoned or wired the news to their home papers. Fulgence Charpentier told them the story was still embargoed. He called Jack Marshall, president of the Parliamentary Press Gallery, to get his co-operation to control the Roy story.

Warren Baldwin believed it would be futile to try to stop coverage of debates in Parliament over Roy's statement. Naval intelligence said it would issue a short press release. But nothing came out of the navy's headquarters, so Baldwin, frustrated again by the foot dragging, told the wire services they could send their stories across the country.

Despite the sporadic leaks, by mid-July, Canadian Press and newspapers in Eastern Canada were sitting on some very dramatic stories. In Sydney, reporters interviewed survivors of the Cap Chat attack but could not have their write-ups published. The crew of the car ferry *Prince Edward Island* arrived at Charlottetown in the second week of July and spun yarns about how they "escaped under forced draught and by the skin of their teeth." Jefferson wanted to pass the Charlottetown stories because the *Prince Edward Island* was not in a convoy, but Eggleston asked him to send the stories to Ottawa, where Lieutenant Commander C.H. Little of the navy tried to kill them. After another argument with Eggleston, the stories were cleared on the condition that references to other ships were removed and the destination of the *Prince Edward Island* was changed from Charlottetown to the ubiquitous "Eastern Canadian Port."

When navy minister Angus Macdonald issued a press release July 13 criticizing Roy's lack of discretion, Jefferson sat in the CP Halifax newsroom and edited the minister's statement as it came across the teletype, "fuzzying up" some of the details. Meanwhile, in Montreal, McMahon eviscerated copy submitted by Joan Capreol of the Montreal *Gazette*, removing facts from an interview with the Greek captain of one of the submarine's victims. A few hours later, the *Montreal Star*'s story based on the interview with the same captain was similarly sanitized. The cuts to these dramatic survivor stories did not deter Capreol, who returned to McMahon's office two days later with a story based on interviews with nineteen survivors of the submarine attack. Capreol strongly argued with McMahon over cuts to her story, thereby salvaging enough interesting material to make it appealing to the seasoned U-boat story chasers at the *Halifax Herald*, who picked up the article from the *Gazette* later that night.

U-517 and *U-165* arrived in the St. Lawrence in late August 1942. On August 27, *U-517* sank the U.S. freighter *Chatham* with the loss of fourteen sailors, while *U-165* sank the USS *Laramie*, killing five men. The two submarines continued their attacks through the middle of September. *U-517*'s kill tally included *Arlyn* (U.S.), with the loss of twelve sailors on August 28; the Canadian ship *Donald Stewart* on September 3 (three killed); the Greek ships *Mount Pindus* and *Mount Taygetus* and the Canadian ship *Oakton* on September 7 (eight men lost); the HMCS *Charlottetown* on September 11 (ten sailors killed); and the Dutch freighter *Saturnus* and the Norwegian *Inger Elizabeth* (four killed) on September 3. *U-165* sank the HMCS *Raccoon* on September 7, with the loss of thirty-six sailors. It sank the Greek freighter *Joannis* on September 16 and damaged the British ships *Essex Lance* and *Pan York* the same day before leaving the St. Law-rence. Two more U-boats arrived in early October to take the place of *U-517* and *U-165*. On October 9, *U-69* announced its presence in the St. Lawrence River by sinking the freighter *Carolus* near Metis Beach, killing twelve men. Two days later, *U-106* sank the British freighter *Watertown*.

Because of censorship and the tight control of information by the navy, the press killed some of the most dramatic local stories of the war. The Canadian public did not know that more than 500 passengers heading to the Goose Bay, Labrador, air-base construction site run by the U.S. air force barely managed to escape from the *Chatham* in the half-hour before the vessel went under in the Strait of Belle Isle between Newfoundland and Labrador. For weeks, the censors killed eyewitness stories that came out of Boston and northern Ontario, spread by construction workers who survived the attack.

HMCS *Raccoon*'s loss did not become public until September 13, when *Le Soleil* published an article entitled "Cinq navires ont été coulées." *Raccoon* had been on the bottom for five days when the *Ottawa Evening Journal* reported on the "daring midday attack" that had damaged SS *Frederika Lensen* the previous July. On September 8, the Montreal cable censors intercepted a tip telegraphed from the National Maritime Federation to the *Toronto Star*, saying there were "developments" in the St. Lawrence River east of Quebec City. On the advice of press censor Ed McMahon, the cable was held "for good." Six days later, Adam Marshall of the Montreal *Gazette* asked McMahon for clearance on a story saying three Greek freighters and a Canadian naval patrol boat were lost on the St. Lawrence. It was the first story of the loss of *Raccoon*. McMahon told him he could not run the time, place, identity, or number of vessels lost, to which Marshall replied, "Oh hell!" The next day, Ottawa censors cleared stories of the arrival in Montreal of eighty survivors of merchant ships sunk in the St. Lawrence, plus survivors of *Raccoon*, without naming any ships or allowing details of their loss. The Ottawa and Halifax censors also finally passed reports of a German torpedo that came ashore on the Gaspé side of the river, blowing out some windows of a waterfront house.

On September 27, Jefferson received a late-night phone call from Baldwin in Ottawa, who reported the new submarine action off the Gaspé. Baldwin told Jefferson to sit on any stories on the attacks until an official announcement was made in the national capital. Baldwin also mentioned that steps had been taken to black out lights on portions of the lower St. Lawrence shores as a prevention against enemy activities in that region. Censorship successfully stifled the story until October 13, when the Wartime Information Board, the government's propaganda arm, organized a reporters' trip to Metis Beach. The *Montreal Herald* and the *Toronto Star* submitted stories to McMahon that were cut to ribbons, and the censor chopped a Canadian Press article so heavily that it was, he said, "quite innocuous and uninteresting."

On the night and morning of October 14–15, 1942, U-69 sank the Newfoundland-to-Nova Scotia ferry *Caribou* in the Cabot Strait, killing 137 people. In the early hours of October 15, Jefferson was told of the attack by a Halifax army public-relations officer. Ottawa censor Warren Baldwin was in town helping Jefferson deal with the U-boat attack stories coming out of the Gulf of St. Lawrence, and neither man got much sleep. Baldwin was awakened by a reporter from the *Halifax Herald* who demanded permission to contact the relatives of the *Caribou* victims. Despite being warned off the story until the next of kin had been officially notified, the *Herald* pressed

on. At 9:30, cable censors reported the *Herald* was trying to get telegrams through to the families of casualties in the Kentville district.
Those telegrams were stopped, so the *Herald*'s switchboard began
placing long-distance calls. The local newspapers created a code
name for the attack, "swim meet," and cobbled together a rough list
of the people who had drowned.

The first day's coverage in the *Halifax Herald* was just a bare-
bones story. The *Herald*'s reporters spent the day looking for eyewitnesses and found two women survivors who had been landed at
Halifax. One of them, Gladys Shiers of Dartmouth, was knocked
unconscious when she went into the water. Her 14-month-old son
Leonard had drifted away in the darkness but was pulled into a lifeboat at the last minute by a sailor. He was the only child, out of
twenty-two aboard the *Caribou*, who had been saved. When the
editors submitted their story, Jefferson cut Shiers's description of
the counterattack by the minesweeper *Grandmère* but let the reporters run the women's dramatic story. A story in the *Halifax Chronicle*
quoted one survivor saying two torpedoes had struck the *Caribou*.
This was left in since other stories reported only one "and this would
confuse rather than inform the enemy."

Life for the censors was made more difficult by the split in jurisdiction between Newfoundland and Canada. The *Caribou* was a
Newfoundland vessel but it had been sunk in Canadian waters. The
Newfoundland censor wanted control over the story. Eventually,
the Newfoundland papers were given first crack, as many of the
victims, including the ship's crew, were from the island.

The attack on the *Caribou* came as *L'Action catholique*, the Quebec City–based mass circulation newspaper, was running a series of
articles on the U-boat attacks in the St. Lawrence. Thousands of
readers across Quebec were told the navy was failing Quebec by
letting U-boats run freely in the St. Lawrence. The journalists did
not understand that the Canadian response to the U-boats—marine and air patrols, and the closure of the river to shipping when
the U-boat threat was clear—was, for the most part, working. The
German successes had come mainly in the first weeks of the campaign when they had the element of surprise. Now, they were being

squeezed out of the river and the Gulf: *U-69* sank the *Caribou* as a parting shot after a frustrating, fruitless cruise into the St. Lawrence. *L'Action catholique*'s series, written by Edouard Laurent, was inflammatory. Quebec premier Adélard Godbout sent the articles to Mackenzie King with a note saying they were "the most complete and objective articles I have yet seen on the subject." Eugène L'Heureux, the paper's editor, said his writer "collected a number of impressions with which he thought the public should be acquainted, in order to stimulate, not maliciously criticize, the men responsible for the defence of our shores and the river."

King's ministers tried to set Godbout straight by giving the Quebec premier accurate information about the Battle of the St. Lawrence. The material sent to Quebec City disproved most of Laurent's and Roy's more inflammatory allegations about weak defences along the Quebec coast. Air Minister C.G. "Chubby" Power authorized the leaking of the dates of the sinkings, names of ships, and places of the attacks to Godbout and to a Quebec Liberal Party organizer in Rimouski. They were supposed to pass this information to the editors of *L'Action catholique* and to Laurent, presumably with the understanding the newspaper would change the tone of its coverage. Historian Nathan Greenfield believes this was a risky decision that may well have backfired against Canada "given *Action Catholique*'s ties with pro-Vichy forces in Quebec and the Vichy government's puppet status." He wondered whether the information Ottawa released to the paper was used in two articles published in the Nazi party newspaper *Volkischer Beobachter* on November 4 and December 18.

At a meeting of the Advisory Committee on the Publication of Military Information on October 20, Eggleston and Lieutenant Commander C.H. Little fought over press coverage of the sub attacks. Little demanded a strict interpretation of the censorship directives. Eggleston said the newspapers would not comply with censorship unless editors believed there were "real security reasons" for the suppression of news. Biggar, who was chairing the meeting, stepped in to try to smooth things over. The navy, he said, had promised to let the censors in on information that would help them understand the situation. Maybe, he said, it would finally get around to doing so.

In the end, the argument made in Parliament by Tory leader Hanson, that rumours would replace the censored facts, turned out to be accurate. Pierre Trudeau was one of the people confused and confounded by the government's news manipulation. In 1943, he hiked into the Gaspé blissfully unaware of the U-boat war along the coast of the peninsula. Fifty years later, when he wrote his memoirs, Trudeau was still ignorant of the Battle of the St. Lawrence. His memory was hazy about German subs, but he recollected hearing the very persistent story that U-boat crews were coming ashore at Quebec towns to buy supplies from friendly merchants. The government tried to kill this piece of wartime urban mythology but it was unstoppable in Ontario and the West. The story was embellished through the fall with details about the food, cigarettes, and chocolate bars the U-boat sailors took back to their subs, which were said to be tied up at municipal docks. The Wartime Information Board, which gauged public opinion by hiring people across the country to report on the spread of rumours, found this story to be unkillable.

The government decided to kill some of the rumours by releasing statistics on the sub attacks. On November 24, Macdonald called a press conference to stop reports that somewhere between thirty and forty ships had been lost in the St. Lawrence. The true number was twenty in the entire region, taking in the St. Lawrence estuary, the Gulf of St. Lawrence, the Strait of Belle Isle, and the Cabot Strait.

The sub-attack stories waned in the late fall of 1942 as the shipping season ended and the U-boats left the Gulf for better hunting in the Atlantic. In December, the Gulf was closed to ocean shipping and stories about U-boat attacks in the St. Lawrence became old news west of Montreal.

The next spring, Quebec nationalists would not let the issue of Quebec coastal defence die: it was raised in the House of Commons in early March 1943, as one Quebec MP after another bid up the number of ships that had been sunk. Onésime Gagnon announced the loss of thirty ships the previous year. On March 15, Roy rose again in the House of Commons to say he had information that thirty-seven vessels were lost. Roy added to his padded numbers with a likely bogus claim to have witnessed a running battle between a submarine and Canadian corvettes. He told the House such sights were common along the Gaspé Peninsula the previous summer. Roy's accusations were reported by most of the major newspapers in the country. Some reporters expanded on Roy's House of Commons statements to tell what they knew of the 1942 attacks in the St. Lawrence. That March, Opposition members of the Quebec Legislative Assembly took up the sub-attack issue. Censors Jacques Girouard in Ottawa and Ed McMahon in Montreal let the stories run, despite McMahon's belief they would be used as German propaganda.

The U-boats did not come back to the St. Lawrence in 1943 but they were active in Canadian and Newfoundland coastal waters. The iron ore port at Wabana, on Bell Island in Conception Bay, Newfoundland, which was attacked twice in 1942, was hit again in February 1943. The U-boat attack at Wabana made the Newfoundland newspapers on February 19, 1943, and Jefferson approved stories on the raid the following day for publication in Nova Scotia. Baldwin, who did not like the tenor of the Canadian stories and recognized their propaganda value to the Germans, imposed a blackout on broadcasting and exporting the story to papers in the United States and Britain.

Meanwhile, strange things were happening in the Arctic. On October 21, 1943, *U-537* moored near Killiniq Island on the north tip of the Labrador Peninsula while crewmen went ashore to set up Weather Station Kurt to automatically beam data to Germany. It may not have been the first time U-boats scouted the region. The previous summer, Inuit in northern Hudson Bay talked about a submarine they had seen in the area. The story was picked up in August 1942 by Jim McLean, a *Toronto Star* stringer based in Winnipeg. It was passed by the censors, who believed the submarine was stalking a ship that carried supplies to the people in the region.

The U-boats made a second major incursion into Canadian

coastal waters in the summer and fall of 1944. The assault began with a German mine-laying foray off Halifax in the late winter and the torpedoing of the ss *Watuka* in convoy sh-125 off Halifax by u-802 on March 22. The Canadian Press did not report on the attack until mid-July. Grand Admiral Doenitz sent four U-boats into the Gulf of St. Lawrence that year. At 2:00 on the morning of October 14, 1944, u-1223 torpedoed hmcs *Magog* as she escorted convoy ons-33 past Pointe-des-Monts, blowing the stern off the frigate and killing three men. On the night of November 24, u-1228, on its way out of the Gulf of St. Lawrence, sank the corvette hmcs *Shawinigan*, killing ninety-one men. Censors slapped a news blackout on those attacks.

In December 1944, Charpentier recommended to the Department of Justice that *Le Soleil* be prosecuted under the *Defence of Canada Regulations* for its story on the sinking of the Canadian National Railways steamship *Cornwallis* off Nova Scotia. This was followed up at a meeting of the Directorate of Censorship's Advisory Committee on Intelligence and Security, where Eggleston said, "It was important that in an open breach of this kind, every effort should be made to punish the offender, since it would be difficult to obtain co-operation from other newspapers if they should come to the conclusion that there was no real strength in the law." The minister of justice, Louis St. Laurent, decided to charge *Le Soleil*, and the paper was fined $50 and $3.40 in court costs. The prosecution of *Le Soleil* was a quiet affair: the other papers in Quebec City did not cover the short trial.

The threat of charges may have deterred the *Halifax Herald*, which contacted Jefferson on January 9, 1945, to protest against continued suppression of stories about the loss of *Cornwallis* and other sinkings. The *Herald*'s editors decided to approach Macdonald, who was in Halifax, to ask him to lift the blackout. By then, the *Herald* was sitting on the stories of the sinkings of one destroyer, one corvette, one minesweeper, and three freighters. More were to come: in the early morning of January 14, 1945, U-boats attacked a convoy "almost within sight" of Halifax, hitting at least three freighters (and, according to Ken Chisholm of the *Herald*, also torpedoing a navy frigate).

The Halifax newspapers believed coverage of the latest U-boat attacks off Halifax's harbour was manipulated by the King government to help the campaign of the defence minister, General A.G.L. McNaughton, in the Grey North by-election scheduled for February 5. McNaughton had stayed in Ottawa through the Christmas season, rather than campaign in what was considered a safe Liberal riding. On January 26, he told a campaign rally near Owen Sound he had been too busy to campaign because "today the North Atlantic is, as it has been for months past, alive with German submarines. . . . We are having ships sunk day-by-day." In frustration, the *Herald* lashed out with an editorial cartoon that ran in its January 27 edition. Entitled "Don't Gag the Right People," the cartoon showed three figures named "Press," "Public," and "Radio" gagged with cloths labelled "Censorship" and held in a darkened room.

Despite the protests from the paper, the cloak of secrecy was not lifted on the Christmas season attacks until February 10. The last major attack, on the minesweeper HMCS *Esquimalt* near Halifax on April 19, 1945, by U-190, killed forty-four sailors. Jefferson, under pressure from the navy, kept the story secret until VE day, knowing it would be lost in the reports of victory (and, as it turned out, in coverage of the Halifax Riots). In the last days of the European war, Jefferson approved a story by Eric Dennis about the possible surrender of U-boats at East Coast ports; on VE day, Jefferson lifted censorship on all of the Battle of the Atlantic material.

Probably few people in Halifax noticed the "now it can be told" stories, even in the newsrooms. Censorship of the submarine war ended just as thousands of sailors rioted in reaction to a municipal edict to close Halifax's beer parlours and liquor stores on VE day. Jefferson took a keen interest in the Halifax Riots—he wandered the city gathering facts for a memo that he would send to Ottawa. Nine months earlier he had predicted the riots, saying in a memorandum that the sailors had legitimate complaints about being exploited by Halifax businesses. He let the newspapers run every word of their coverage of the trouble, and believed they missed many details. He also passed all of the stories submitted about the explosion of an ammunition depot on an island in Halifax harbour on July 22, 1945, an event that brought back bad memories of the much larger Halifax Explosion of 1917. By then, the focus of the war had shifted to the West Coast in anticipation of a long fight with Japan.

There was little real need for censorship on Canada's West Coast until the attack on Pearl Harbor. In the spring of 1941, censorship in the West focused on the armed merchant cruiser *Prince Henry*'s successful raid on German shipping along the coast of Central and South America and another armed merchant ship, the RCN auxiliary cruiser *Prince Robert*, which stopped the U.S. liner *President Garfield* off Hawaii and removed four German airmen. The Toronto censors were able to keep the name of the *Prince Robert* out of the newspapers, but several Toronto radio stations and CBC's national newscast aired it on April 30, 1941.

Japan's thrust into the Central and South Pacific immediately placed British Columbia's ports in the war zone, both as potential attack targets and as clearing houses for news from the fighting theatres. In those first months of the war, that news was invariably bad. The first major challenge on the West Coast was to keep a lid on news of the sinking of the Canadian troop ship *Empress of Asia*, which was shattered by Japanese bombers on February 5, 1942, at Singapore. Don Mason, marine editor of the *Vancouver Sun*, had the story March 9, 1942, but Vancouver press censor Lew Gordon refused to clear it. The censors wanted to release the story—certainly the Japanese knew they had wrecked the transport—but they continued to suppress it on the advice of Captain Brand of naval intelligence, who was "not very impressed with the [censors'] argument that there was no need to withhold information from the enemy merely because we had proof that the enemy knew more than we did." A complete and vivid description of the loss of the ship, written by Gordon Sinclair, was shelved by the *Toronto Star* after the censors demanded the removal of the ship's name and the ranks of the men who were interviewed. However, vague survivor stories carried by the Canadian Press, describing a dive-bombed ship sunk in the South Pacific but failing to mention the vessel's name and nationality, were approved.

The censors also suppressed all news of the presence of Soviet ships in B.C. ports. The Soviets made the request for censorship to prevent friction between their government and the Japanese, with whom they were at peace. Lew Gordon ordered the *Vancouver Province* to change the caption under the picture of what he called a "mangey-looking Siberian bear" that was a mascot aboard a Russian ship from "Siberian bear" to "a seagoing bear." The censors also turned down requests from the Vancouver newspapers for permission to mention the presence of Soviet ships in the city's repair yards and complained when newspapers quoted anonymous sailors from unnamed ships spouting the "Russian party line." This ban lasted until the fall of 1944.

The censors did suppress stories of complaints by boat and ship owners about the trigger-happy shore batteries at Vancouver firing shots across their bows as they entered Vancouver harbour. The closest Vancouver came to any real naval action was the bombardment of Estevan Point on Vancouver Island by a Japanese submarine on June 20, 1942. The submarine's deck gun targeted a lighthouse on the isolated northwest corner of the island. The attack, which caused no injuries and no real damage, was one of a number of ineffective Japanese raids along the Pacific Northwest coast that caused a sensation in the press. The censors kept a lid on the story until military officials in Ottawa released it on June 22.

In the Great Lakes area, censorship focused on U.S. defence installations at Sault Ste. Marie and the U.S. government's ban on stories about ore carriers' movements. On November 5, 1940, the *Toronto Telegram* published a story reminding its readers of the Rush–Bagot Agreement, which limited Canadian and U.S. naval strength on the Great Lakes. With British and Canadian acquiescence, it was being ignored by the States, which used Lake Michigan for naval training. That night, the British United Press was warned by the censors not to pick up the story. The news agency moved a story anyway, and the next day was told "there had been no change, nor would there be any, on this issue." The article was removed from the wire soon afterwards. The *Toronto Star* tried to run a story November 6 saying the *Telegram*'s speculation that the Rush–Bagot Agreement would be renegotiated was inaccurate, but the censors killed that story, saying, "It was undesirable that any further publicity be given to the Rush–Bagot treaty affair." External Affairs officials concurred with the decision.

Some censorship of East Coast and Great Lakes naval issues continued in the days after the European war ended. Just after VE day, Perry turned down a request from Russ Whitely of Canadian Press to write about the barrage balloons that floated above the Sault Ste. Marie locks, saying these were U.S. installations and clearance should come from stateside. All Canadian naval censorship ended on VJ day, August 15, 1945.

The Atlantic Coast of Canada was a vital theatre in the war against Germany. Hundreds of Canadian, British, and other Allied sailors and civilians died in the fighting. Censors were called upon to control coverage of some of the most compelling local stories of the war. In selecting Bruce Jefferson for the job of Halifax censor, the Directorate of Censorship made one of its best decisions. He turned out to be strong enough to resist the pressures of both the Halifax media and the city's powerful contingent of military officers. Jefferson was also able to maintain consistent censorship of the U-boat war off the East Coast while allowing some important stories of ship losses to be published, sometimes after a relatively brief waiting period.

Still, any coverage of the Battle of the Atlantic and the U-boat attacks in Canadian waters drew criticism from the navy, which sought a complete news blackout of marine actions on both of Canada's coasts. Despite Jefferson's tight censorship, relations between the navy and the censors were strained at best, and the navy usually left the censors ignorant of important events. This placed the censors at a disadvantage when dealing with reporters, who often knew more about the Battle of the Atlantic than the censors.

The naval censorship system broke down in the St. Lawrence, where things were out of Jefferson's hands. There were more media competing for news, and political factors were often at cross-purposes with the military's need for secrecy. Canadian newspapers and radio stations also took a much more intense interest in the St. Lawrence submarine attacks because they brought the war into Canada. In Quebec, the censorship system never operated with the consistency of Jefferson's Halifax office. In fact, the nationalist press in that province, which opposed participation in the war and had strong sympathies with the fascist regime in Vichy, sometimes made a mockery of the naval censorship system—a situation that reflected a larger pattern in Quebec.

CHAPTER 5

"These Little Treacheries": *Censorship and the Quebec Media*

DURING WORLD WAR TWO, Quebec's nationalist media published articles and commentary that rivalled the fascist propaganda carried by the government-controlled newspapers in Hitler's puppet state, Vichy France. The resemblance is no coincidence: some of that material came directly from collaborationist France, and the federal government knew it. William Lyon Mackenzie King and his two wartime justice ministers (and Quebec lieutenants), Ernest Lapointe and Louis St. Laurent, were afraid of the elite francophone media in Quebec, especially *Le Devoir*, *L'Action catholique*, and *L'Événement-Journal*. Because of the Liberals' political needs, the censors were a joke among the isolationist Quebec media. Once extreme nationalist editors realized censorship was an empty threat, they published isolationist, pro-Vichy, and anti-Semitic articles with impunity.

Important parts of the Quebec press had opposed Canadian involvement in World War One. Of the four "mainstream" papers shut down in Canada during that war, two were from Quebec: *Le Bulletin* of Montreal and Quebec City's *La Croix*. During the Great War, chief censor Ernest Chambers also wanted to close *Le Devoir* but his recommendations were ignored. Prime Minister Robert Borden knew that Henri Bourassa, the Quebec nationalist icon who founded and owned the paper, would eagerly embrace martyrdom if the federal government did anything to rein in *Le Devoir*.

Eventually, though, Bourassa gave in. *Le Devoir* was blamed by some English-Canadian newspapers, including the *Vancouver Sun*, for instigating the Easter 1918 anti-draft riots in Quebec and for the censorship crackdown that followed them. Bourassa issued a press release in May 1918, saying he would "submit" articles to Chambers and let the future "decide whether it [was] in conformity with the best interests of the country." He told the acting editor, Georges Pelletier, to let the censors vet all controversial copy. During World War Two, Pelletier, now armed with a law degree, was the managing editor of the paper, and in this war he was not letting anyone cut his stories.

The new press censors knew the nationalist Quebec press would fight them. Still, it is unlikely they went into the war suspecting Mackenzie King's government would so completely surrender to *Le Devoir*, Quebec City's *Le Soleil*, and *L'Événement-Journal*, and to the fringe Quebec journalists who would publish some of the most racist and pro-fascist material ever to run in commercial Canadian newspapers.

At the outbreak of the war, Claude Melançon, a popular member of the Canadian National Railway's public-relations team, became responsible for censorship of the French-language press. He opened an office on Place d'Armes in Montreal and visited all of the newsrooms of the city, meeting editors and distributing copies of the censorship regulations. At first, he was treated well, but that genteel situation did not last long. Premier Maurice Duplessis, believing Quebecers opposed the war as much as he did, plunged into one of the roughest provincial elections in Canadian history.

Even before the German attack on Poland, *Le Devoir* and other, less important, French-language papers and magazines had come out against Canadian participation in a war against Hitler, or any other foreign conflict. And, in the Depression, the mainstream Quebec press, especially *L'Action catholique*, often published anti-Semitic rants and sang the praises of Mussolini and Franco.

In the first days of September 1939, between Britain's declaration of war and Canada's parliamentary vote, Quebec nationalists packed meeting halls in Montreal to show their opposition. RCMP officers were in the crowds. At least one of these meetings, a gathering of about four thousand people that filled St. Jacques Market Hall in Old Montreal, was violent, with fights breaking out in the crowd.

Phillippe Girard, president of the Syndicats Catholiques de Montréal, an umbrella group of trade unions, said the Nazis would not destroy democracy. Representative government would die, he said, because of "Judeo-International finance." Addressing some French-Canadian World War One veterans in the crowd, Girard said only English-speaking soldiers had been given pensions and jobs. He ended his speech by saying, "Don't worry, we will have something to eat without going to war. Let's send the Jews to the war."

The Montreal *Gazette* demanded the federal government use its *War Measures Act* powers to shut down the meetings. "It will not do to play at this war business," the *Gazette* editorial said. "It will not do for the Government to ignore any overt act designed or calculated to give comfort to this country's enemies." The Mounties agreed, asking the censors to stop any mention of the meetings in the press or radio. Thompson, still setting up his temporary office in the Ottawa train station, called *Le Devoir*'s Pelletier on September 8 to ask him to help.

Pelletier complied this time, but he started his own campaign to turn Quebec public opinion against Canadian involvement in the war. Pelletier signed an editorial that ran in *Le Devoir* on September 16 blaming Britain for not nipping Nazism in the bud in the mid-1930s. He asked if Britain and France went to war to protect Poland because "for centuries the cities of Poland have harboured thousands of Jews whom England does not want to be dispersed." England had never fought for Quebec, except in 1759, "and that was to take us over."

The provincial campaign that began in the third week of September 1939 was vicious. The provincial Liberals were led by a nonentity, Adélard Godbout, and were portrayed in the Duplessis-supporting press as a pack of Ottawa stooges. Here, the nationalists were on solid ground: federal ministers Ernest Lapointe, Charles G. "Chubby" Power, and P.J.A. Cardin staked their House of Commons seats on the outcome and seemed to do much more campaigning than Godbout.

A few days after Duplessis called the election, *Le Devoir* came out blaming Lapointe for tough new radio censorship rules that were a direct interference by Ottawa. "We believe [Duplessis] will make use of this argument," Pelletier predicted with the sharp foresight of an insider.

The radio censorship rules had not been created to stifle Duplessis. They had been written and were in envelopes, waiting to be mailed, when the election was called. Simply, the federal government did not want any political speeches, interviews, or editorials to be broadcast without being cleared by radio censors. Usually, this was simply a matter of running a script past the station manager, the same kind of vetting that was used in peacetime to keep smut off the air. In a one-off move, the Censorship Co-ordination Committee appointed federal lawyers as broadcast censors in Quebec, placing them in Montreal, Quebec City, Rimouski, and New Carlisle. Certainly, there were political fingerprints all over these decisions: radio censorship was, in the fall of 1939, under the control of the minister of transport, not the justice minister, but it was Lapointe who picked the censors. The lawyer-censors stayed busy by making deletions to approximately 250 of the scripts submitted during the election campaign.

Quebec City's *L'Événement-Journal*, co-owned by lawyer and former provincial Liberal cabinet minister Jacob Nicol, reacted to the new rules. How, the editors asked, could the federal government question the loyalty of Quebecers and their government when, just a few months before, Quebecers had cheered the King and Queen during their visit? "Mr. Lapointe and his colleagues will have to bear the brunt of their revolting decision," the paper editorialized.

At the same time, the paper carried a series of long articles under the standing headline "Daily Letter from Adolf Hitler." In the first letter, supposedly written to his sister, the bogus Hitler wrote, "This news that Canada declares war on me has caused me great sorrow. For, after all, those Canadians, I have done them nothing. In the past, their country belonged to France; later, England grabbed it; the Germans have never mixed in this squabble, now forgotten, anyway." Hermann Goering, the writer claimed, was trying to find any linguistic, cultural, or political affinities between the Poles and the Canadians. The writer wondered "what in the world has urged the government of His Very Canadian Majesty to declare war on me. If it is another country which has forced her hand, I shall protest, on the principle that peoples have the right to dispose of themselves."

In the next letter, the imposter Hitler said he could understand why England and France had declared war, "But the Canadians! They know, the Canadians, that never shall I go to war against them at home. I had decided not to bother them, for the good reason that I even ignored their existence, but, if they declare war on me, who has done them no wrong, I will certainly have to make them pay for it." The writer claimed Hitler craved nothing in North America and knew, in any case, the United States would intervene if Canada was attacked.

By September 14, "Hitler" was no longer writing to his sister but to a friend, "Baptiste," in Canada. "Dear Mr. Baptiste," the pseudo-Hitler wrote, "you have indeed reason not to want to get killed in Europe, as Europe would not want death in America for your sake— not even England." Two days later, "Hitler" thanked Britain on the editorial page of *L'Événement-Journal* for selling Germany steel and machinery before the Labour Day weekend attack on the Poles: "We will give it all back to them, in the shape of bombs or other things, in the garden of France." The writer said Mackenzie King's slogan was "Canada first . . . at war" which meant "England, once more, would fight to the last Canadian. It is, I am told, the application of one of the principles of economic warfare."

The censors had the "letters" translated and circulated in Ottawa. Montreal-based censor Claude Melançon took the train to Quebec City and visited the paper's editor, Bruno Lafleur, to complain. He got a promise of co-operation, but the letters kept running well into the election campaign.

Meanwhile, *Le Devoir* made a bizarre claim that men were being fired from good jobs across Canada to compel them to enlist. That lie was picked up by Duplessis's candidates across the province, who sometimes added a local angle to the story.

In the last week of the campaign, *Le Devoir* carried a story that used quotes from isolationist American aviation hero Charles Lindbergh, who had spoken out against Canada's declaration of war.

L'Événement-Journal used Lindbergh's statement as a cudgel to beat the federal government and the censors. Lapointe might be able to stifle the Quebec press, *L'Événement-Journal* said, but it was afraid to censor comments made by a U.S. celebrity. The Quebec City paper editorialized, "Mr. Lindbergh has stated that Canada had no business to enter this war. By preferring the British Crown to America's independence, Canada has broken the continental peace, says Lindbergh."

L'Événement-Journal argued Lapointe was willing to tear Canada apart to beat Duplessis. Voters had the right to use the election as a referendum on the King government's war policies and should be able to read and hear debate, argued the editors, "from the declaration of war itself through the war measures, censorship and the loan of $200,000,000 [to Britain], up to the means employed by Mr. Lapointe to gag public opinion in view of conscription. No power on earth can now prevent the French-Canadian voice from being heard." For his part, Duplessis promised to let the newspapers "publish all that they want: popular liberties shall be re-established."

The press in the rest of the country turned against Quebec and its media. Even the Montreal *Gazette* was attacked by papers in English Canada. The *Globe and Mail* claimed the *Gazette* supported Duplessis's "active treachery" because the *Gazette*'s editorial writers had questioned the censors' powers to vet Duplessis's radio speeches. The *Globe and Mail* said the *Gazette* was wrong: No politician, even the premier of Quebec, had more rights to criticize the war effort than other members of "the common herd." (Nine days later, the *Globe and Mail* was singing a different tune about radio. The Conservative-friendly Toronto paper briefly made common cause with the leftist Co-operative Commonwealth Federation [today's New Democratic Party] when the CCF attacked censorship of CBC Radio's English service, one of *Globe and Mail* publisher George McCullagh's favourite whipping boys.) Even the Communist Party paper *Clarté*, which Duplessis wanted shut down, carried a cartoon showing a figure of Lapointe towering over a cringing censor.

Despite political pressure on the owners of the paper, it soon printed an editorial attacking Lapointe for his "revolting procedure" of gagging the Quebec media. Broadcast censorship, *L'Événement-Journal*'s editors charged, was Lapointe's "air raid."

Ten days later, Thompson complained about an anti-censorship article by Bruno Lafleur illustrated with a cartoon of a pair of scissors and a gagged CBC microphone. Lapointe, the editor wrote, made young French- and English-Canadian men "cannon fodder." In breach of a censorship directive that was supposed to keep meteorological data from U-boat captains, *L'Événement-Journal* printed the day's weather forecast, stating sarcastically that it had not been officially notified of the "stupid" new rule. The editors said they "hope this will in no way affect the success of His Majesty's and the Allied armies, nor the health of Honourable Ernest Lapointe, Minister of Censorship in Canada."

Still, the Union Nationale got its message onto the airwaves. Duplessis's people simply ignored the censors' cuts. The ban on mentioning censorship was one of the first rules they broke. On October 4, a Mr. C. Coderre, representing the Union Nationale, told listeners of the Montreal station CBF that he would not give his radio speech because his party would not submit to censorship. The station immediately switched to recorded music.

In at least one instance, a CBC station manager literally pulled the plug on a Union Nationale speaker. This was an October 7, 1939, broadcast by Noel Dorion over CBV, Quebec City's CBC station. The studio operator cut the power to the microphone when Dorion began reading parts of his speech that had been cut by censors. Dorion said Duplessis had told him to ignore the rules.

The next day, Jean Blais of the Union Nationale repeated Dorion's actions. This time, chief radio censor R.P. Landry ordered his employees to use scissors to cut out parts of radio speeches that violated the censorship rules. The reaction was predictable: speakers now told their audience their scripts had been cut by "the censorship of Mr. Lapointe." CBF Montreal tried to limit the damage to its reputation by announcing at the end of each political broadcast that it was not censoring of its own accord, but on orders from Ottawa.

Ottawa sent a telegram telling station managers to read a statement over the air if a speech was cut off in mid-sentence. In English it read, "We regret to inform you that we have been obliged to discontinue the address of Mr. X by virtue of the *Defence of Canada Regulations* and the directives issued there-under." Another telegram went out on October 19 warning stations not to broadcast anything about the provincial election in the two days before the vote.

On election night, there were no interviews of candidates or broadcasts of the victory and concession speeches of the leaders. Announcers read the results and reporters had to stick to pre-censored scripts. Even though one of the country's most controversial premiers had been tossed out of office, it made for a dull evening.

Duplessis and his friends in the media would not forget. Their party had suffered a crushing defeat, winning only fifteen seats while the Liberals took seventy (one independent was elected). Quebec City's *L'Événement-Journal*, in its post-election issue, quoted Duplessis saying Lapointe's censorship had "insulted" Quebec. "Hitler in Germany was favoured by the CBC," the ex-premier said, "to the detriment of the Province of Quebec.... Under Mr. Lapointe in this province, one cannot sing, play the piano or the violin."

It would not be long until the Quebec press got another chance to take on the King government's censorship. In November, *Le Devoir's* writers tried to debunk a news release from the French High Command, sparking a protest from Count Robert de Dampierre, France's ambassador to Canada, who said the *Le Devoir* article was written in Berlin. Pelletier, the paper's editor, told the Montreal censor *Le Devoir* had not meant to impugn the honesty of the French. The wording, Pelletier said, was innocent but a grammatical error had crept in. "I warned him that the defaitist [sic] attitude of his newspaper might lead to serious trouble," Melançon told the Ottawa headquarters, "and he re-expressed his desire to avoid any kind of trouble." Censorship was, just temporarily, getting under Pelletier's skin. On December 9, 1939, he wrote a long article about the difficulties of publishing a paper under the censorship regime. Within a few months, however, Pelletier would take the measure of Ottawa's willingness to push his newspaper around, and he would find the censorship regime, at least in its dealings with Quebec media, was hollow at its core.

The front-line censors were about to learn the same lesson from their masters. In February 1940, just as Canada headed into a federal election, Melançon wrote to J.F. MacNeill, deputy minister of justice, enclosing several clippings from *Le Devoir* to show "the insidious way" the paper conducted its campaign against Canadian participation in the war. MacNeill reminded Melançon the paper's articles "could be a good deal worse."

That spring, Hitler's armies overran Denmark and Norway, then ruptured the borders of the Netherlands, Belgium, Luxembourg, and France. The government of the Third French Republic accepted a humiliating peace. German troops marched into Paris on June 14 and power fell into the hands of Marshal Philippe Pétain, who had saved France in World War One. During the intervening years, Pétain had come to hate the Third Republic for what he viewed as its socialism and its insistence on the separation of Church and State. In the resort town of Vichy, Pétain erected a conservative corporatist state with strong ties to the Roman Catholic Church. At the same time, Charles de Gaulle, who had escaped France ahead of the German blitzkrieg, built the nucleus of the Free French armed forces out of survivors from Norway and Dunkirk who were cooling their heels in English camps. For a time, de Gaulle considered making Montreal his capital-in-exile, but the city proved to be unwelcoming.

Had de Gaulle set up his headquarters in Montreal, he would have found that Quebec nationalists and their newspaper, *Le Devoir*, hated him. They, of course, were not alone: President Franklin Roosevelt loathed de Gaulle and, along with much of the U.S. press, believed he was a poseur whose only real goals were the creation of a personality cult and the seizure of power. Churchill believed he was the only available alternative to Pétain, since, unlike the rest of the governments in occupied Europe that had either fled to London or struggled to survive under Nazi rule, France's Third Republic had voted itself out of existence. De Gaulle was recognized by the major Allies as leader of the Free French forces, but his real desire, the official leadership of the French provisional government, eluded him until September 1944, when he was already ensconced in liberated Paris and was assuming control of the bureaucracy in the Allied-held areas of France.

Still, while the Allies were suspicious of de Gaulle, they knew better than to trust Vichy as anything more than a Nazi thrall. In early July 1940, *Le Devoir*'s Pelletier lashed out at Vichy's critics. In a confidential letter to chief French-language censor Fulgence Charpentier, Pelletier said the English-language press had no right to denounce the Pétain regime as treacherous, as had the *Ottawa Journal*, the *Winnipeg Tribune*, and the *Winnipeg Free Press*. Quebecers would be affronted, he said, if *Le Devoir*, which represented the majority of Québécois, reprinted those editorials. Pelletier said he could see no reason for the francophone press to moderate its tone while the English-language press indulged in French-bashing.

Charpentier replied that the English-language press was simply reacting to support for Pétain's collaborationist regime and the (rather short-lived) movement among Quebec anti-war activists for annexation to the neutral United States. At least the English-Canadian papers had, unlike *Le Devoir*, followed the censorship regulations. A few days after this exchange, *Le Devoir* ran a front-page editorial praising Vichy for formally ending France's alliance with Britain. The censors recommended the Department of Justice lay charges, but nothing came of their complaint.

Through that summer and fall of 1940, *Le Devoir* continued its guerrilla war with the censors. Léopold Richer, the paper's parliamentary correspondent, denounced England for its past iniquities, aggressions, and conquests in an article that Charpentier believed should have resulted in charges. He had already warned Pelletier that the paper's articles would be censored before publication unless it stopped publishing anti-British and isolationist material, but Pelletier kept up his isolationist campaign. *Le Devoir* raised the stakes by publishing a series of anti-British letters from Vichy senator Alcide Ebray in the summer of 1940.

Le Devoir was not alone. *L'Action catholique*, distributed in parishes across the province, used the departure of the first Canadian contingent to warn its readers that anyone who volunteered for the army was unlikely to return. Willie Chevalier, who worked part-time for the censorship system and was probably its most enthusiastic employee in Quebec, wrote to Charpentier that "anyone who like myself has to read the paper daily could tell you that these little treacheries appear daily in *L'Action catholique*."

Not all of the brush fires began in the French-language nationalist press. The Montreal *Gazette*, second-largest English-language paper in the city, was glad for anything that embarrassed King's government. On June 21, the day before France surrendered, Parliament passed the *National Resources Mobilization Act* (NRMA). This law gave the federal government huge powers to requisition property and manpower, but only within the borders of Canada. The law required adults to register with the federal government at centres in communities across the country, usually in post offices and town halls.

Montreal mayor Camillien Houde opposed the use of Montreal's city hall and other municipally owned buildings. On August 2, he said publicly, "I declare myself peremptorily against national registration. It is unequivocally a measure of conscription, and the [federal] government recently elected last March, declared through the mouths of all its political chieftains, from Prime Minister Mackenzie King to Premier Adélard Godbout of Quebec . . . that there would be no conscription in any form whatsoever. . . . If the government wants a mandate for Conscription, let it come before the people, without this time fooling them." Three days later, after a special night cabinet meeting attended by Thompson, who gave advice on handling the expected press reaction, Houde was arrested under the *War Measures Act*. He stayed locked up at internment camps in eastern Ontario and New Brunswick until August 1944.

The censors later claimed to have been bound by an opinion given by lawyers at the Department of Justice that newspapers should not report subversive speeches. Publishing them would actually "enlarge the offence." The censors did not like the opinion, which, they said later, "proved to be a most embarrassing and impractical one from the very beginning, particularly in the Province of Quebec." Still, they felt bound to enforce it.

The Montreal *Gazette* carried a long story on Houde's speech in its first edition of August 3. Warren Baldwin called the newsroom and ordered the story killed in the later editions. Soon afterwards, the censors issued a statement to the Canadian Press wire service, for distribution to all its members, that said: "Re: Houde: Editors may safely report factual developments and carry editorial and outside comment provided offensive material is neither reproduced nor defended. Editors are asked to refrain from 'material likely to aggravate harmful controversy between groups in Canada.'" The president of the *Gazette*, Tory stalwart John Bassett, phoned two cabinet ministers, Defence Minister J.L. Ralston and Secretary of State Pierre-F. Casgrain, the minister responsible for press censorship. The *Globe and Mail* had already picked up the story for its first edition and a Montreal radio station broadcast Houde's statement in its 10:30 newscast.

Houde's comment and arrest generated the kind of publicity that any reasonable person would expect when the mayor of the country's largest city is carted off to prison without anything resembling due process for making a public statement that a sizeable number of his constituents agreed with. The mass-circulation newspapers like *La Presse* believed Houde was a victim of Ottawa's pro-conscription lobby, though *Le Devoir* thought the mayor had brought his troubles down on himself. Still, most major papers, even those that supported Houde's arrest, condemned what they saw as a crude, politically motivated attempt to censor coverage of Houde's statement.

The morning after the mayor's arrest, a Saturday, Bassett called the federal Opposition leader, R.B. Hanson, and read him Houde's statement. That afternoon, debate opened in the House of Commons on Houde's arrest and the censorship of the *Gazette*. Hanson asked, "Have we any longer a free press in Canada?" Prime Minister Mackenzie King stood up for the censors, saying it should have been obvious to any newspaper editor that the mayor's words were subversive.

In an editorial, the *Gazette*'s editors said, "(T)he Prime Minister's belief [that] 'any newspaper office' should have suppressed the story on its own initiative, suffice to say that this opinion was not shared by either the *Gazette* or the *Globe and Mail*, the only newspaper offices affected on Friday evening." The *Gazette*'s editors believed publication of the story was in the public interest and no valid reason existed for its suppression.

The *Globe and Mail* editorialized against the "arbitrary and unwarranted actions of civil servants whose duty is to protect the lives of soldiers, sailors and airmen, and not to save the skins of politicians," adding that misdirected censorship zeal was alien to Mackenzie King's "lifetime policy of trusting the people." The paper insisted the publishers of Canadian newspapers were as well qualified as anyone in the government to decide what is in the public interest. The paper had co-operated loyally in the suppression of naval and military intelligence and would continue to do so it said, but the editors would not agree to censor news and opinions which were merely embarrassing to the politicians. Publishers could be trusted to maintain "British ideals of freedom of speech and freedom of the press" and people should insist upon their right to discuss "fairly but fearlessly the shortcomings of politicians. Failure, corruption, sabotage of the war effort and other misdeeds of malefactors and Quislings must be dragged into the light of day."

Later, the censors made their own case in a letter to the prime minister. The two big papers had not asked for a ruling on their Houde stories, and, in fact, it was not the censors' job to save the papers from themselves. Baldwin had warned the *Gazette* that it risked breaking the *Defence of Canada Regulations*, but he had no power to force the paper to stop its presses. On August 8, the censors issued Directive 61, which allowed the reporting of the facts of Houde's case as long as the statement itself was not repeated. Two days later, the *Globe* warned the censors to be careful "about playing with political fire in the future . . . The task of the Censors is easy if they remember that the acid test in any instance must be: 'Does it help the enemy?' The politicians will look after themselves."

The *Ottawa Citizen* made the issue personal, saying, "Montreal's supreme demagogue," Mayor Houde, had, through the actions of the press censors, received far more publicity than if the censors had not interfered. The paper singled out "Messrs. Eggleston and Charpentier" and implied they were now creatures of Mackenzie King.

It took two years for the censorship rules to be loosened to allow for the publication of "subversive" statements made in public. Even then, the media could not agree with, or sensationalize, them. Meanwhile, Houde stayed on ice, first at the army base at Petawawa, Ontario, then in a camp in rural New Brunswick. In 1943, the censors allowed *Le Petit Journal* and *La Patrie* to run ads for a fund to help pay for a campaign to gain Houde's release. He was set free in August 1944. Finally, the voters of Montreal had their say: Houde was re-elected that fall.

This sloppy performance gave further proof to *Le Devoir* and the rest of Quebec's newspapers that the federal news-management system was toothless. The censors knew they were weak. On September 11, 1940, Charpentier explained to Jack Pickersgill, King's private secretary, that *Le Devoir* straddled the borderline of the censorship rules but "it is wise enough not to overstep the mark." Warning letters, phone calls, and personal confrontations with Pelletier had not worked.

Instead, *Le Devoir* and its friends embraced Vichy. Some of Quebec's conservative francophone elite believed Pétain was determined to create in France the type of society that was already idealized in Quebec. Legally, they were on firm enough ground: Ottawa had diplomatic relations with Vichy, although a "cold war," with some fighting, existed between Britain and occupied France. And the French-Canadian editors could point to the federal government's own inconsistent policies. When the British attacked the French fleet in Algeria, sinking one battleship, crippling two more, and killing nearly 1,300 French sailors to keep Vichy's navy out of the hands of the Nazis, King backed the British but also praised the Vichy French sailors for gallantly defending their ships. King opposed the British–Free French invasion of the French African territory of Dakar. King thwarted a British plot to seize $100 million in Vichy government gold on the *Emile Bertin*, in Canada with French bullion for deposit in the Bank of Canada, and turned down British requests to capture Vichy vessels off St. Pierre and Miquelon.

Some federal ministers from Quebec were, at first, willing to give Pétain a chance. Lapointe, in September 1940, told the cabinet's

War Committee that Free French leader Charles de Gaulle "had no prestige" and his broadcast to French Canadians on August 1 "had been regarded as an insult" while Marshal Pétain was respected by French Canadians for his "courage and integrity."

Canadian policy changed in early 1941 as Vichy proved to be a puppet of the Nazis. The evolution of Ottawa's attitude was fairly subtle, and Vichy's supporters in Quebec may well have misread the situation, at least in the short term. Canada's senior diplomat in France, Georges Vanier, fled the country in 1940 just ahead of the Germans, but Ottawa sent a diplomat to Vichy on special assignments. Canada also had mail service with France, a situation that would vex the censors. Charpentier and Eggleston warned the prime minister that banned pro-German, anti-British papers published in France, such as *La Croix d'Auvergne, La Dépêche vendéenne, Le Messager de la Haute Savoie, La Croix de la Haute Savoie, La Chronique de Fougères, L'Avenir de la Loire, Le Patriote des Pyrénées, Gringoire, Le Petit Marseillais, La Croix de l'Aveyron,* and *Le Soleil de Marseille* circulated throughout Quebec. Despite the ban, *Le Devoir* continued to get *Gringoire* and use material from it.

Even Liberal papers like *Le Soleil* initially supported Pétain, preferring to lay blame for Vichy's more fascistic policies on the young rising star in the regime, the reptilian Pierre Laval. By 1941, *Le Soleil,* disheartened by Pétain's toadying to Hitler, switched its support to de Gaulle. The Vichy regime continued to have the support of *L'Action catholique,* the province's largest Roman Catholic newspaper. On April 18, 1941, the paper angered the censors by covering a speech by Father Pierre Gravel at St. Roch, praising the leadership qualities of reactionary Quebec social historian Abbé Lionel Groulx and linking his ideals with those of Vichy: "Our people will not be saved by learning English. They will be saved the day each citizen becomes conscious of his duties and has a national conscience. [Marshal Pétain] is a saviour for France in spite of his old age and is admired by all judicious persons. Those who criticize him and persecute him are traitors," the clergyman said.

In April 1942, *Winnipeg Free Press* parliamentary journalist Grant Dexter analyzed the situation in Quebec. Most of the material in his memorandum probably came from his friend Norman Robertson, the senior bureaucrat at External Affairs who was, at the time, surveying the Quebec media to gauge opposition to conscription. The newscasts of the French-Canadian stations were not a problem, as they were word-for-word translations of the English CBC newscasts, Dexter wrote. The issue was the Vichyist leanings of people who were invited by the CBC to read on-air editorials. "The commentators are either Vichy men or are under the impression that it is quite impossible to criticize Vichy or to praise the Free French." Dexter claimed August Frigon, the network's president, was perceived by the King government as pro-Vichy. King didn't want to fire one of his few prominent francophone managers, so, Robertson told Dexter, the government built a second managerial structure around Frigon's deputy, Gladstone Murray, a Free French supporter. The government, Dexter said, was afraid to help Murray too much because of the reaction of Quebecers if the situation became public.

The federal government believed Vichy short-wave broadcasts were popular in Quebec, especially among the province's nationalist francophone intellectuals. In his memo, Dexter claimed Vichy's chief broadcaster ran a college in Paris that was popular with wealthy francophone Québécois, so he was very well known to "some hundreds of key people in Quebec." The Catholic Church in Quebec believed Vichy's argument that France had replaced the worship of God with the love of money and had been in a state of sin since the Revolution. "The French people became materialistic, Godless, lost," Dexter wrote. "Now God has punished them for their sins . . . they must repent and turn back towards the light."

Quebec was flattered by being touted within Vichy France as an ideal state, one that had not been ruined by the French Revolution and the Third Republic. It had survived English occupation by reaching back to, and nurturing, its rural, Roman Catholic roots and its strong family ties. "Quebec is a shining light to them," Dexter explained. "Quebec never turned away from God, never forsook the church, never lusted for Babylonian gals. Quebec stayed good and Quebec is reaping the reward. The golden era of France—prior to the revolution—has continued in Quebec and Quebec must help

France recover her lost soul." Pétain was seen as the great leader who was guiding the French race to a new golden age. "This line of broadcasting is a ten strike in Quebec. It fits right in with everything the Quebecers have been taught . . . de Gaulle and the Free French are a projection from the age of sin. . . . You see, all of this ties in with all that the clergy have been preaching for the past hundred years."

Father Julian Peghaire, writing for the *University of Ottawa Quarterly Review*, argued Pétain was saving his country from disaster. His education reforms were so successful that they had been adopted in German-occupied France. (Peghaire may not have realized Vichy and the Church ran the schools throughout France.) Obviously, Charpentier concluded, the changes to the system bore "the stamp of German approval." The Ottawa censors decided it was not in Canada's interest "to have the public listen to that kind of propaganda, even more so when the province of Quebec is in danger from that source." Charpentier said he read the article and diplomatically wrote to the editor that it "constitutes direct propaganda, which is not denied at all by its author, in favour of a non-ally government, at the present time under German control." Soon afterwards, the editor of the journal phoned Charpentier to say he would not publish the article.

The issue seemed dead until November 28, when Charpentier saw a notice in *Le Devoir* that Peghaire would speak at a meeting of L'Alliance Française at the Ritz-Carlton Hotel in Montreal. Charpentier asked the Montreal censor to notify L'Alliance Française that the gist of the lecture had been submitted to Charpentier as an article and had been turned down. RCMP "witnesses" would be in the audience at the Ritz, and while censors would not prevent the priest from speaking, they warned L'Alliance Française they would act aggressively against any breach of the *Defence of Canada Regulations*.

Tetrault claimed he knew nothing about Peghaire's subject, or of the speaker himself. "A Mr. Ristelhueber" (who was, in fact, Vichy's lead diplomat in Canada) had recommended Peghaire. L'Alliance Française finally decided to cancel the meeting. Ristelhueber called Claude Melançon, now the federal government's associate director of public information, to complain the priest's opinions were harmless, and that he had every right to speak at a public meeting.

Ristelhueber's currency with the censors dropped precipitously when, in early November 1941, *Le Devoir* ran a letter to the editor that said Mr. Henri-Haye, Vichy's ambassador to Washington, accused the British of stealing $100 worth of children's vitamins that Henri-Haye had sent back to his hometown of Versailles. The censors told Casgrain the government needed to do more than just send letters of warning to *Le Devoir*, which, "since the inception of the war frequently and unmistakably opposed our national effort and has persisted in publishing subversive material despite our repeated warnings to its editors." It was time, the censors said, to charge *Le Devoir*, perhaps even to shut the paper down.

Soon afterwards, the government received the same advice from the RCMP in Montreal. On December 4, Inspector C. Batch, assistant intelligence officer, wrote to the commissioner of the RCMP, sending a carbon copy to the press censors, contending, "*Le Devoir* is aggressive in its writings which do not appear to be at all sympathetic to the British, Russians and Free French." Its defeatist attitude, Batch believed, did not promote French-Canadian unity.

In February 1941, Willie Chevalier, assistant press censor in Montreal and a former reporter for the Liberal newspaper *Le Canada*, complained of yet another isolationist article in *Le Devoir*, calling the piece "clearly fifth column work" and telling his superiors in Ottawa "everyone I meet in Montreal is amazed at our tolerance of this German paper published in French." Less than five days later, the censors complained to Pelletier again, this time for reprinting an article from the fascist *La Nacion* of Buenos Aires, praising the work of L'Action Française, which supported Pétain. Later that month, Chevalier wrote a memo to Ottawa listing *Le Devoir*'s anti-war articles. An article in the July 13, 1940, edition headlined "On a Chapter of History" denounced the British for the attack on the French fleet in language that, Chevalier wrote, "could have been written by one of Mr. Goebbels's hack writers." Chevalier said *Le Devoir* "carries German communiqués on p. 3, buries British ones at the bottom of the sports or financial pages." The paper's standing commentary section, "Le Carnet de Grincheux" (The Notebook of a Grouser), was a daily attack on the war effort.

Much of the anti-war writing, Chevalier said, was done by Richer, who constantly argued the war was unnecessary, would bankrupt Canada, and would result in conscription. *Le Devoir*, "which flatters itself on being a very good Catholic paper," had ignored the "impressive" Mass for Victory, held at Notre-Dame Cathedral on February 9, 1941, even though it was covered by almost every daily and weekly newspaper in the province. "Altogether," Chevalier wrote, "there can be no doubt that *Le Devoir*, systematically and with gross misrepresentation and distortion of facts, continually sabotages the Canadian war effort." People who relied on the paper for their news were "potential if not actual fifth columnists." *Le Devoir* had gone far past the boundaries of legitimate criticism to become "a most subversive paper."

Eggleston decided something must be done to stop *Le Devoir*, agreeing with the Montreal censors that the paper should get a warning from the secretary of state, then, if needed, a one-week suspension. Again, nothing happened. In mid-March 1941, Chevalier sent a memorandum to Ottawa explaining his frustration with the paper, which had not toned down its coverage. It was hardly worth the bother to censor or criticize other Quebec papers, he said, "so long as *Le Devoir*'s bias is tolerated."

Federal opposition politicians, especially Conservative leader R.B. Hanson, thought chief press censor Fulgence Charpentier was weak. Hanson did not realize Louis St. Laurent, the justice minister, was the real protector of *Le Devoir*. He refused, time and again, to accept Charpentier's advice to charge the leaders of the Quebec nationalist press.

Knowing he was being attacked in Ottawa, Pelletier wrote to Charpentier to deny the paper opposed the "efficient prosecution" of the war. Yes, he had quoted Charles Lindbergh's anti-war speeches, but he had never declared his support for them or claimed they represented the bulk of public opinion in the United States. His paper's main attacks on the Roosevelt administration were caused by

Pelletier's alarm at the pro–birth control propaganda issued by the U.S. government and carried in major U.S. magazines.

A month later, Pelletier wrote to the censors to deny that he published Vichy propaganda. Not enough news came from France over the Canadian Press and the Associated Press wire services, Pelletier wrote, so he had to hunt for it elsewhere. To force him to stop carrying news from France would be tantamount to the "encircling of French Canada by the press, information and literature of English or American origin." Charpentier replied that he could see no reason why anyone in Canada "should help in their nefarious work those who are crushing France." The censor hinted he had secret details of German agents using Vichy as a propaganda pipeline, and offered to show proof to Pelletier. That appeal didn't work, so, in July 1941, the censors once again recommended to Casgrain that he shut *Le Devoir* down.

Through intercepted mail, the government knew that in July 1940 Henri Coursier, Vichy's consul in Montreal, wrote to René Ristelhueber, Vichy's chargé d'affaires in Ottawa, to say *Le Devoir* had negotiated a deal with him for an "alternative news service" to provide news from Vichy. The RCMP also found evidence that Vichy diplomats collected surveys of Quebec public opinion to help Vichy tailor its short-wave propaganda broadcasts.

In November, Colonel R.B. Gibson, the director of military operations and intelligence at the Department of National Defence, gave Eggleston a clipping from the October 13 issue of *Le Devoir*. The writer of the article asked readers to listen to short-wave radio broadcasts from German-occupied France. "Under the guise of Frenchmen or French-Canadians in France speaking to their friends and relatives in Quebec, this programme . . . [is] a direct appeal by the Germans to the French-speaking Canadians of Quebec, urging them to collaborate more closely with the Vichy regime," Gibson wrote. Charpentier appealed to Pelletier, telling him Canada's diplomatic relations with France did not create a licence to distribute Axis propaganda, just as the country's new alliance with Russia did not legalize Communist propaganda.

Pelletier responded to yet another complaint by assuring Charpentier that "when the day comes where the Canadian Government breaks relations with the Vichy Government we will cease to champion the Vichy Government." Censorship, the editor said, had become a tool of Gaullists trying to take over control of the Quebec press. All of this nastiness played into the hands of anglophone troublemakers like Toronto Baptist pastor T.T. Shields, who toured the country speaking at Loyal Orange Lodges, whipping up hatred of all French Catholics. The censors were able to keep most of his rants out of the English and French press.

There were other, smaller, newspapers and magazines in Quebec that the censors found equally frustrating. *L'Oeil*, a monthly magazine, printed a stream of Pétainist material after it started publishing in September 1940. Its editor, Alfred Ayotte, held a full-time job on the editorial staff of *Le Devoir*, and believed France had always suffered from its relations with Great Britain. *La Voix de Gaspé* published a brief, scathing description of *L'Oeil*, calling it Duplessite, neo-fascist, and anti-Semitic. It was, the paper said, an eye that needed glasses. Ayotte answered the charges of Vichyism in a letter to Charpentier dated November 4, rubbing Charpentier's nose in the fact that Justice Minister Lapointe had recently made a speech expressing his "affection" for the "men of Vichy." Lapointe's speech, he said, proved "it is at least permitted to express sympathy to the people we love." Montreal censor Willie Chevalier wanted *L'Oeil* shut down, but Charpentier recommended to Louis St. Laurent that the paper be allowed to stay open under strict supervision of its political content.

Louis St. Laurent asked the censors to make a special study of the publication and "to forward to me those issues which would appear to be most dangerous." The magazine was violently anti-Semitic, but this was not actionable under the *Defence of Canada Regulations*. In one editorial it claimed "the Jews wanted conscription for overseas. Shall they be the first to leave?" In another issue, *L'Oeil* mocked the idea of the creation of a Jewish army. "Up to now, the Jews have found it more heroic or more profitable to make soldiers' uniforms than to put them on." De Gaulle, Ayotte wrote, "is mostly supported by the Jews, the Free Masons and the Communists." Charpentier explained Ayotte's anti-Semitism as a ploy to attract advertising from French-Canadian merchants. It was not Charpentier's finest moment. The censors somehow clung to their belief Ayotte could be brought into line with threats that he would be charged, even after it became obvious that the government would not touch the mainstream Quebec press.

The paper continued its Pétainist campaign until the Vichy regime collapsed and the old marshal was trucked off to Germany to await his fate. It then focused more of its attention on the Jews, publishing, on February 15, 1945, a full-page letter under the heading "Les Juifs: racistes invétérés," written by someone with the pen name Un Qui Les Connait. The writer claimed the Jews were parasites, the Québécois were their victims, and the Jewish race was damned.

Jacob Livinson, honorary director of the Canadian Jewish Historical Society, complained to the censors. F.E. Joliffe, acting director of the Censorship Branch, asked the legal opinion of F.P. Varcoe, deputy minister of justice. Varcoe said the anti-Semitic article did not contravene Regulation 39 of the *Defence of Canada Regulations.* In a letter written on VE day, Livinson demanded to know from Joliffe what was being done to stop *L'Oeil.* "You who are so well aware of the injurious implications of this type of poisonous journalism of which 'L'Oeil' of Montreal is a ready and willing partner," Livinson wrote, and reminded Charpentier he was "in a key position, in times of war or in peacetime, to put a stop and halt these bad acts in print! Thousands of law-abiding Canadian citizens rely upon you and hope that you will render justice to them."

There were Catholic publications, such as *Vers Demain,* edited and published by Quebec Social Credit Party leader Louis Even, that were even farther out on the fringe. It said France had been betrayed by the Freemason-Jewish politicians of the Third Republic but, after the Nazis took Paris, "God bent down to the France he loved, and God spoke to Pétain. The victory of 1918 left irresponsible men at the head of France, [and] the defeat of 1940, by Divine Mercy, gave France a responsible chief. Responsible to France. To God. Compare this with democratic parlance: responsible to Parliament, people, electorate."

The main target of the censors, however, remained *Le Devoir*. By February 1942, *Le Devoir*'s status had evolved to "less objectionable." Still, the paper indulged in "suspicion and chiding for everything British, approval and praise for anything related to Vichy and Pétain."

During the April 1942 conscription plebiscite, Quebec nationalists took up their radio censorship cudgel from the 1939 election, demanding equal time from the CBC. *Le Devoir*, Charpentier wrote, could be blamed for violence in Montreal during the plebiscite campaign because of its anti-British propaganda. On March 2, 1942, the paper carried a long article on the Ligue pour la Défense du Canada's mass meeting at Maisonneuve Market. One of the headline speakers told his listeners, "when the Germans and the Japanese are already at our gates . . . the best policy is to laugh it off." On March 16 and May 18, 1942, Charpentier wrote long memoranda to Louis St. Laurent detailing *Le Devoir*'s anti-conscription coverage and recommending sanctions against the paper, but again nothing happened.

After the plebiscite, in which Quebec voted 73 per cent against releasing the government from its pledge of no conscription for overseas service (compared to the rest of the country that voted 80 per cent yes), nationalist journalists in Quebec went back to their pumping for Vichy. L'Heureux of *L'Action catholique* was warned by Charpentier not to publicize Radio Vichy broadcasts, which, he said, used Canadians interned in France to broadcast propaganda to Quebec in return for a few days' leave from confinement. Responding to a series of flattering articles in *L'Action catholique* on occupied France by André Laurendeau, Charpentier wrote L'Heureux on October 19, 1942, "I am afraid that Mr. Laurendeau in attempting to show his portraits of these gentlemen [Vichy leaders Pétain, Laval, and Darlan] . . . inserts some of his own fancies so dangerous in wartime to our equilibrium." The following December, the paper carried an article praising Salazar's fascist regime in Portugal.

On December 17, 1942, Charpentier wrote a ten-page memorandum on *Le Devoir*, hoping to get the newspaper shut down temporarily, or, even better from his point of view, for the duration. He compared *Le Devoir* to Britain's Communist *Daily Worker*, which had been suspended because of long-term opposition to the war. *Le Devoir*, Charpentier charged, used the conscription plebiscite to "redouble [the] virulence [of] its opposition to the success of our armies." Pelletier, the paper's editor, was a driving force of the Ligue pour la Défense du Canada, which opposed sending any Canadian forces overseas.

When the Allies invaded French North Africa in November 1942, *Le Devoir* supported Admiral Darlan, the unscrupulous Vichy stooge who governed the colony. The paper had mocked de Gaulle, whose men wanted to oust Darlan (and were likely responsible for his assassination on Christmas Eve of that year). The censors also had to deal with Vichyite propaganda closer to home.

The paper repeated its vitamin pill accusations that November, publishing a letter from an Abbé E. Galtier, of New York, that claimed Great Britain's navy murdered French-Canadian children by requisitioning Quebec's supply of vitamin pills. This was an urban myth that took hold in Quebec during the war.

In the viciously fought Outremont by-election of November 30, 1942, the paper had supported nationalist, isolationist candidate Jean Drapeau against Liberal star candidate (and future war services minister) Léo Laflèche. It printed anti-Semitic statements and extremist isolationist rants by Drapeau and his supporters, including a claim by the future Montreal mayor that French-Canadian women would be drafted for overseas war service. *Le Devoir* said a Liberal victory would be a defeat for French Canada and a "Judeo-Anglo-Saxon" victory. Charpentier did not get an answer when he asked the federal justice minister to intervene.

On January 19, 1943, Charpentier wrote to *Le Devoir* staff writer Roger Duhamel, who would later be appointed Queen's Printer for Quebec, to complain to him about the newspaper's January 16 reprint of a book excerpt by Paul Mousset, *Quand Les Temps Travaillait Pour Vous*, that claimed French survivors from Dunkirk were treated like POWs in England and described the British government as "comfortable plutocrats" who did not care about anything but money. The clippings were sent to Justice Minister St. Laurent with a short note saying the censors considered them enemy propaganda.

On February 11, 1943, *Le Devoir* printed a long transcript of a Henri Bourassa barnburner in which the elderly nationalist icon condemned Canadian participation in the war and praised Vichy. The following day, Charpentier wrote to his boss, chief censor O.M. Biggar, to again ask for action against the paper for printing the speech, which he said was "a pacifist, isolationist and anti-participationist plea against the war effort." The censors' complaints were answered by F.P. Varcoe, the deputy minister of justice, who said the government would not lay charges against *Le Devoir* for this piece or others about which censors had recently complained.

Varcoe's letter came four days after Charpentier sent him a piece headlined "Les Nageurs de Hong-Kong" which *Le Devoir* reprinted from the Vichy publication *La Revue françaises*. The story praised two Olympic champion Japanese swimmers who were said to be instrumental in defeating the Canadians and British at Hong Kong by swimming across the harbour and destroying important defence works on the island. It was, the censors wrote, "excellent propaganda for the Japanese."

The paper's coverage moderated somewhat through 1943, but early the following year *Le Devoir* was the focus of an investigation by military intelligence and censorship officials who wanted to know how Nazi-controlled Radio Paris was able to get the text of a *Le Devoir* article that was used in a propaganda broadcast less than seventy-two hours after *Le Devoir* was on the streets of Montreal. Radio Paris quoted a *Le Devoir* editorial predicting the Soviets would set up a puppet "commonwealth" in occupied Eastern Europe that was similar to the British Empire, where countries like Canada were shackled. Cable censors were asked to check wire copy of foreign journalists, including those from the Soviet Union, to determine if the text of the editorial had been sent to Europe by a foreign news agency.

Le Devoir's competitors in Quebec picked up the Radio Paris broadcast and turned it against the paper. One, *Le Canada*, gleefully reported on February 22, 1944, that the Nazis used a *Le Devoir* radio broadcast to divide the Allies with suspicion, "hoping to win diplomatically a war they had lost militarily."

Even after the Nazi collapse, the censors continued their running battle with Quebec nationalists. By then, no one could argue that *Le Devoir* and its friends were giving much aid and comfort to the enemy. The fight was now blatantly political. There was some mild censorship of radio speeches leading up to the June 11, 1945, federal election. The censors cut a line from a radio speech of André Laurendeau that was to be broadcast two days before the election that claimed King had thrown the country into war "to obey the orders of British Imperialists." Laurendeau would later go on to edit *Le Devoir* and become (with Davidson Dunton, former head of Canada's propaganda agency, the Wartime Information Board) co-chair of the Royal Commission on Bilingualism and Biculturalism. In the 1950s, he broke with Duplessis and regretted his opposition to Canadian participation in the fight against Hitler.

The elements of Quebec's press that were anti-participationist were on the wrong side of history. They either misjudged the threat of Nazism to the world or chose to ignore it. Having at first hitched itself to U.S. isolationism, to the point that some extremists actually floated the idea of annexation to a neutral United States, some of the Quebec nationalist press soldiered on through the war in support of the Vichy regime in France. The Vichyists in Quebec were not a fringe group. They included many of society's most influential people: senior Catholic clerics; the province's most important Catholic newspaper (*L'Action catholique*); and its most influential political newspaper (*Le Devoir*). Some of Vichy's vocal supporters—André Laurendeau and Jean Drapeau among them—went on to be very important members of the journalistic and government elite in the 1950s and later. One is left wondering how, when he made his famous *"vive le Québec libre"* speech at Montreal's city hall in 1967, de Gaulle felt about nationalist Quebec's wartime attitudes concerning the Free French.

That said, it would be wrong to argue that Quebec gave unanimous support to Vichy and to the segment of its elites that supported the regime. The censors were not in the business of administering praise for coverage that was loyal to the war effort. Many large, commercially driven papers like *La Presse*, which vastly outsold

Le Devoir, never drew complaints from the censors. It is also important to note that the battle between isolationists and the government was a fight between French Canadians: Charpentier scolding
Pelletier; Willie Chevalier advocating the suspension of *Le Devoir*
before heading to Africa to work against Vichy on behalf of British
intelligence. Still, the failure of the federal government to effectively
rein in the worst excesses of the nationalist, anti-participationist
press left a stain on the nation's war record. In many ways, King's
government, especially its justice minister, St. Laurent, deserves the
blame for this. In treading so carefully to maintain domestic political peace, it allowed Canada's Vichyist press to engage in anti-Semitic and pro-fascist propagandizing that has remained an embarrass-
ment to Quebec and to the rest of this nation.

CHAPTER 6

• The Hong Kong Cover-up

MIDWAY THROUGH THE WAR, Mackenzie King's more effective and fearless critics were not in the House of Commons. They were two rich, glamorous Conservatives headquartered in Toronto. George McCullagh was the self-made founder of the *Globe and Mail*, a man who despised party politics and came close, with the help of his unstable, alcoholic creature Premier Mitchell Hepburn, to establishing a perpetual one-party provincial coalition government in Ontario. When the wheels finally came off both Hepburn's mind and his political machine, McCullagh ditched him and settled the paper's support on the media-savvy leader of the provincial Conservatives, George Drew. Handsome, wealthy, and urbane, Drew was a World War One vet, a lawyer and political comer who had written for *Maclean's* magazine during a brief time of underemployment in the 1930s. With McCullagh's help, Drew quickly became leader of the Ontario Conservative Party. But his aim was higher: George Drew wanted to be prime minister of Canada.

McCullagh was suspicious of the press censorship system, but he gave it a few months' grace at the beginning of the war, and the paper actually praised the government for hiring Thompson as chief censor. The first signs of trouble for the censors came in November 1939, when one of the *Globe and Mail*'s opinion columnists, Judith Robinson, launched a public fight with them in her popular column. Through the late fall of 1939, she was involved in a running battle with Toronto censor Bert Perry over small military details that showed up in her column. The censors went after her for an article accusing the government of neglecting soldiers' families. Robinson mocked the system when one of the censors killed a brief, rather obscure article about passenger ship service in Argentina that had already run in the *New York Times*: "That's the way (Nazi) secret agents always work; just study censored news in Canada to find out what's doing in Argentina. It's as easy as that. Ask the censors in Ottawa if it isn't," she wrote, under the headline "Keeping Secret Agents Baffled." Later, Robinson took up the cause of a Communist convicted and jailed under the *War Measures Act*. Perry told Ottawa that Robinson had "made an extreme attack on constituted authority" and someone in the government, almost certainly without the censors knowing about it, put an RCMP tail on the columnist.

The *Globe* seemed to speak with various, often confusing, voices that the censors can hardly be blamed for being unable to fathom. In its December 11, 1939, editorial, "Newspapers and the War," the *Globe* argued, "While the right to criticize is one of democracy's priceless privileges, self-imposed censorship in the name of patriotism is also a priceless privilege obtainable only in a democracy. Its free exercise is a more valuable demonstration than grudging concession to the censor's rules." The next day, the paper's anonymous editorial writers changed their collective mind, saying Canadian censorship rules had been found "stupid and irksome by journalists in Toronto and Ottawa who have been forestalled by absurd and anomalous decisions. One cynic has defined a censor as a person who suppresses in Canada what the enemy already knows."

If the censors despaired over that scolding, comfort awaited them in the next day's paper. The *Globe and Mail*'s senior political columnist, J.V. McAree, wrote that the censorship in World War One had been much more oppressive and, for the most part, this time around, the system was in good hands. At the same time, the paper's editors supported the government's prosecution of eight people in Montreal who were charged under the *War Measures Act* for distributing anti-war leaflets. (They were vigorously prosecuted by Gérald Fauteux, who later went on to found the University of Ottawa law school and to sit on the Supreme Court of Canada.)

The *Globe and Mail* changed course again on January 10, 1940, when both Drew and still-premier Hepburn, in one of the most dramatic and strange moments in Canadian politics, rose in the Ontario legislature to attack Mackenzie King's handling of the war. King used the attack as an excuse to call an election in the dead of winter, an unusual event in Canada. By the end of January, the *Globe and Mail* had taken the same position that the majority of the Quebec press had embraced the previous fall when Maurice Duplessis had sprung an election on his province: censorship of opinion had no place in a political campaign. In editorials printed during the campaign, the *Globe* accused the King government of using censorship to gag its opponents with "a radio Gestapo" that was "an insult, not only to the candidates, but to the people who nominate them." It asked, "Why not go the full way with a dictatorship, as with a blacked-out Parliament, and have it over with?" The criticism of broadcast censorship brought results. On February 7, chief radio censor R.P. Landry cancelled the rule that all opinion pieces had to be submitted to censors before they could be broadcast. Instead, radio station managers were made responsible for ensuring that nothing in breach of the *Defence of Canada Regulations* went over the airwaves, but the paper, and especially Robinson, kept finding convincing evidence that the censors were leaning on Mackenzie King's critics. When the Toronto radio and newspaper censors issued conflicting rulings on a major nationwide radio speech by George Drew, the *Globe* began working hard to make censorship a major issue in the campaign. It carried stories quoting Drew that the censorship system was "nothing more than a political machine for preventing effective correction of Mr. King's misstatements." The prime minister, he said, was creating the "machinery of a dictatorship" with censors who were really "a Canadian Gestapo whose duty it is to prevent just criticism of the Government reaching the ears of the public." But the fact remained, he said, that "Canada went into the war unprepared," and he maintained that "any defence preparations that were made were done by Gen. McNaughton during R.B. Bennett's (Conservative) administration." The next day, Drew accused King of establishing "a political censorship quite as effective as that imposed on Germany." King, the Ontario Tory leader said, had "learned something about the Nazi technique" when he had visited Germany before the war.

Judith Robinson warned her readers on March 6 that "the war for liberty is only six months old, and already the system set up by the Federal Liberal Government can get away with freedom's murder." Robinson was angry that the *Globe and Mail*'s censorship fight had not been taken up with vigour by any of the major English-language newspapers in Canada and by the national Tory leadership. The paper hunted around to find celebrities who would help the cause and found Arthur "Roy" Brown, the Canadian pilot credited with shooting down German air ace Manfred von Richthofen in World War One. "The very idea of Mr. King restricting you and me as to what we may say is embittering," Brown told an Ontario Conservative rally. "What did Mr. King ever do for his country in the face of the enemy that gives him any right to dictate to you and me what we shall say in a democratic country? Everybody who criticizes the Government today must pull his punches due to the censorship of the *Defence of Canada Regulations*, which, by their use might better be called the *Defence of Mackenzie King Government Regulations*."

In the end, King won a landslide victory despite Drew and the *Globe and Mail*'s campaign. Tommy Church, one of the few Toronto-area Conservatives to win a substantial majority, blamed censorship for what he saw as his party's inability to get its message to the voters. "The people of Canada want the facts about the Canadian war effort," he said. "They did not get the truth through the election campaign." Church, now a member of the Conservative front bench, returned to Ottawa determined to clip the wings of the press censorship system.

The following year, the *Globe* ran a weekly series of large advertisements supposedly paid for by an "Informal Committee on Publishing" that claimed freedom of the press in Canada was in constant jeopardy from unnamed enemies. The *Globe*'s motivation for its attack on the censors is difficult to determine. McCullagh did not write an autobiography before he killed himself in 1953 and the newspaper did not keep records of the discussions of its editorial board. They were probably motivated by a genuine concern about the erosion of press rights, and they may have been motivated partly by the knowledge that the RCMP was targeting two of its writers, Judith Robinson and Oakley Dalgleish (who went on to be editor and publisher of the paper). R.B. Hanson, the leader of the federal Conservatives, claimed in the House of Commons that the police and the government were abusing their powers to intimidate journalists who had been critical of the Liberals.

Other reporters did not take up the issue of the rough handling of journalists by the RCMP. Even in the pages of the *Globe and Mail*, coverage of the RCMP's unhealthy interest in the two reporters seems to have been overtaken by events: the conscription plebiscite the following month, the restructuring of censorship, and the controversy over the publication of a scathing letter written by George Drew that condemned the training and equipment of the Canadian troops lost at Hong Kong at Christmas 1941.

Hong Kong had been vulnerable to a fast Japanese attack since 1938, when Emperor Hirohito's troops occupied the Chinese territory of Guangzhou, which surrounds the territory. Still, the British added little to the defence of the colony until the arrival on November 16 of "C" Force, made up mainly of the Royal Winnipeg Rifles and the Royal Rifles of Canada. Two ships, the *Prince Robert* and the *Atawea*, carried 1,975 infantrymen, support troops, and headquarters officers to the Crown colony. The Canadian troops had seen garrison duty in New Brunswick, Newfoundland, and Jamaica. They arrived with small arms, but their heavier weapons and vehicles had been left behind in Vancouver because of logistical snafus. Combined with British troops and local forces, the Allied strength at Hong Kong stood at about 15,000 men. They faced 50,000 Japanese troops, most of them seasoned veterans of the ongoing Sino-Japanese war and of a brief fight with the Soviets in 1939.

Eight hours after the first strikes at Pearl Harbor, Japanese troops violated Hong Kong's borders. Enemy bombers quickly disposed of the handful of Allied military planes, leaving the Japanese with uncontested air superiority. The Japanese fought their way across the mainland territories, and, five days after the invasion began, the British forces were hunkered down on Hong Kong

Island. On the evening of December 18, Japanese troops began their assault on the city. For a week, Allied troops put up a strong fight. The Canadians proved their bravery, which was recognized later with a flurry of decorations, including a Victory Cross to Sergeant Major John Osborn, who threw himself on a grenade to save his men. The Canadians, led by poor senior and mid-level officers, had suffered from low morale since leaving Vancouver. Without vehicles, they could not be supplied with the ammunition they needed. With their backs to the sea and no hope of rescue, most of them fought hard to buy a few days' more freedom from whatever the Japanese had in store. Their training could later be criticized, but not their bravery. The Canadians fought harder than the seasoned British garrison at Singapore, and they did it mainly under the command of non-commissioned officers who proved to be better soldiers than most of their superiors. Canadian Brigadier General John Lawson, commander of Allied forces on the western side of the island, had let his officers treat the NCOs and enlisted men like curs. The trouble began on the troop ships, Hong Kong expert Brereton Greenhous has shown, where officers lived in swanky first-class cabins while their men, forbidden to smoke on most parts of the ships, were crowded into the hold and fed unappealing rations that included tripe (cattle stomach) soup. Perhaps Lawson redeemed himself with his men when he was gunned down December 19, the first day of fighting on Hong Kong Island, as he ran from his surrounded pillbox headquarters with pistols blazing in both hands.

On Christmas Day, the British governor accepted the inevitable and surrendered the garrison to the tender mercies of the Japanese, who engaged in an orgy of rape and murder against the Chinese and British people in the colony. General Takashi Sakai let his men slaughter, bayonet, and decapitate wounded soldiers in the military hospitals, rape nurses, and treat the Chinese residents with cruelty and contempt. After the war, Sakai would face a firing squad.

Most Canadian soldiers were held at North Point Camp, a filthy hole of a place, where they suffered grievously from malnutrition and disease. Some were sent to even more brutal captivity in Japan, where, given starvation rations, they worked as slaves in mines and factories.

Almost immediately, Canadians looked for people to blame for the disaster. At the same time, the country was involved in yet another partisan drama. Sir Arthur Meighen, the newly chosen Tory leader, resigned his Senate seat in January and ran in a by-election for the House of Commons. This gave him a soapbox to push for conscription, and the undermanned Hong Kong garrison proved to be useful to this campaign. King's government, not knowing how many men were in captivity or the number that had been killed and wounded, had tried to stall the Parliamentary opposition when they asked for those figures in the early months of 1942. George Drew, a skilled amateur military critic who was now the leader of the Ontario provincial Conservative Party, waded into the fight. He found interesting friends on the federal socialist Co-operative Commonwealth Federation (CCF) benches, including Tommy Douglas, who would soon leave Ottawa to become premier of Saskatchewan. Winston Churchill visited Ottawa at the end of December, making his "some chicken, some neck" speech in the House of Commons and trying to drum up morale as the Japanese picked off the British, Dutch, and U.S. possessions in the Pacific. Once the British PM left the city for Washington, the opposition parties began sharpening their knives, realizing the casualty figures were just a small part of the information that King wanted to keep secret. Members of the CCF, especially those in Manitoba and Saskatchewan, were receiving troubling information from families of "C" Force members who believed their sons and brothers had been recklessly sent overseas without training. Tories were getting the same messages, along with some leaks from the military and bureaucracy. They focused on the poor training of the troops, their lack of equipment and the failure of the government to ship the troops' vehicles. In the early weeks of February 1942, after Meighen had lost to the CCF candidate in York South, the issue came to a head in the House of Commons, and King did a very King thing: he launched a Royal Commission to study the Hong Kong deployment.

In Canada, Royal Commissions are a handy way for governments to say they are doing something about problems while actually hoping that public and media will lose interest in the issue during the months or years that the commission is doing its job.

King would later say he had never liked the Hong Kong deployment. At the time, though, he saw things very differently. In mid-November, as his private railway car moved through the farms and marshes between Ottawa and Montreal, King worked on a press statement about the arrival of "C" Force. Halfway to Montreal, he added a paragraph that, he wrote in his diary, made it clear "that defence against aggression anywhere was defence of any country enjoying freedom today. Also cleared up what is meant by defence of Canada, to be equivalent of defence of freedom anywhere in the world. That much has come out of the welter and confusion of the last few days. . . . For Canada to have troops in the Orient, fighting the battle of freedom, marks a new stage in our history. That too is a memorial."

In fact the expedition was the brainchild of the army's chief of staff, General Harry Crerar, who had accepted a British request for garrison troops and sold his minister, J.L. Ralston, on it. King went along with it because he believed British promises that the nationalist Chinese on the mainland and the U.S. fleet would come to the rescue if the Japanese attacked. Like his political and military colleagues in the Western world, King severely underestimated the fighting skills of Japanese troops and Tokyo's ability to launch simultaneous invasions in the Pacific. The Japanese were seen as small, near-sighted, bandy-legged, rather comical people instead of the tough veterans of years of fighting in China that they were. Crerar had picked the Royal Rifles because many of its officers, including Francis Power, the son of air defence minister Charles Power, were well-connected Liberals itching to see some action. (Power survived his captivity and went on to a distinguished legal career. He served one term as a Liberal MP in the 1950s.) In a typically Canadian decision, he chose the Winnipeg Rifles as the second regiment because he wanted some regional balance in "C" Force.

Paul Douglas Dickson, Crerar's biographer, claims the controversy over Hong Kong had a tragic consequence. Rather than examine the real failings in Canadian training, Crerar, now posted in England as head of the Canadian military contingent, sought to win back Canada's fighting reputation. He cast around for a chance to have Canadian troops assigned to a raid, and, in the spring of 1941, began negotiations with Lord Mountbatten to have Canadian troops lead the attack on Dieppe.

King spent a couple of weeks trying to stonewall the Opposition but he soon realized he had been given the opportunity to turn the situation against his many enemies in the military high command—most of whom hated King's anti-conscription stance. He launched an inquiry that he knew would be a political cover-up, but not even King could have seen that the "inquiry" would also whitewash the military's role. Earlier, he had told his defence minister Ralston that he was afraid "Crerar may slip out from under his responsibility by seeking to have it appear that the matter was one of political decision, though the records were clear that it was referred to the Chiefs of Staff for their approval before any action was taken." Later, he told his diary the inquiry

> might well show where the onus really lies, how ready we were to meet a British request, and will put the blame where it ought to be on those responsible for taking some men overseas who should not have gone. Instead of helping the Tories in their determination to have conscription at all costs, it is going to react against them. The public will see that our whole war effort being what it is, that mistake is being made in pressing matters so far. I hope the Defence Department will see the same. They have themselves to blame for getting this off right at the start.

At the time, King's critics asked how any inquiry could be effective when all of the members of "C" Force were dead or in Japanese hands. There was only the thinnest anecdotal account of the Canadians' stand against the Japanese. Yet King went ahead, hoping the appointment of a Royal Commission would make the problem go away.

King appointed Sir Lyman Duff, the 76-year-old chief justice of the Supreme Court of Canada, to be a one-man Royal Commission to investigate whether the troops sent to Hong Kong were adequately trained and equipped, and if the government knew there was a real risk of war with Japan when "C" Force was deployed. Duff had recently been given a term extension by King, and the prime minister probably knew that Duff had recently burned Supreme Court records on World War One draftee appeals rather than let them fall into the hands of pro-conscription forces. His inquiry, held during the run-up to the 1942 conscription plebiscite, was a farce. The hearings were held in secret. The lawyers were ordered to turn over every note, submission, and transcript at the end of the inquiry. Lawyers and witnesses were not allowed to talk to the press, a blackout that was backed by a special censorship rule passed by the federal cabinet.

The big political question that hung over King and his government was whether the cabinet and the bureaucracy knew the Japanese were planning an offensive against the British, American, and Dutch colonies in the Pacific. The evidence is clear that there was, at least, wilful blindness in Ottawa. We have King's intriguing conversation with the *Winnipeg Free Press*'s Grant Dexter in early November 1941, when King told Dexter that Roosevelt expected a Japanese attack within a month. In early October, when Hideki Tojo manoeuvred for power, the British and Americans came to the conclusion that the Japanese would accept the imperial navy's pressure to attack southwards, rather than the army's plan for an attack on the Russians. This was a pivotal decision that probably sealed the fate of both the Nazis and the Japanese militarists.

On October 16, two days before Tojo was officially appointed Prime Minister, Washington sent a message to its military installations in the Pacific, including Pearl Harbor, warning of the deteriorating political situation and of a possible attack. In Ottawa, military intelligence officers, who had close connections to their British counterparts, believed from early September 1941 that the Japanese would come into the war and attack British colonies. Colonel W.W. Murray, the chief cable censorship officer in Ottawa, was so sure of a Japanese assault that he became a pest to Norman Robertson, the top bureaucrat in the Department of External Affairs, who was also one of King's closest advisors.

After several weeks of hearings in Ottawa, Duff decided the Canadian forces that faced the Japanese on December 8, 1941, had been fit to defend Hong Kong, and that their officers had not let them down by failing to train them. Duff either invented, or someone fantasized for him, a telegram from the Chinese government that, in effect, guaranteed the Canadians would be rescued by the nationalists who, in fact, could barely hold the territory under their control. The chief justice seemed to think Chiang Kai-shek's word, if it had actually been given to the Allies on paper or in conversation, actually had some value. He tossed some blame for the disaster on quartermaster officers who had lacked "energy" in finding a way to ship the vehicles along with the troops. No one else in the upper ranks was criticized. Crerar, who was in England, didn't bother testifying at Duff's inquiry, although he did send written answers to questions posed by the commissioner, his counsel, and Drew. Duff did not make any recommendations to prevent a similar failure, probably because he wasn't asked to.

The Royal Commission looked like a cover-up because that's what it was.

In the days leading up to his appointment, Duff had talked to King about the political fallout of the Hong Kong defeat and had told King he believed Drew and "certain groups" in Toronto were using the loss of "C" Force as evidence that Canada needed to bring in a military draft and spend more money on training. Before the hearings began, Duff asked King for help choosing a lawyer to be commission counsel. In March, Duff had told King the hearings should be secret so they could not be used as a soapbox by Drew, who had been appointed Opposition counsel. Duff had told King that Drew's public criticism of the Hong Kong deployment made Duff ashamed of the legal profession. On April 8, while the inquiry was adjourned to allow counsel to write their submissions, King and Duff went to a dinner for the Australian external affairs minister, who was visiting Ottawa. King gave Duff a ride home. Duff told King he "has his mind all made up on the Hong Kong matter. . . .

He gave me no hint of what his opinion would be, but I think the fact he mentioned it at all makes clear he is satisfied with the Government's position. He makes no bones about his feelings towards Drew." In fact, Duff's report was already written and was probably at the printers.

On June 5, as U-boats hunted in the St. Lawrence River and the country licked its wounds from the bitter conscription referendum campaign, King released the Duff report to Parliament. Drew quickly realized Duff's report was a whitewash (an opinion shared by most postwar historians). Having failed to influence the chief justice's report, Drew took his objections to the people. First, he made a public speech, published by the *Globe and Mail*, attacking Duff and his report. He said in an interview in the *Globe* that the "actual facts brought out in evidence were so blood-curdling that the public have a right to know what did take place." The evidence showed "inexcusable blundering, confusion and incompetence had been hidden from the public." King, Duff, and justice minister Louis St. Laurent met at the chief justice's house and decided to charge Drew under the same section of the cabinet orders made under the *War Measures Act* that gave the government its press-censorship powers. Charges had to be approved by a provincial attorney general or by St. Laurent. First, King's men approached the attorney general of Ontario, who turned them down. St. Laurent decided to do his own dirty work, and on June 23, Drew was served with a summons to appear in court. His charges carried a maximum penalty of five years in jail and a $5,000 fine. Drew made it clear he would use his trial as a platform to make the case that he had presented behind closed doors to the Duff inquiry. King quickly backtracked, and in the first week of July the charges were dropped.

On July 11, 1942, the Ontario Tory leader sent a thirty-two-page letter to King that eviscerated all of Duff's conclusions and accurately assessed the failures of leadership, training, and equipment of the doomed Hong Kong force. Had it been published, it would have saved the Hong Kong veterans years of struggle to have their story told. Drew gave copies of his letter to the leaders of the two opposition parties in the House of Commons, the Canadian Press wire service, and members of the Parliamentary Press Gallery.

At last, Drew had an issue that would give him national publicity. King met that day with federal Conservative leader Hanson, who told the prime minister he and many Tory MPs did not agree with what Drew was doing. Hanson told King he was caught in the middle: squeezed by the *Globe and Mail* for not demanding enough evidence of the fitness of the Hong Kong force, while the *Toronto Star* criticized him for hurting the war effort by asking for too much. Hanson said Drew was simply out to make political capital as he could. The national Tory leader probably knew Drew was after his own job. Hanson did say Drew's claim that he was counsel for the "public," rather than the "Opposition," showed disloyalty to the Conservative Party, but, at least publicly, King was on his own.

It was a very busy day in Ottawa. The same afternoon, the new director of censorship, O.M. Biggar, a close friend of Chief Justice Duff, was called into a federal cabinet meeting for a three-hour session on the Drew letter controversy. King asked Biggar, Defence Minister Ralston, and Justice Minister St. Laurent whether newspapers that ran the letter could be sued for libel. Some ministers argued Drew and the newspapers would be safe if the letter was tabled in the House of Commons, giving its contents parliamentary privilege. King took a copy of his father's book *Libel and Slander* from a shelf and read passages from it that convinced him Drew and the press could, in fact, be sued. Still, the government chose to use the censorship system to stifle Drew's criticism rather than drag Drew into a courtroom. King had learned his lesson the month before.

By then, the rest of the national press had come around to Drew and *Globe and Mail* founder McCullagh's position. At 9:30 p.m. on July 14, Andrew Carnegie, a Canadian Press reporter on Parliament Hill, had finished his story about the Drew letter. He submitted the article to the Ottawa office of the Directorate of Censorship and asked that it be approved because King had made a promise to the leader of the Co-operative Commonwealth Federation that the letter would be tabled in the House. Jacques Girouard, the first frontline censor to work on the issue, was wary, saying he should wait until the letter was submitted to the House. The immunity would begin only after the tabling. Girouard's instincts were right. King changed his mind about giving Parliament the Drew letter, claiming that it violated secrecy promises that the Canadian government had made to the British.

Still, the Canadian Press sent the letter out on its wire, along with analysis of its contents, with a warning that it was not yet cleared for publication. Editors across the country wanted to run the letter in their next editions: they worried about being scooped on a story they already had in their hands. At the same time, Canadian reporters were sending telegrams to London and New York trying to sell the story to foreign newspapers. The censors were willing to approve articles saying the letter existed and describing the controversy, but the contents, Drew's scathing criticism of Duff's whitewash, could not be divulged.

The Montreal *Gazette* probed the boundaries of the Drew letter ban in its editorial of July 16. When a journalist with British United Press and the Southam newspaper chain's parliamentary reporter "Torchy" Anderson wanted to file stories based on the *Gazette* editorial, Biggar turned them down. At 8:00 p.m. on July 16, the *Globe and Mail*'s first edition for July 17 hit the streets carrying a story saying censors had suppressed the entire Drew letter. That day, McCullagh left for a fishing trip to ponder whether he was willing to risk jail by publishing the letter.

Meanwhile, the censors worked to protect themselves against the gathering storm. Eggleston sat down to write a chronology of the controversy, while his boss, Biggar, wrote a detailed memo to the minister in charge of press censorship, apparently hoping the government would relent. Still, the censors did the government's bidding. Eggleston sent a telegram to all of the regional offices telling them the Directorate was refusing to pass for publication articles based on that morning's *Gazette* editorial. The *Vancouver Sun* submitted a story that used Canadian Press's Drew letter material. When Lew Gordon refused to approve parts of it, the *Sun* ran, in bold text on its front page of July 18, a statement saying, "In Vancouver today, Lew Gordon, British Columbia Press Censor, ruled that no part of the letter could be published." In a memorandum to his head office, Gordon said he had been misquoted: "This office never made any ruling that no part of the letter could be published, as alleged in the *Sun*."

The same day, Gordon did clear stories to Canadian Press about the Calgary Trades and Labour Council's telegram to King condemning "an attitude of suppression of information" about the Hong Kong report. The Calgary unions called for a secret session of the House of Commons to deal with the allegations in the Drew letter. In Toronto, local censor Bert Perry used cable interceptions to follow the strategizing between John Bird, editor of the *Winnipeg Tribune*, and Bob Farquharson, the *Globe and Mail*'s managing editor. Stories in the July 17 editions of the *Globe* and the *Ottawa Citizen* criticized the censorship system and encouraged other major newspapers to further test the boundaries of the censors' policy.

The censors believed the two papers, especially the *Citizen*, had treated them unfairly, so Charpentier and Eggleston sat down to draft a letter to make the censors' case to all of the country's newspapers. Partway through that process, they tore up the letter and started writing a new one. They decided to write a defence to the executives of the Canadian Press wire service. They had never spiked the *Citizen*'s Drew letter material because they had never seen it, they claimed. Their defence was not convincing: the Canadian Press's Montreal-based editor John Dauphinee soon phoned to say he was submitting all of the agency's material on Drew's criticism of Duff and his report. The censors read the 7,500-word dispatch and stamped it "Publication Not Authorized." The Canadian Press's wire service carried a note to this effect shortly afterwards.

Late that afternoon, Norman MacLeod, the parliamentary correspondent for the British United Press, a commercial news service that competed against Canadian Press, called Eggleston to say Drew had written a second letter analyzing the failures of the Hong Kong mission and his news wire wanted to carry a story on it. Eggleston reviewed the material over the telephone and, at first, was willing to pass all of it except one paragraph that the censor believed drew on secret parts of the military's evidence at the Duff inquiry. Cable censors were ordered to prevent any news stories on this Drew letter from being sent to the United States.

The *Globe and Mail* and many of the rest of the major Canadian newspapers published long stories and editorials on July 18 criticizing the way King's government handled the controversy. The *Winnipeg Tribune* devoted nearly a full page to publishing the first Drew letter, with big *X*s showing sections that editors had cut to conform to the censorship rules. The *Globe* printed a long editorial explaining the background of the Drew letter controversy (without actually spelling out his criticisms of the Hong Kong deployment) and argued, "The press of Canada has not opposed what it conceived to be censorship for public protection, to safeguard military secrets from the enemy." King, the paper told its readers, had made a promise to table the letter in the House of Commons, and then broken it, and the press still showed its loyalty to Canada by refusing to leak the document. There was no need for threats of tougher censorship, since, "from the beginning of the war newspaper publishers and editors in general have accepted their responsibility, leaning backward to do it, not because of fear of the big stick, but because they wished to do their full duty." The *Vancouver Sun* and the *Province* also published editorials that day criticizing King's handling of the Drew letter, the latter newspaper saying, "It is futile, of course, to attempt to hide what so many people know. It is also the height of folly, because when news is suppressed, where there is news, rumour takes its place, and rumour has a way of spreading and expanding—literally feeding upon itself."

That afternoon, King refused to table both Drew letters in the House of Commons. Through the evening, the censors were pressed by reporters and editors to release at least some of the material in the second letter. Biggar would have passed most of it, removing a paragraph that referred to secret messages passed between the British and Canadian governments telling of the deteriorating situation in the Pacific that should have been a warning to Ottawa not to send soldiers to Hong Kong unless they were trained and battle-ready. Eggleston, however, believed the letter had to be dealt with as a whole, not carved up and offered in pieces to the various offices of the Directorate of Censorship. He argued successfully that the entire second letter—the one he had been willing to pass, except for one small cut, the day before—should be stamped, "Not Approved for Publication."

The cable censors set out to create their own press censorship. They tried to disrupt the newspapers' communication by refusing to pass telegrams between the editors of the *Globe and Mail*, the *Vancouver News-Herald*, and the *Winnipeg Tribune*. Biggar called Girouard and cable censor Major McEvoy into his office and warned the cable censors to stay off censorship's turf: they had no right to suppress material that was not military secrets. In this case, they had killed messages that were simply a recounting of what had been published in newspapers. McEvoy claimed his agents had proof of a conspiracy among parliamentary reporters, CCF leader M.J. Coldwell, and Drew, and that reporters had extensive information as to what Coldwell proposed to do in the House with the Drew letter. Biggar, a smart lawyer who, this time, did not let his friendships with the prime minister and the chief justice cloud his judgment, did not feel that this had any relevance. Girouard agreed, saying there was a real danger of censors appearing to be involved in politics. McEvoy angrily restated his position, but finally gave in to Biggar's ruling that communication between the country's newsrooms should not be disrupted.

Two days later, the Canadian Press's Andrew Carnegie submitted the original Drew letter to Eggleston for a ruling. Eggleston started to look for a way out of the quagmire. He reminded Carnegie that approval of the document would allow it to be published without risk of prosecution, but the refusal by censors to approve a story did not *guarantee* that charges would follow its publication. This was, in fact, the basis of the "voluntary" Canadian press censorship system. "This seemed to strike Andy as a new idea, although we have frequently tried to make it clear to all parties concerned, and he asked whether I could write something for them as guidance," Eggleston told his colleagues.

On the evening of July 21, Blair Fraser of the Montreal *Gazette* phoned Jacques Girouard to get clarification of the censors' position on Drew's first letter. Girouard told Fraser the censors would not give immunity to publish the entire letter or portions of it because they continued to believe the material violated the *Defence of Canada Regulations*. Five minutes after the call ended, Fraser called Ed McMahon, the Montreal censor. Fraser was, McMahon believed, "fishing for material" to be used in the *Gazette*'s defence if the newspaper ignored the censors' advice. McMahon ended the call quickly by telling Fraser to contact censorship's head office in Ottawa.

At the same time the Montreal censors were fending off Fraser, *Globe and Mail* publisher George McCullagh and his managing editor Bob Farquharson were in the Toronto office of the Directorate of Censorship asking if the press censors would pass Drew's first letter to Mackenzie King. Bert Perry refused to give in. McCullagh wanted to know what was censorable in it. Perry did not know, since he had not read Drew's original letter. When McCullagh asked what would happen if the *Globe* published the letter without censorship approval, Perry told him the newspaper was liable to be prosecuted under the *Defence of Canada Regulations*. Perry drew the conclusion that McCullagh was not afraid of being charged. He was wrong. George McCullagh, who suffered from bouts of serious depression and may well have been bipolar, would not, perhaps could not, choose jail.

Instead, he and his colleagues let the country know that the King government was sitting on serious allegations about the Hong Kong deployment, and it was using censorship to prevent the people from knowing what the critics of the Duff report had to say. On July 24, the *Globe and Mail* published a roundup of critical editorials from across the country under the headline, "Gagging Process of Censorship Draws Protest Across Canada." The Toronto-based Tory magazine *Saturday Night* said the "argument of possible assistance to the enemy has completely ceased to be used in defence of the policy of suppression," while the *Financial Post* accused King's government of a "wanton abuse of wartime censorship." The criticism had spread to smaller papers like the *Brantford Expositor*, which said, "There must be no countenancing of any procedure which might stifle the right to free and proper expression and inquiry," while the

Vancouver News-Herald declared, "It is impossible to gag a free people or shackle a free press in an alert democracy. If all the people stand together to maintain their right of free speech, no Government can succeed in depriving them of it." The *Ottawa Citizen's* editors argued that "a re-examination of their ruling on the part of the press censors seems to be in order. Any censorship for other than the proper and legitimate purposes for which it was established is . . . something that is both alarming and dangerous and ought to be vigorously contested." The *Toronto Telegram*, in one of its few editorials on censorship, warned, "If the newspapers remain silent under the official ban on publication and fail to urge with all of the power at their command a full investigation by Parliament of all evidence they will go far to forfeit the trust of the public and to demonstrate that the boasted freedom of the press is a right to which they are not entitled." The *London Free Press*, a Conservative paper, believed wartime censorship was a "necessary evil" but added, "It is a dangerous infringement on the liberties for which we are fighting when censorship is used for other than its proper and legitimate purposes. Unfortunately, this is the impression which has been given in the present instance." Popular columnist Elmore Philpott, writing in the *Vancouver News-Herald*, said, "Colonel Drew's accusations are so astounding in many other respects that they demand complete publicity in Parliament."

On July 22, Biggar and Eggleston met with reporters of the British United Press wire service and frustrated senior journalists in the Parliamentary Press Gallery. The Hill reporters demanded that the censors stop issuing recommendations and begin promulgating clear orders about what could and could not be published. Eggleston objected to that idea, saying, "In effect they were asking us to assume responsibility" that a free press "should properly exercise itself." Biggar warned journalists that they might not like an "involuntary" censorship system: "It would mean a censor in every newspaper office with dictatorial powers to order material expunged even if already in type or on the page. This smacked a good deal of the sort of disastrous censorship which France had in the fall of 1939 and in the early months of 1940."

On July 26 and 28, Parliament debated the Duff report. Some of Mackenzie King's backbenchers tried to smear Drew as a fascist, using as "proof" Drew's flamboyant Italian wife Fiorenza. King released some information that Duff had suppressed. He was set upon by Tommy Douglas, who had worked closely with Drew to collect information that undermined Duff's conclusions.

By then, King was living at his farm in the Gatineau Hills, where Parliament seemed very far away. Maybe King could read a calendar and knew that the story would wither away in the summer news doldrums. Maybe he realized the press would eventually run out of things to say about the Drew letter and Hong Kong and would move on to something else. In early August, the Hong Kong fallout had moved from the front pages. By the end of the month, the papers were filled with the casualty lists from Dieppe, and no one wanted to hear any more stories about military failure. Drew and the *Globe and Mail* took one last shot in November, when the paper published Drew's allegation that the federal government had tapped his telephone lines and opened his mail during the controversy. "The time has come," Drew said, "for Canadians to assess the general condition of their country and express themselves openly on the degree to which freedom of the press and freedom of the expression of opinion have been curtailed in Canada." The government denied the allegation.

Meanwhile, the survivors of the Battle of Hong Kong struggled to live. In Canada, the press was warned by the censors to stop publishing stories of the atrocities committed against them, partly to prevent violent retaliation against ethnic Japanese in Canada. In September 1945, the real cost of the Hong Kong deployment struck the prime minister when King met some of the survivors in Montreal and was aghast at what he saw. And these men had been eating steadily for a month, trying to regain the weight they had lost since Christmas 1941. After the war, the press had a strong dislike for the Hong Kong story, and many of the veterans were dead before the men of "C" Force got the recognition and financial compensation they deserved.

A year from the height of the Hong Kong controversy, George

Drew was on the hustings, winning the premiership of Ontario. For years, he struggled to get his analysis of the Hong Kong disaster on the public record. During the years he was premier, Drew received handwritten letters from soldiers and their families begging him not to lose interest in their fight for the truth. He also received a steady stream of information from military insiders who confirmed Drew's argument that the government had recklessly sent untrained men to Hong Kong when they should have known the Japanese were preparing to attack. In 1948, when he was federal Tory leader, facing off against King and the PM's hand-picked successor, St. Laurent, Drew fought to get the letter tabled. This time, King used a novel excuse: the letter had been shared with the British, and King would be breaking a diplomatic confidence if he allowed it to be entered into the parliamentary record. By then, the British had their own official inquiry on Hong Kong that directly contradicted Duff's conclusions. Canadians now knew the chief justice's report was a whitewash. According to Duff's biographer, Hong Kong would haunt Duff until he died in 1955 at the age of ninety.

George McCullagh went on to buy the *Toronto Telegram* just after the war. His astounding success in business seemed to give him no inner comfort, and he spent the last years of his life fighting depression. He was forty-eight when he killed himself in 1953. Mc-Cullagh's widow later married George Drew. In 1948, Drew beat John Diefenbaker to become leader of the federal Progressive Conservatives, but he was hammered in the next two elections by Louis St. Laurent, the man who tried to send him to prison. Diefenbaker, who finally led the federal Tories out of the wilderness, made Drew Canada's high commissioner to the United Kingdom, the country's most coveted diplomatic post.

The Canadian deployment to Hong Kong was one of the most controversial decisions of the war. There were people in Ottawa who were paid to know that the situation in the Pacific was deteriorating and there was a serious threat that "C" Force would be attacked by the tough Japanese veterans on the Chinese mainland. King and Duff's decision to spare the army and the government from accurate criticism deserved to be exposed for what it was by the press and Opposition politicians. This was certainly a case where the army needed to learn from its mistakes. Drew had done the job that journalists should have performed, but his efforts were stifled. When he did need support from the press, they were not willing to fight King and his censors.

The Japanese treated their Canadian prisoners with unconscionable cruelty: one in four who surrendered at Hong Kong would never see Canada again, while the death rate for Canadians held by the Nazis was one in twenty-five. Most of those who did return from Japanese captivity were barely alive, racked by starvation and untreated diseases. Their captivity did lasting damage: few of them lived past middle age. The Hong Kong veterans' long fight for fair compensation has kept them in the public mind since the end of the war. George Drew did the right thing when he criticized King's government and Sir Lyman Duff for trying to cover up the planning failures of the Hong Kong deployment, and the *Globe and Mail*, which may well have become Drew's megaphone for partisan political reasons, still deserves credit for taking its stand. The *Globe* fought to the very edge of the law, its Drew letter campaign being one of the great moments in Canadian media history. Perhaps it would have been an even more shining moment if McCullagh had chosen jail. This certainly would have saved the Hong Kong veterans and Drew the years of postwar struggles to put the truth on the record. Still, the *Globe*'s tenacity may well have dampened the King government's temptation to harness censorship to its own partisan agenda.

CHAPTER 7

The Battle of Bowmanville

WHILE THE CENSORSHIP SYSTEM was "voluntary," there were a
few occasions when the censors issued outright bans on stories. This
was the case in October 1942, when the censors ordered a news
blackout on stories about the shackling of German prisoners of war
at Camp 30 in Bowmanville, Ontario. Just after the collapse of
France, the censors had issued a ban on reporting on the small number of enemy POWs who, almost by sheer bad luck, had fallen into
Allied hands that spring and had been shipped to camps in Canada.
The following April, the censors told Canadian newspaper and radio
reporters the ban covered any claims by German and Italian POWs
that they were mistreated or brutalized by their Canadian guards.
That included any whistle-blowing by the guards themselves. The
government did not seem to fear public outrage against abuse of
enemy soldiers, although there would be some, especially from journalists and clergy. Mackenzie King's government didn't want German
retaliation against Canadians held by the Nazis.

Canadian soldiers would, especially through the Normandy
campaign, be reluctant to accept the surrender of German soldiers,
partly in retaliation for the murder of Canadians by the 12 SS Panzer Division *Hitlerjugend* in the early days of the invasion. Canadians
shared this trait with Americans, who would sometimes shoot prisoners out of hand in the heat of battle or if guarding the prisoners
hurt their combat effectiveness in any way. By the time of the Battle
of the Scheldt Estuary, Canadian troops were more likely to accept
German surrenders. Canadian war correspondents knew about the
Canadians' reputation for cold-bloodedness and did not report it.

After the raids on Dieppe (August 19, 1942) and the Channel Island of Sark (October 4, 1942), the German military issued press releases claiming bodies of German soldiers who had been taken prisoner by the Canadians and British were washing ashore on the French coast with their hands tied. The Germans stopped short of alleging the soldiers had been bound up and murdered, although the implication was there. The Germans displayed orders taken from Canadians captured at Dieppe which said German prisoners were to be tied up or handcuffed until they could be taken to a secure holding area. Germany claimed these orders breached the 1927 Geneva Convention's prohibition of the binding and public humiliation of prisoners of war. The German position seems ridiculous, considering its deliberate murder and brutalization not only of Russian prisoners but also of POWs from France who were made to work in mines and munitions plants. Still, with so many Canadians now in German POW camps, the Canadian government had to take the Nazis' complaint seriously.

After the Sark raid, German officials announced they would shackle British and Canadian prisoners in retaliation for the binding of Wehrmacht soldiers. Their decision was to drive a wedge between Ottawa and Whitehall, with Churchill's government taking a very public hard line against the Germans that would prove difficult to retreat from.

Churchill's war cabinet decided on October 8, 1942, to order German military prisoners held in Britain and Canada to be shackled if Germany carried through with its threat. The Canadian government and Canada's military were not consulted. Instead, the country's leaders learned from the BBC they would be chaining up Germans. Two days later, London announced that the Germans had shackled 1,376 Allied prisoners, mostly Canadians, and that retaliation would be taken against the same number of Germans in Allied camps. Rather than publicly fight with Churchill, King's government agreed to handcuff or shackle German POWs, but Ottawa had no enthusiasm for the idea, nor did most of the soldiers in charge of guarding the captive Germans.

The press in Britain and Canada despised the idea of breaching the Geneva Convention, and some Protestant ministers saw the violation of the treaty as a moral failure and the beginning of a downward spiral that would cause suffering to ordinary soldiers on both sides. Canada had its own reason for treading very, very carefully. The Germans had been given a propaganda gem just after Dieppe, one they could have used to justify dropping all Geneva Convention protection for Canadian troops. Canadian Press reporter Ross Munro had gone into Dieppe and managed to survive the raid. The Wartime Information Board, the government's propaganda arm, hired Munro to tour Canada to recount the heroics of the botched attack. On September 4, 1942, Munro told a packed rally at the Montreal Forum that Allied forces had shot German soldiers out of hand when they had surrendered. The commando unit, headed up by Simon Fraser (Lord Lovat), captured a German coastal battery and took 150 defenders prisoner. "Some of the Germans had been killed in the skirmish but many of them were left," Munro told the Montrealers. "Then," he continued, "in an aristocratic tone Lord Lovat said to the remainder, 'I'm sorry, but we will have to erase you' and erase them they did."

This was murder, even in wartime. Why did Munro, only twenty-eight years old but still one of the sharpest minds among the Canadian reporters stationed in Britain—he was to have scoop after scoop until the last days of the war and went on to a distinguished peacetime career—make the allegation? Killing 150 POWs in cold blood would, if true, be a war crime. The allegation, carried on the front page of the second section of the next day's Montreal *Gazette*, was made only once by Munro, and does not appear in the articles and books Munro wrote during and after the war. Lovat, who had inherited the title of the last aristocrat beheaded in the United Kingdom for treason, was one of the toughest commando leaders in the British forces, and he was awarded the Distinguished Service Order for his actions at Dieppe. The day after the Montreal Forum rally, Canadian military intelligence agents scrambled to shut down coverage of Munro's claim. (Munro later said he could not remember making the statement, which seems rather bizarre considering the details of the *Gazette*'s quote.) Newspapers across the country were warned not to use anything about Lovat's supposed actions. The newspapers obeyed, but the *Gazette* story was already on the streets of Canada's largest city and nothing could be done to take it back. So the Canadian government had good reason to fear German retaliation against the Canadians captured at Dieppe.

Concern for the safety of the Canadian soldiers in Nazi hands would be an important motivator of Canadian government actions during the shackling crisis. The press, too, disagreed with Churchill's decision. The *Globe and Mail*, along with several other newspapers, editorialized that the moral high ground taken by the Allies was undermined when authorities mimicked Germany's breach of the Geneva Convention.

The German and British decisions to engage in tit-for-tat abuse of POWs appear to have been taken in haste and regretted almost at once. Indirect negotiations, facilitated by the Swiss government, began immediately. Still, neither side would publicly back down until some sort of face-saving deal was crafted.

The shackling of German POWs began on the Canadian Thanksgiving weekend. On Saturday, October 10, 1942, Lieutenant Colonel James Mason Taylor, commandant of Camp 30 in Bowmanville, requested General Major Georg Friemel, the highest-ranking German army officer in Allied custody at the time and the official spokesman for the prisoners, to solicit a group of POWs to volunteer to be shackled. Friemel, who had been captured on May 10, 1940, in Holland when Dutch troops counterattacked elite German airborne soldiers at Ypenburg, refused the order. Senior German army officer Generalleutnant Hans von Ravenstein, senior air force officer Oberstleutnant Hans Hefele, and senior naval officer Korvettenkapitan z.S. Otto Kretschmer were asked to co-operate with shackling. They, too, refused.

Like Friemel, Kretschmer was quite a catch. He had skippered U-23 and U-99 off the British coast for just over a year and a half, but sank more tonnage than any U-boat skipper in the entire war. He had developed a reputation as a chivalrous sub captain who went out of his way to save the lives of sailors whose ships he destroyed. On March 13, 1941, Kretschmer and his fellow U-boat stars Fritz-

Julius Lemp in *U-110* and Joachim Schepke in *U-100* took on the warships escorting Halifax-to-Liverpool convoy HX-112 in a ferocious fight. Schepke was crushed to death in his conning tower when a British destroyer rammed *U-100*. Kretschmer got into the middle of the convoy, sank three tankers, two freighters, and damaged a fourth tanker. Out of torpedoes, *U-99* submerged and tried to slip away. It was Kretschmer's misfortune to run up against a skipper of his own calibre, Captain Donald Macintyre of HMS *Walker*. Kretschmer could not shake off *Walker*, and when *U-99*'s hull began to crack apart, Kretschmer returned to the surface. Kretschmer made sure all of his men got off the sinking sub before offering his hand to a sailor from *Walker*. His interrogation had been conducted by a British admiral in a London townhouse over bottles of Scotch. The admiral came away from the little party hoping there were no more Otto Kretschmers lurking out there. When he arrived in Toronto, Canadian naval officers threw him a party. The German navy desperately wanted Kretschmer back and made several bids to break him out and rescue him.

Kretschmer was quite comfortable where he was. Until the time of the shackling dust-up, Camp 30 had been more like a university residence than a prison. Its clusters of buildings, centred on a boys' reform school, were new and comfortable. The "camp" had private rooms, a swimming pool, decent food, plenty of recreation, and a full calendar of social events. While the inmates of the camp did devise several escape scenarios, none was particularly serious. Very few of the prisoners were dedicated Nazis. They were, in the main, from regular army and navy units that had fought professionally and with distinction. There was very little animosity between the captives and their guards.

On October 10, Lieutenant Colonel Taylor followed Ottawa's orders and told his men to handcuff 100 German officers. The guards were told to use force if necessary. German prisoners did not report for roll call and approximately 150 POWs, armed with hockey sticks and steel bars, were seen to be barricading themselves in their rooms and the camp's kitchen. Canadian guards at Bowmanville, mostly middle-aged World War One veterans, asked for reinforcements from army training camps around Kingston, Ontario. Before help arrived, the guards, carrying unloaded rifles with fixed bayonets, stormed the German command centre (the camp's kitchen) in the late afternoon of October 10. The Germans fought back for more than an hour, until the Canadians brought in a high-pressure fire hose. The last holdouts surrendered at roughly 6:00 p.m. The fight was more sport than warfare, and pictures of the brawl show most of the participants laughing. However, the Canadian officers went too far. After they surrendered, the German prisoners were forced to run a gauntlet of Canadian guards who beat the POWs with rifle butts. The Germans especially despised being hit with the walking stick of Lieutenant G.E. Brent, who led the assault, and Brent was now a marked man.

Before dawn the next day, some German officers were awakened and marched to a satellite camp. A roll call at 6:40 a.m. showed that two officers escaped from this group, but they were recaptured within half an hour when the Canadian guards saw them running and fired a couple of shots in their general direction.

Back at Camp 30, the German prisoners answered the morning roll call, but Kretschmer warned the guards to keep Lieutenant Brent away from his men. At 9:00 a.m., Brent arrived and sought out Kretschmer. An argument broke out and Kretschmer struck Brent in the face. The Canadian officer was jumped by German soldiers and sailors, who dragged Brent into one of the prisoners' barracks and tied him up. A Canadian guard sounded the alarm. That was enough to win the Canadian lieutenant's freedom: Brent was unceremoniously chucked out the door of the barracks. Guards firing at Brent's captors missed the Germans, but a ricochet sent a piece of cement into the barracks, which lightly wounded one of the German officers. After a lull, the Germans waved a truce flag and the wounded POW was evacuated to a local hospital.

On the morning of Monday, October 12 (Thanksgiving Day), the young Canadian trainees arrived from Barriefield, near Kingston, to spell off the exhausted older guards. They deployed in the camp before dawn, armed with empty rifles sporting fixed bayonets. Many of them were also carrying clubs and clutches of Canadian soldiers attached fire hoses to the Bowmanville water system.

Hungry for action against real Germans, the Canadian recruits stormed the POW barracks and the main camp building, where they fought Germans armed with fire axes, rocks, hockey sticks, and sections of pipe torn from Camp 30's plumbing system. The brawl, involving 400 Canadian soldiers and an equal number of Germans, lasted until early evening, when the last German holdouts surrendered. Injured people on both sides received first aid. The Germans suffered the most severe casualties: one officer lost an eye and a second suffered a serious bayonet wound. After the riot, about 100 German soldiers were marched out of the camp in handcuffs. That night, the POWs returned to their own barracks, where they found their personal belongings had been ransacked and some of their decorations, including a Knight's Cross (probably Kretschmer's), had been stolen.

At least thirty reporters, mostly from Toronto newspapers, worked the long weekend and watched the fights. They were backed by teams of editors at the three major papers in the city. The *Toronto Star* had booked space at a local hotel and set up a mini-newsroom to handle the mass of copy and the photographs. The journalists hadn't missed much: they had the entire story except the allegations that Canadian soldiers had stolen German decorations.

The *Globe and Mail* had the competitive advantage, as, unlike the *Toronto Telegram* and the *Toronto Star*, it published on Thanksgiving. The first editions of the *Telegram* and the *Star* were not on the street until Tuesday afternoon, so it appears the latter papers planned to make up in volume what they lacked in exclusivity. Reporters, photographers, and at least one sketch artist filed their work in time for the *Star*'s deadlines.

However, none of that material was published. On October 10, the first day of the riot, Ottawa-based censor R.W. Baldwin sent a telegram to all newspaper editors and radio news managers in Canada, saying the censors "urgently request [a] complete blackout [of] any incident which may arise in prison camps as a result [of] Canadian actions."

In a follow-up memorandum to Wilfrid Eggleston, Baldwin explained his news blackout. Any news about the shackling of Germans in Canadian custody or stories about the camp brawl might get back to Germany and upset "the delicate balance of negotiations."

On Sunday, *Globe and Mail* managing editor Bob Farquharson called Bert Perry (the Toronto newspaper censor), described the riot, and asked for clearance to print the story. Perry turned him down "because of the dangers involved, and in consideration for our men in German camps." Farquharson was not happy with this decision, but was willing to live with it as long as no other paper beat the *Globe* on the story.

That Monday afternoon, Ken Edey, the *Toronto Star*'s news editor and liaison with the censorship department, phoned Perry to ask if any of the copy filed by the *Star*'s team of sixteen reporters and photographers could be used. Perry said the Directorate of Censorship wanted the entire riot story suppressed. Edey told Perry the *Star* had a sketch of the riot scene and asked the censor whether he should "destroy it, send it [to Perry's office] for safe keeping, or put it in a safety vault so that enemy agents would have no access to it, in case they want to engineer a wholesale escape of the camp occupants. We were somewhat puzzled by this request, as it sounded very much like sarcasm, or as if we were being kidded." In a ruling sent to the newspaper, Perry said the *Star* could print a story on the Saturday morning escape attempt, but only if it was "disassociated with the shackling incident" and "there should be no mention of the [escaping] prisoners being fired upon." On the same day, Perry approved a story written by a *Star* stringer in Espanola saying the shackling of prisoners in a camp near that northern Ontario town had taken place without incident. At the same time, the Montreal censorship office noted the *Globe and Mail* had used an Associated Press photograph in its first edition showing Pittsburgh, Pennsylvania, police collecting extra handcuffs and shackles to be donated to Canadian POW authorities. The Montreal censor phoned the Montreal *Gazette* to ask it not to use the picture.

Meanwhile, at Bowmanville, a compromise was worked out between Canadian Camp 30 authorities and German POW officers to allow a token shackling of prisoners. The Swiss consul in Toronto visited the Bowmanville camp, took statements from the Germans about the alleged brutality and the theft of the decorations, and forwarded his report to Germany. In the ten days after the riot, the embargo on Canadian coverage of the Bowmanville brawl was maintained. Meanwhile, in Ottawa, King was resisting pressure from Churchill to increase the number of prisoners who were shackled.

On October 22, a new issue of *Time* magazine, carrying an eight-inch story on the Bowmanville riot, appeared on newsstands and in subscribers' mail. The article, which, like most *Time* stories of the period, ran without a byline, was a "brightener," a story written in a flippant style that was supposed to give some humour and colour to the pages of dreary war coverage. The writer suggested the German prisoners of war were finally getting some of the punishment their comrades had dished out to Europe. The story had the bare bones of the incident: the Germans' refusal to submit to shackling and the brawls that occurred over the long weekend. The *Time* story did contain errors, the most serious of which—to Canadian censorship authorities—were the writer's claims that Canadians used a machine gun and tear gas to suppress the riot. The censors also objected to the reporting of the fact that one German prisoner had suffered a bayonet wound. They do not appear to have been relieved (or simply may not have yet known) that some of the more egregious actions of the Canadian soldiers were not reported by *Time*: the fact that Canadians forced the German POWs to run a gauntlet after the first day's riot was subdued; and the claims by the Germans that Canadians had stolen their decorations.

Prime Minister King was horrified by the breach of censorship. "A very sensational statement appeared, which may do great harm. Gives Hitler just the kind of ammunition he wants. All goes to show the folly of shackling prisoners at the outset and the wisdom of our decision not to attempt it on more than the present scale," he wrote in his diary. The Ottawa censors sent telegrams to all of the radio stations and newspapers in the country ordering them not to report on the *Time* article or the information in it while Canadian officials considered sanctions against *Time*. When officials realized the Canadian press was furious at *Time*, they began to approve stories on the breach of censorship.

Baldwin and Eggleston, as well as officials in the Department of External Affairs, considered seizing the issue from newsstands or temporarily banning it from Canada. They decided not to act on that impulse, but did send a report to RCMP deputy commissioner R.L. Cadiz and asked him to begin a criminal investigation to root out the author of the story. Sent over the signatures of Eggleston and Charpentier, the censors' memorandum requested "every possible effort should be made to determine and apprehend the guilty party who transmitted this information to the United States, and that every appropriate action should be taken to deal with him."

Directorate of Censorship officials began their own search. In mid-afternoon of October 22, Toronto censor Bert Perry confronted Eddie Phelan, the *Globe and Mail*'s telegraph (news wire) editor and asked him if he knew who had written the *Time* article. Phelan, who had just received the magazine in the mail, said he did not know the source of the item. Phelan shared the censorship staff's indignation for two reasons: his newspaper had sat on several major exclusive stories during the Bowmanville clash; and Phelan was *Time*'s regular stringer in Toronto. Whoever had written the story had trespassed into Phelan's sideline.

In a memorandum written the same day, Baldwin told Eggleston the *Time* article "may conceivably endanger the lives of Canadian prisoners in Germany." Preliminary steps, Baldwin said, had been taken in Washington to prevent the information in the *Time* article from reaching the Germans. Canadian authorities had taken on a daunting task. *Time* was the largest-circulating news magazine in the United States. Copies were on the newsstands and arriving by mail at the homes of hundreds of thousands of subscribers. The German government would have no trouble getting a copy if it wanted one.

Eggleston tried to shape domestic and foreign coverage of the riot and of the *Time* article. When British United Press, which carried stories to newspapers in Canada and the United Kingdom, submitted copy at 11:00 a.m. on October 22 quoting "a high Government official here as saying that the *Time* story was the most serious censorship incident in Canada since the beginning of the war and that a full investigation was under way," Eggleston asked them to delete a suggestion that *Time* might be banned from Canada but allowed the rest of the statement to stand. The Hearst-owned International News Service wired the *Toronto Star*, asking for a story on the riot and the reaction to the *Time* article. A *Star* editor told Perry he would reply "Canadian censorship definitely forbids story." Perry told the *Star* not to answer the message at all: "We did not like the idea of it going out in that form, as this might lead to I.N.S. sending out a story to the effect that Canadian censorship had clamped down on the story, thereby verifying the facts as published by *Time*."

That night, Defence Minister Ralston issued a statement acknowledging the violence at Bowmanville and denouncing the *Time* story. The Canadian Press carried the story, with an Ottawa dateline, that was to be used by newspapers across the country. The Canadian news agency explained how all of the country's major papers had suppressed the story to protect the Canadians taken prisoner at Dieppe and attacked *Time* for running an error-filled account of the POW riot in blatant disregard for the Canadian censorship rules.

Toronto Star editors were not satisfied with the minister's press release. Believing the core of the Bowmanville story was now in the public domain, they wanted to publish the stories and pictures gathered by their corps of reporters on the scene. On the morning of October 23, *Star* sub-editor Dave Griffin brought the *Star*'s complete mass of copy covering the Bowmanville story to Perry's office, demanding that the material be passed for publication. For the first time, the censors saw all of the *Star*'s material. The photos shocked Perry, who not only spiked the *Star* material but made sure the two other dailies held their stories and pictures from Bowmanville.

The following day, Ottawa censor Baldwin backed Perry's action, issuing a statement to his staff requiring them to maintain censorship on the Bowmanville riot but allowing coverage of the errors in the *Time* story. The same morning, U.S. censors told Baldwin that an NBC listening post had picked up a German broadcast of the original Ralston statement on Bowmanville. The broadcast had kept strictly to the minister's press release, showing either the Germans did not have the *Time* story or were choosing to ignore it. Either way, Baldwin did not want any more attention drawn to it.

Maurice Pope, architect of the censorship system, later became a Lieutenant General and Ottawa's liaison with the Pentagon. *(Library and Archives Canada)*

Lawyer Oliver Mowat Biggar, a friend of Mackenzie King, was brought in to fix a broken censorship department. *(Smart and Biggar LLP)*

Camillien Houde, Montreal's mayor, spent most of the war interned at Canadian military bases. It turned out to be a boost to his career. *(Life Magazine)*

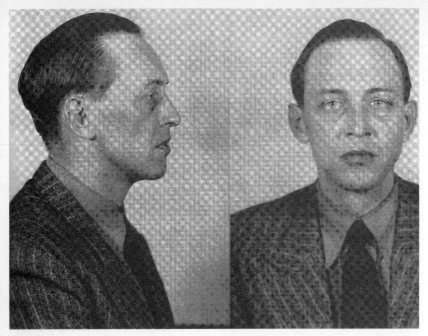

Werner von Janowski, a German spy dropped by sub in the Gaspé, was likely a triple agent. The leak of the story of his capture was one of the major failings of the censorship system. *(Library and Archives Canada)*

Like Janowski, Langbein was a German spy who conned Canadian intelligence officers. Unlike the capture of Janowski, Langbein's surrender was kept secret from the media.
(Library and Archives Canada)

Prominent journalist Wilfrid Eggleston was the head of English-language press censorship through the war.
(Carleton University Archives)

The bizarre French monitor submarine *Surcouf* leaving Halifax for St. Pierre just before Christmas, 1941. The picture was taken by Halifax press censor H. Bruce Jefferson. *(Nova Scotia Archives)*

War correspondent Peter Stursberg said reporters agreed to have their work checked by censors because they did not risk jail, alienation of their comrades, or being seen as disloyal.
(CBC Archives)

From his perch in a penthouse of the Lord Nelson Hotel, Halifax censor H. Bruce Jefferson watched the naval war unfold. *(Nova Scotia Archives)*

Sub skipper Otto Kretschmer sank more allied tonnage than any U-boat commander. He spent most of the war as a POW in Canada, and the Germans desperately wanted him back. *(Library and Archives Canada)*

Fulgence Charpentier was the head of French-language press censorship. He fought an ongoing battle with *Le Devoir* and other prominent Quebec newspapers. *(Canadian Parliamentary Press Gallery)*

New Canadian editor Tommy Shoyama later rose to the highest level of the federal bureaucracy, after helping Tommy Douglas establish Medicare in Saskatchewan. *(Library and Archives Canada)*

Very few soldiers saw as much action as Ross Munro of the *Canadian Press*.
(CBC Archives)

George McCullagh, the *Globe*'s erratic owner, fought several battles with censorship but backed down when he was threatened with jail. He is seen here with Ontario Premier Mitchel Hepburn (left). (*Library and Archives Canada*)

The *Globe and Mail* responded to the Drew letter controversy with this cartoon attacking Justice Minister Louis St. Laurent.

Maybe They Don't Gag The Right People

Near the end of the war, the *Halifax Herald* lashed out at the censorship system and General Andrew McNaughton, who was running for a seat in Parliament.

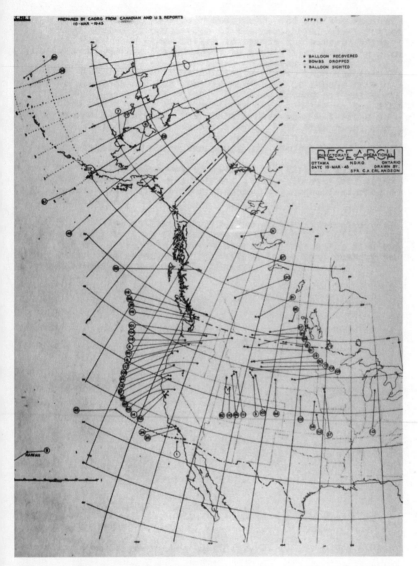

This map, published here for the first time, shows some of the balloon bomb landings in Canada. *(Department of National Defence)*

Baldwin was being disingenuous. The German government had a complete account of the riot, including aspects that were known to the Toronto newspapers (and the censors, through Perry's belated reading of the *Star* coverage) and not published in *Time*. As well, Berlin was aware of the theft of the decorations and the beating of the prisoners after they had surrendered. All of this material was in the hands of the Swiss consul, who had a duty to quickly dispatch the facts to Germany. The German government chose not to use this information for its propaganda value, perhaps because doing so would cause a new round of retaliation on both sides and endanger the ongoing negotiations. The British, noted Lester Pearson (Canada's senior diplomat in Washington), asked the United States government to do what they could to damp down press comment on shackling while negotiations continued in Switzerland. The State Department, whose point person in Geneva, John Foster Dulles, had the ear of the Swiss government and ranking Nazis in the country, said they would do what they could.

In Washington and New York, Canadian officials tried to learn the name of the Canadian stringer who had sent the story to *Time*. Lester Pearson wrote a long memorandum to Secretary of State Cordell Hull outlining Canada's objections to the *Time* article, hoping to generate enough anger in Washington to elicit some action. Pearson was able to solicit help from the U.S. Office of Censorship to put pressure on *Time* magazine to name its author. The U.S. censors obtained some clues. They told Pearson the stringer was a daily newspaperman ("probably from Toronto although this is not certain") who had been sending stories to *Time* for two years. He tried twice to get a job with them in New York and had also tried to be appointed their regular salaried Canadian correspondent, but in both attempts he had failed. He simply "sent them stories in the hope that they will be used and has been paid for the ones used."

Eggleston and Charpentier were certain the *Time* story had somehow been filed by one of the Toronto daily newspaper reporters on the scene. In a memorandum to Chief Censor O.M. Biggar, they said senior editors of the Toronto newspapers assured the Directorate of Censorship they would conduct internal investigations to find the writer. The censors believed identifying the culprit would put an end to the issue. Attacking *Time* would be a mistake. Stopping the magazine at the border would have little financial impact on *Time* but would inconvenience its readers in Canada. There was no point in making an enemy of *Time*, which had a circulation of two million in the United States. The Luce magazines had been isolationist in the first years of the war, but *Time* had quickly come around after Pearl Harbor, and, so far, no malice by the publication had been proved.

The strategies of the Directorate of Censorship drew both criticism and praise from editors of major Ontario newspapers and senior journalists. Robert Owen, managing editor of the *Kingston Whig-Standard*, wrote to Eggleston October 23 to complain that censorship of the Bowmanville riot had allowed rumour to fill the void created by the censorship of the facts, and now rumour had turned up in one of the world's largest magazines. The Kingston editor was sure Berlin knew at least as much about the riot as he did. Owen's paper had, despite its better judgment, gone along with the censors and now, because of the weakness of their system, the *Whig-Standard* had been beaten on a local story by a U.S. magazine.

Baldwin, rather than Eggleston, answered Owen's letter. He did not address Owen's assertion that the details of the riot were almost certainly known to German authorities. Instead, he defended the way the Directorate of Censorship had tried to manipulate coverage of the *Time* article. Baldwin saw the problem not as a matter of suppressing news from the enemy, but as one of keeping the Germans from using Canadian newspapers as authoritative sources that could be quoted in propaganda broadcasts. It was, then, not a matter of the management of secret information, but one of packaging. The *Ottawa Journal* supported Baldwin's position in an editorial published October 24. In response, the *Journal* received a letter to the editor from B.T. Richardson, the vice-president of the Parliamentary Press Gallery and a *Winnipeg Free Press* reporter. The letter was printed in the November 6, 1943, edition of the *Journal*. Richardson noted the author of the *Time* story still hadn't been identified and speculation as to his criminal guilt, motives, and ethics was premature. He said the anger directed at *Time* "seems to me to be part of a trend of attack on the press of Canada, which, strangely enough, the press itself encourages." The Bowmanville fiasco showed Canadian censorship was inept and unimaginative, and had ignored the fact that the Swiss consul had submitted a report to Germany. If, Richardson said, the censors knew the Germans were in on the secret of the Bowmanville riot, just who, in fact, were the censors hiding the facts from?

The letter was followed by an unsigned Editor's Note claiming the *Time* article's errors "will doubtlessly be used by Hitler, Goebbels and Co. even though they have the Swiss consul's report."

Most speculation in the Canadian media centred on the motivation of the *Time* writer. Invariably, profit was considered the primary motive. *L'Action catholique*, on October 29, headlined a short item on the *Time* article "Faire sensation pour gagner des piastres" ("Make a big deal to earn a few dollars") and said the writer had jeopardized Canada's war effort for the sake of an exclusive story and a few dollars. Quebec City's *Le Soleil*, on October 26, said *Time*'s breaking of the embargo was proof that censorship was a waste of time.

Various bits of information, including one American official's reference to the *Time* article's author being a semi-regular stringer who sent the copy to New York by mail, led investigators to the author of the *Time* story. N.R. Howard, the U.S. assistant director of censorship, met Eric Hodgins, editorial vice-president of *Time*, at Rockefeller Center on October 24 and was able to extract more details about the article's writer. While Hodgins would not disclose the journalist's name, he did drop hints

> that the correspondent was not the regular *Time* correspondent for Canada; that the correspondent was a "stringer" who occasionally submitted articles on speculation and was paid for whatever *Time* used; that this correspondent has said he was one of a number of Canadian newspapermen who were eyewitnesses of the Camp Bowmanville disturbance, and that what he wrote was written as eyewitness material; that he had sent the correspondence by mail and had said in the accompanying letter that he was uncertain as

to whether this material would reach *Time* in New York or whether it would be suppressed or deleted by censorship.

The break in the case may have, however, come from inside the newsroom of the *Toronto Star*. The author of the *Time* story was also a stringer for that newspaper.

On November 1, the RCMP told the Directorate of Censorship the name of the author. Unfortunately for the Canadian government, freelance writer Ed Rohrbough (based in Barrie, Ontario) was a poor candidate for the role of scoop-hungry, greedy, unpatriotic reporter. While he came from a privileged background (his father was a Republican congressman from West Virginia), Rohrbough's situation in Canada was more likely to engender sympathy than contempt from the public. Toronto censor Perry, in a memorandum to his superiors in Ottawa, made it clear that they should quietly let the matter drop. Even the RCMP, in private meetings with Perry, came out against charging the struggling reporter. He was just a kid who had come north to join the Canadian army before Pearl Harbor. Rohrbough had lost an eye in a boxing match during basic training at Camp Borden and had been honourably discharged. Once out of the service, Rohrbough had moved to the nearby town of Barrie, where he scraped out a living as a news freelancer while looking after his sick wife.

There was concern, too, in the Department of Justice that Rohrbough could not be successfully prosecuted. F.P. Varcoe, the deputy minister of justice, wrote a November 4 memorandum for Justice Minister Louis St. Laurent, beginning with the line, "I have doubt that the above mentioned free-lance reporter for the *Toronto Star* can be convicted of any offence for transmitting to *Time* the information published concerning the fracas at the Bowmanville Prisoner of War Camp." Varcoe noted that Regulation 16 of the *Defence of Canada Regulations* prohibited the communication of information "which might be useful to the enemy or of which the dissemination might prejudice the successful prosecution of the war" but all of the facts in the story were available to the Germans through the Swiss consul's reports. Prosecuting him for the errors in the article (information that, because it was wrong, was not known to the enemy) would be difficult, Varcoe noted, because none of it was particularly useful to the Nazis. Instead, Varcoe offered a political solution which, he believed, would quickly and efficiently put the issue to rest, spare Rohrbough from prosecution, and keep the government from going to court with a risky, and potentially embarrassing, prosecution. He suggested a statement be issued by the government assuring the public and the Canadian media that the *Time* story was a foolish mistake by an inexperienced but patriotic young man.

The government, however, did not take that advice. On St. Laur-ent's orders, Varcoe instructed the RCMP to lay charges in Barrie against Rohrbough under Section 16 of the *Defence of Canada Regulations*. The government appointed J.C. McRuer, a federal prosecutor, to the case. Varcoe instructed McRuer to stress in court that Rohrbough's breach of the embargo had a "regrettable effect" on the relationship between the Directorate of Censorship and the press: "The result of individual newspapermen or publishers trying to beat the gun is its tendency to make the only system of control which fits our institutions unworkable, and at the same time constitutes a betrayal of their colleagues." Rather than be an example to the Canadian media, Rohrbough was to be punished for betraying their solidarity.

As well, Varcoe said, Rohrbough had to be held to account for errors in the article that could be used for propaganda by the Nazis. The censors were not informed of the government's decision, and, in fact, were tipped off to the charges by the Canadian Press.

Very few Canadian newspapers came to the aid of Rohrbough, and none offered the reporter anything more than moral support. The *Glace Bay Gazette* in Nova Scotia was one of the rare publications that wanted to back the freelancer, but the censors killed its editorial.

The case went well for the government. Rohrbough pleaded guilty to the charge. An agreed statement of facts was entered into evidence, thereby limiting the amount of information placed on the court record to a bare minimum.

The government did not challenge Rohrbough's assertion that *Time* had rewritten and sensationalized his copy, and it acknowledged Rohrbough had co-operated with the police once they had identified him as the author. "No one regrets more sincerely than he does the fact that his action may have caused any harm to the state," his defence counsel, J.R. Cartwright of Toronto, told the court. Rohrbough was given a one-year jail sentence, which was suspended.

Rohrbough's prosecution contrasts sharply with the treatment of Arthur Cross, a well-connected Ottawa-based journalist who recklessly leaked a major war secret entrusted to the members of the Parliamentary Press Gallery. Cross was a staff reporter at the *Montreal Star* with a lucrative sideline selling stories to London's *Daily Express*. On August 2, 1942, Cross was one of the reporters who received a secret directive saying the government would "shortly and for a limited time" be taking over the Château Frontenac Hotel in Quebec City "for war purposes" and warning against reporting or speculating on the reasons for it. Journalists quickly assumed the requisitioning of an entire hotel the size of the Château Frontenac could mean just one thing: a summit of Allied leaders.

On August 6, Cross tried to send a telegram to the *Daily Express*: "Chateau Frontenac being taken over temporarily." The cable censors held the telegram and informed Ottawa. Cross went to another cable agency in Montreal and sent a second telegram to the *Daily Express*. This one, saying "Our two friends believed meeting down river from here," was inadvertently passed by cable censors who did not pick up on its meaning. It was, however, intercepted by MI5, who contacted the Canadian mission in London to complain. Not only did the cable hint at the secret Quebec Conference, it had been forwarded through the main telegraph office in Dublin, in neutral Ireland, a place believed to be thick with German spies. London was enraged. Whitehall's secretary of state for dominion affairs wrote to Britain's high commissioner in Ottawa on August 7: "This being *en clair* is certain to have been picked up by enemy.... Please ask Canadian authorities to do all they can to stop messages of this kind."

Cable censors were instructed to watch all of Cross's cable messages, but on August 9 another Cross telegram made it to the

Daily Express. This one said, "Will look for hastier if eye go and looks now as if that's what will happen stop hear unclue joe arriving." Cross clearly knew what he was doing and had worked hard to evade censors on both sides of the Atlantic.

Confronted by Eggleston, Cross lashed out. "The way things are hurled at me, I seem guilty of some heinous crime," Cross wrote to Eggleston. "Actually, I want to reproach both myself and you, or censorship generally, in this." Eggleston's offence, according to Cross, was tipping the journalist's employers at the *Montreal Star* to their Ottawa man's creative use of the telegraph system, "a tattle-tale gesture, even though I am sure you had nothing of the kind in mind." As a friend, Cross argued, Eggleston should come to the aid of a former colleague. Eggleston wasn't buying Cross's act. He was a federal employee with "serious responsibilities and pledged to perform his duties without fear or favour," and, within a few days, he recommended charges be laid against Cross. If Rohrbough was to face charges, so should Cross, Eggleston told his superiors.

In the end, the Ottawa old-boys system prevailed. Biggar told his minister in the fall of 1942, "I formed the opinion that he was rather a fool than a knave, and that he had already been fairly heavily punished for his improper course of action by the deprivation of special press privileges which he might have otherwise enjoyed." In the end, Cross's connections had saved him while Rohrbough, an obscure freelancer with no powerful friends in his corner, was the only individual journalist charged under censorship laws during the entire war.

On December 9, 1942, Baldwin issued a directive to Canadian newspapers that they could report on an announcement that would be made in London, Ottawa, Berne, and Berlin that shackling of POWs would be stopped. In keeping with the delicacy of the negotiations, censors were told it was "important [that] follow-up stories should not overly attack [the] German current position in [this] matter."

It was in neither side's interests to continue inflicting systemic punishment or humiliation on the prisoners of war in their custody. Therefore, they engaged in a remarkable indirect negotiation in the fall of 1942 to extricate themselves from hastily made decisions to shackle POWS. Publicity of shackling, and of the riot in Bowman-ville of German prisoners who resisted shackling, not only would have embarrassed the Canadian government but could have also prevented German authorities from being able to make an agreement that would allow them to save face. The Canadian censorship system was one of the mechanisms used to dampen down the shackling controversy.

Nevertheless, one freelance reporter easily breached the censorship system by mailing an article to the United States, which was not directly involved in the shackling dispute and had not directed its censorship system to watch for articles on the issue. Canadian journalists and censors had a complex relationship, and most censorship actions relied on a close working relationship between the parties. Rohrbough was able to file his article to *Time* magazine because he worked outside this system. Also, as a freelance writer, he was not part of the chain of communication that linked censors, newspaper editors, and reporters. In the end, Rohrbough's *Time* article was ignored by German state-controlled media outlets and had no obvious impact on the negotiations between the Allies and the Axis to end shackling, but, because he had disrupted the working relationship between the Directorate of Censorship and the highly competitive Toronto media, Rohrbough was hauled into court.

At the end of the war, the *Toronto Star* asked for permission to run its stories, pictures, and sketches of the 1942 brawl. The censors approved the material after VE day, but by then, people were tired of war stories and most *Star* journalists' work never saw the light of day. Some of it was mined for POW history books that were published in the latter half of the twentieth century. Meanwhile, the Bowmanville buildings stayed empty for decades while Toronto's sprawl spread toward the once-quiet little town. When a developer applied to the local municipality to tear down the buildings and redevelop the property for subdivisions, the story of Camp 30, its illustrious prisoners, and its famous fight made the papers, and the local council tried to protect the derelict property. In late March 2009, a number of suspicious fires broke out simultaneously in several of the buildings.

Meanwhile, the most famous of Camp 30's prisoners returned to Germany after the war, although a few enjoyed life in Canada so much that they decided to stay. Otto Kretschmer, untainted by serious Nazi connections or sympathies, resumed his service in the German navy in 1955 and rose to the top of its leadership before assuming a senior position in NATO. He retired in 1970 with the rank of flotilla admiral. By the 1990s, he was a consultant on U-boat-themed computer games. Kretschmer died in 1998, while celebrating his fiftieth wedding anniversary. He drowned when his sailboat capsized in the quiet blue waters of the Danube River.

CHAPTER 8

Censoring News from
the Front Lines

ON JANUARY 14, 1944, *Globe and Mail* war correspondent Ralph Allen sat down at his typewriter and began a column that, back in Europe, would not have made it past the censors. Allen had covered the Canadian campaigns in Sicily and the Italian mainland. Less than six months later, he would go ashore with the Canadian army at Juno Beach on D-Day. Back in Canada to see his family and to check in with his publisher, George McCullagh, Allen took the opportunity to launch a sneak attack on the censors who handled the copy of Canada's small colony of war correspondents.

Material written by reporters who were attached to Canada's fighting forces was vetted by military censors on the battlefield and at the Allies' chief headquarters in London. Reporters like Allen found the military censors to be arbitrary, illogical, and more concerned with the reputation of Allied generals than with the truth. In his January 15 column, Allen described the ways the army spoon-fed war correspondents with press releases and communiqués that were parroted back as news copy. The stories, in turn, were censored on the spot by army and navy officers before going out on the wires under the bylines of people who were being paid to cover the war.

But the reporters at army headquarters got something that resembled a complete picture of the military situation, even if it was doled out by army officers and filtered by military censors. The closer a reporter got to the fighting, the more confused the picture became. Modern warfare had created giant battlefields that were far too big for one person or even a team of journalists to begin to understand.

Someone covering the Battle of Waterloo from the British side could, if able to make things out through the clouds of smoke, watch the day's action from the high ground at the north end of the field, understand the importance of each of the major moves of the armies on the battlefield, and send a report that night with a fairly accurate description of the fighting. Almost fifty years later, a reporter at Gettysburg would have needed three days to see the battle. The field was larger and there was no vantage point that would have provided a view of all the fighting, but a hard-working correspondent could probably piece together the entire story by using personal observations and by talking to some foot soldiers and officers. By the time of World War One, the battles lasted too long, the field was too large, the reach of weapons was too great, and the fighting too intense for any eyewitness to understand what was happening unless they were taken in hand by military officers who had the benefit of the reports that moved up the chain of command. This didn't happen.

In the previous century, the military had grasped the power of the press. Journalists had embarrassed the British government during the Crimean War, but for the little colonial conflicts in the latter half of the nineteenth century, scribes were still an essential part of any ambitious general's retinue. (Reporters like Winston Churchill made fortunes sending war correspondence back from British imperial outposts and its British reporters watched most of the big battles of the American Civil War.) Coverage of the Boer War, however, provided Britain's enemies, including Kaiser Wilhelm's government, with a steady stream of propaganda. By the outbreak of World War One, the British high command treated war correspondents as spies: any caught near the front without permission could be shot, and only the most trusted senior Fleet Street correspondents got close. The rest, even the famous correspondents such as Philip Gibbs, settled for covering sideshows like the Balkans and Salonika. No Canadian reporters were allowed near the trenches during the first two years of World War One. The handful of Canadian journalists who went to France in 1917 missed Canada's victory at Vimy Ridge.

Reporters covering World War Two had a different set of obstacles. After the revelations of Britain's ruthless propaganda and censorship campaign in the Great War, readers and listeners back home demanded better coverage of the war this time. The military, however, had developed subtler ways to manipulate coverage. Even if, somehow, reporters got a true picture of the fighting in World War Two, they were still burdened with the difficulties of filing their stories. Those journalists who covered the Canadian advances in Sicily and on the Italian mainland had no choice but to rely on the army in order to get their stories out of the fighting theatre and back to Canada. Often, that meant typing up the story in a quiet place away from the front, giving it to an army dispatch rider who carried the copy on a motorcycle, a horse, or, as sometimes happened in Italy, a donkey to divisional headquarters and its censors, then hoping that the copy made the plane to London, where it was censored again and either telegraphed or put on a news wire. Photographs had to be developed in London so the British censors could look them over, and either flown back to Canada or sent over a very primitive fax machine. Some correspondents tried using carrier pigeons from the Normandy beaches, carrying coded messages that told editors and readers back home that the D-Day assault was successful. This romantic and somewhat medieval tactic didn't work: pigeons carrying weird messages like "Beer is Best, Drink Guinness" were showing up in coops along the southern English coast weeks later.

Radio reporters at the front line had their own technological challenges. A CBC reporting unit went overseas in December 1939 with the First Canadian Division. To get around some of the recording problems, the CBC commandeered an army truck for a mobile studio. Some CBC reporters went into the fighting in Western Europe using a hand-cranked, five-kilogram machine that could cut a recording disc holding about three minutes of sound. The machine was undependable. Often, the reporter risked his life, had the disc shipped back from the front and flown to England, only to learn that the CBC technicians in London had found the disc to be blank. Tape recorders were new, rare, and didn't deliver the recording quality of the old disc systems. Despite being handicapped by technology, CBC reporters covered the 1940 Blitz (the building that housed its offices took a direct hit) and went on to distinguish themselves in Europe. Their reports were a combination of journalism and show: CBC star Matthew Halton practised his lines and got as close as he could to the fighting to record the noise of it, but, if the battle did not provide enough colourful sound, special effects of fighting were added in the studio.

Allen explained most of these problems to his readers. He could accept all of them, except the censorship. "To tell the truth," he wrote, "I am no more capable of writing a fair or reasonable sentence about censors than composing a brochure in praise of Brussels sprouts." Allen larded his column with anecdotes of unreasonable and unfathomable decisions made by the military censors. In the first story he had filed from the Mediterranean theatre, Allen described sitting in North Africa under a date palm. The words "date palm" were cut. "From that moment on, I attempted to govern my actions by the conviction that all censors are maniacs, a hypothesis that has stood the test of time faithfully and well," he wrote.

> One time the censor passed the names of three towns which our troops had captured on the same road. The towns don't matter anymore, but let's say the sentence read: "The Canadians today took Capello and Broccoli and the intermediate village of Ravioli." The only cut here was the word "intermediate." My contention was that, although the information that the Town of Ravioli lay between the Towns of Capello and Broccoli might well have been of use to the enemy, the enemy very likely had the information already, in view of the fact that he had lived in the vicinity for generations and probably had a map.

He recounted how Major Bert Wemp, the correspondent of the Toronto *Telegram*, and Wallace Reyburn of the *Montreal Standard* had fought with the censors about the illustrious history of the 48th Highlanders. Wemp had mentioned in a story that the 48th Highlanders "had fought at Vimy Ridge in the last war." The censor removed the words "Vimy Ridge."

Then Reyburn had joined the fight, writing a paragraph for his own paper about Wemp's censorship troubles. He tried to tell his readers about the strategic cut to Wemp's piece, but he failed to take the censors into account. They hacked up Reyburn's account of Wemp's troubles. Allen admitted there was little he could do about the military censors, "aside from sitting here and gnawing on a steel filing cabinet for the sheer pleasure of it."

Allen believed correspondents should be allowed to report on the courage of Canadians, even those who had been recently killed. He made a somewhat unconvincing argument that the military should let war reporters file stories naming Canadian soldiers, even if their families had not been officially notified. Perhaps, he argued, Canadian mothers would be shocked to learn from newspapers of their sons' deaths, but at least the articles would give those deaths far more meaning, maybe even dignity, than if the news of them was conveyed by messenger boys carrying the official regrets of the Department of National Defence. A front-page story of heroism, Allen said, was worth much more to a family than a government form letter. He wrote of a group of fifteen Canadian soldiers who attacked a company of German infantry. Six of the Canadians died quickly in the fighting. A seventh soldier, who was dying from his wounds, held off the Germans with a Bren gun until his comrades escaped. The names of the eight survivors could be published but, Allen argued, the mother of the soldier with the Bren gun would probably never know of her son's bravery because military censorship would not allow his name to be used in Allen's dispatch. If he did receive a decoration, the war correspondents were forbidden from writing about it until the official announcement was made, usually weeks or months later, in the *Canada Gazette*, the government's official "newspaper."

But there was another side to this coin. It might have been folly for the war effort and cruel to mothers to let Canadian war reporters loose. Quite simply, even discounting the effects of censorship, Canadian war reporters and their editors were fairly good at covering simple stories but terrible with the big picture. Day after day, week after week, the papers carried sensational headlines that were flat-out wrong: Rudolf Hess had committed suicide (he hadn't, at least not for another fifty years); the battleship *Prince of Wales* was unsinkable (the Japanese air force proved otherwise during the Singapore campaign); the Canadians had taken Caen on the first day of the Normandy invasion (the city would be flattened by bombers weeks later before the Canadians could get inside); SS chief Heinrich Himmler and Luftwaffe leader Hermann Goering had been attacked in August 1944, and possibly killed by the same people who had tried to blow up Hitler the month before (they would both survive the war and kill themselves in jail); Parisians had slaughtered the German garrison when the Resistance and the Americans liberated their city (it fell fairly bloodlessly). Newspaper competition was intense in the 1940s and editors were willing to rush the wildest rumours into print while, at the same time, allowing censors to cut facts out of stories that dealt with reality. There were no real consequences for these mistakes, and, in the end, they seemed to do very little harm, although Canadians who cared about current events must have spent a lot of time after the war relearning them.

At the same time that domestic newspapers were garbling coverage of the war in Europe, front-line coverage that arrived in Canada from other countries was twisted, shaped, and censored. Canadians didn't know of the big U.S. naval defeats in the Central Pacific because they weren't reported by the U.S. newspapers and wire services. Even the amount of damage at Pearl Harbor had been downplayed, and disasters like the Battle of Savo Island (off Guadalcanal, August 8–9, 1942), which cost four U.S. heavy cruisers and more than 1,000 American sailors, were barely mentioned at all. The battles on the Russian front might as well have been taking place on Mars, for all Canadian newspapers knew: almost all coverage of them was filtered through Stalin's propaganda machine to remove the details of Soviet defeats and the Red Army's appalling losses.

The British, who had led the way in media manipulation in World War One, not only operated sophisticated propaganda and censorship departments, they also employed seedy Fleet Street journalists at a "Morale Office" to invent believable rumours, including the story that circulated in Italy saying Mussolini had stashed away a fortune in Switzerland and was preparing to flee the country as soon as the Allies landed on the Italian mainland. That piece of fiction helped knock Italy out of the war.

The Canadian military made sure that its own record of events was accurate. Its field historical officers were given access to military reports and front-line officers that was far beyond the reach of war correspondents. Colonel Charles P. Stacey was allowed to see the papers of army commanders A.G.L. McNaughton and H.D.G. Crerar during the war and in the years afterwards, and Stacey's work would later lay the foundations for all subsequent official and popular histories of the Canadian army in World War Two.

Stories from the fighting fronts had two audiences: Canadians back home and the hundreds of thousands of soldiers, sailors, and air force personnel serving overseas. The soldiers at the front lines were keen analysts of censorship. They were, and the surviving veterans continue to this day to be, voracious readers of wartime accounts and very protective of their reputations and their versions of events. The British papers were so heavily censored that, for almost a month, soldiers fighting in Normandy and Italy did not know the Germans had unleashed a blizzard of v1 cruise missiles in the weeks since D-Day. Still, they had a fairly good idea of the situation in their own theatres of operations, and they searched the British and Canadian papers for news about themselves. They were also avid radio listeners, tuning into broadcasts from Britain and listening to the English-language shows on German radio. Both the Germans and Japanese propagandists made the very clever move of broadcasting the latest hits, tailoring their shows to a demographic of young, single, and/or lonely men whose taste was quickly reflected in popular culture back home. It's no accident that the top pop singles of the war years were maudlin ballads about separation, old-fashioned white Christmases, and dreams of the girl left behind. Often, because of military censorship, the fighting men were disappointed and angry that stories of their most bitter battles weren't showing up in the media.

The Canadian forces reacted by starting their own paper, *The Maple Leaf*, and hired Lieutenant J.D. Macfarland, who would go on to edit the *Toronto Telegram* and help found the *Toronto Sun*, to run it. The paper was more than just a public-relations sheet, and Macfarland sometimes pushed back at the military censors and his superiors. He would cross the army one time too many when, in 1946, he criticized it for being too slow to demobilize the troops. (He was not alone in generating military rage: General George Patton, furious at 23-year-old GI Bill Mauldin's *Willy and Joe* cartoons, which were very popular with soldiers because Mauldin understood their problems and spoke for them, bawled out Mauldin and threatened to have the cartoonist of the U.S. armed forces newspaper *Stars and Stripes* tossed in jail if he was caught in Patton's Third Army sector again.)

The army tried to shape civilian press coverage by having military public-relations officers (sometimes called press-relations officers; either way, they were PROS) guide reporters at the fighting front and shadow them at military headquarters. Most of the PROS, like the domestic press censors, were journalists. Some, like Canadian Press executive Gil Purcell, easily slipped back and forth over the line between journalist and PRO. Purcell, working for the army, lost a leg during training exercises in England. He finished the war in Canada, running his news agency and dealing with many of the people who had been his colleagues in the army.

Public-relations officer Richard Malone, the former circulation manager of the *Winnipeg Free Press* (Malone would later own it, the *Globe and Mail*, and several other important papers), wrote two books about his wartime work. He ran the Canadian press and public-relations office during the Sicilian and Italian campaigns, then held a similar post in Western Europe after D-Day. In his first book, published just months after the end of the war, Malone admits the army was reluctant to accept and co-operate with reporters, who, for the first time in history, had the ability to file material in something that resembled real time.

Malone, like the domestic press censors, says he found himself caught between reporters and the army brass. The army, both Canadian and British, slapped news blackouts on most bad news, holding stories until they were so old that no one cared anymore. Sometimes, the military issued orders to officers and men not to talk to war correspondents. (After Dieppe, the British kept the worst details of the botched raid out of its papers through censorship and a news blackout. Ross Munro, who survived the raid, had to use Benzedrine to keep himself awake for three days in the hope that he could finally file his stories.) Journalists were angry that so few of them were allowed near the fighting front, especially in Sicily and on the Italian mainland, and, even when they could see the fighting, the army couriers and censors sometimes "lost" their articles if they thought the coverage might be unflattering. Most of the army brass, mimicking their British colleagues, despised the press. They believed reporters were biased, sloppy, and inaccurate, and that their presence was a drag on military units. Junior officers who worked around correspondents saw them as dilettantes who wore unearned rank and demanded special privileges. Senior officers were stung by criticism they saw coming from people they believed were amateurs in matters of war. Malone says many reporters arrived in the field not knowing the difference between a company and a platoon and utterly ignorant about the weapons used by the soldiers. For months, these neophyte war correspondents would file copy riddled with factual errors. The soldiers they were covering would be embarrassed and annoyed.

By the time of D-Day, some of the Canadian correspondents were much more battle-tested than the men who went ashore with them, but by then, many senior officers had made up their minds about war journalists. Correspondents could redeem themselves by proving their courage. Many of the correspondents were willing to take serious risks, but they had to work hard to match the daring of two army film unit photographers who went in with the infantry at Bernières in the teeth of German resistance and took photographs and film footage that were world scoops. Nine non-military reporters—Ross Munro and William Stewart of the Canadian Press; Marcel Ouimet and Matthew Halton of the CBC; Ralph Allen of the *Globe and Mail* (acting as pool reporter for Canadian daily newspapers); Lionel Shapiro of the North American Newspaper Alliance (whose Jewish religion placed him in added danger); Charles Lynch of Reuters; Roland Clark of the British United Press; and Joseph

Willicombe of the International News Service—went ashore with Canadian troops on D-Day, knowing, should the invasion be another Dieppe, some of them would not come back. The army made them wait offshore until the German machine guns overlooking the beach were silenced. Soon after they got settled ashore, the Germans shelled the press camp in the Juno beachhead. People back home could hear the sounds of the Normandy campaign because the CBC team brought a mobile studio. By the end of the war, it would be seriously shot up.

Matthew Halton and Marcel Ouimet of the CBC were there for the Paris Liberation. By mid-September, Halton was broadcasting from the small Allied foothold on German soil, just forty-eight kilometres from Cologne. He missed Operation Market Garden, the failed lunge for the Arnhem bridges, but he still managed to file radio broadcasts that put the best face on the fiasco. Even with Halton's positive spin, Field Marshal Montgomery's censors held Halton's main report on Operation Market Garden for three days, making it old news by the time the Canadian public heard it. Stanley Maxted, a Canadian working for the BBC, had been much closer to the action. He went into Oosterbeek, on the outskirts of Arnhem, with Britain's First Airborne Division, watched the fighting for ten days from dugouts and shattered buildings, recorded the sound of German anti-aircraft guns firing at Allied supply planes, and fled the battlefield as the Germans were about to cut off the last escape routes to the south bank of the Rhine. Before destroying his recording equipment, Maxted managed to make several discs that he carried out at night across the Rhine in the teeth of enemy fire. Still, Canadians only heard Field Marshal Montgomery's verdict of Operation Market Garden: that it was, for the most part, successful. In fact, it was a bad plan, poorly executed, that resulted in one of the last big German victories of the war and wasted the lives of thousands of troops.

Through the winter of 1944–45, the Canadian correspondents covered their country's soldiers during the tough fighting in the Scheldt Estuary, the key to the vital port of Antwerp, where Canadians fought ferociously against German positions that were often manned by Soviet deserters who knew surrender meant repatria-tion and death at the hands of the NKVD, Stalin's secret police. The winter's Dutch campaign was an important sideshow that was a matter of survival for the local people. The bulk of the German army in the west was on the far side of the Rhine, being mauled by the British and Americans pushing toward Hamburg and Prague.

The line between journalist and soldier was so faded that, look-ing at a Canadian war correspondent in World War Two, a person could easily mistake him for an army officer. That's because Cana-dian correspondents wore the country's uniform, held an honorary rank (usually captain), and were provided with a soldier-chauffeur and a jeep. They lived in military-issue housing and were subjected to military justice while overseas. Often, they lived better than the officers they covered. CBC reporter Peter Stursberg was given the captain's cabin on the U.S. destroyer *Hambleton* for the invasion of southern France, though the captain, who ran a dry ship, did relieve Stursberg of a bottle of whisky that he brought for the trip.

In many ways, they were as embedded into the Canadian forces as the war reporters of the Afghanistan and Iraq conflicts, although they pretended to be officers instead of enlisted men. Very likely, there was far less of a philosophical gulf between soldiers and cor-respondents in World War Two than in most modern wars. Ross Munro, who covered all of the major campaigns and would become the most famous of the Canadian correspondents, wrote, "I was committed to the war completely and utterly, right from the start. Maybe it was jingoism, chauvinism and stupidity, but we felt that the Germans were going to wreck this world of ours and we would have to stop them." He later reflected, "I never felt, except on the Dieppe raid, that I was really cheating the public back home." Other reporters had no illusions about their work. "It's humiliating to look back at what we wrote during the war," Charles Lynch told author Philip Knightley in the 1970s. "It was crap—and I don't exclude the Ernie Pyles or the Alan Mooreheads. We were a propaganda arm of our governments. At the start the censors enforced that, but by the end we were our own censors. We were cheerleaders. I suppose there wasn't an alternative at that time. It was total war. But for God's sake, let's not glorify our role. It wasn't good journalism. It wasn't journalism at all." Stursberg later wrote that reporters who challenged the official line faced "dis-accreditation, disgrace, even imprisonment." At the very least, no Canadian journalist (in English Canada) wanted to be labelled as unpatriotic. The generals knew journalists would eventually realize the value of playing by the army's rules. The ones who criticized too often would eventually be moulded into conformity and would come to understand "that he was himself part of the show."

Still, these reporters did give the Canadian public a very vivid and accurate account of the war, within the boundaries and restrictions placed around them. The front-line action reports were solid journalism, and much of the analysis was insightful. Ralph Allen's analysis in the *Globe and Mail* of the British failure to clear the Scheldt estuary at the time of the capture of Antwerp was extremely critical of the British for shifting their strength to the Arnhem offensive, leaving the bloody fighting in the Belgian and Dutch polder country to the Canadians. However, the correspondents did succumb to pressure to make heroes of the Canadian and British commanders. The British disappointment at the quality of senior Canadian officers was covered up, while even Allen succumbed to the pressure to write puff pieces about controversial commanders like Arthur "Bomber" Harris, whose planes were systematically bombing German cities to rubble.

There was no one like Eggleston and the domestic press censors running interference for the press or agonizing over the role of war reporters in civil society. Only the PROs stood between the generals at National Defence Headquarters and the war correspondents in the field, and they could always be counted on to obey orders. Anything that embarrassed the army was to be cut by the military censors before it left England or Europe for Canada. Correspondents were always aware that their stories would be censored to take out "defeatism" and details that might help the enemy determine Allied plans. They, like war reporters in the Nazi and Soviet forces, usually reacted by showing extreme, sometimes foolhardy, personal courage and getting as close to the front as possible.

To make up for their inability to understand the big picture, reporters went looking for the stories of ordinary soldiers. They understood the power of stories of individual heroism. These were popular at home, but they were also ingratiating to the front-line troops. Most war correspondents wanted to be like Ernie Pyle, the American reporter who became one of the war's new media celebrities and an honoured guest of any unit he visited. Pyle came to detest the war and would, in 1945, die in it, but he was the soldier's friend, one of the people who, like Mauldin (who would be rewarded for his work with a Pulitzer Prize), gave voice to the cynicism, egalitarianism, and war weariness of the enlisted men at the front.

War, for some people, is an opportunity to show talent and rise quickly. This is the case for reporters as well as soldiers. Young reporters who might have toiled away covering police news and city hall now found themselves in the midst of battle, with huge readerships at home and the chance to quickly become truly famous. Most of the Canadian reporters who did find fame during the war went overseas as unknowns. Almost all of them landed speaking tours, book deals, and better jobs. The fame that they won during the war tended to stay with them most of their lives, while most soldiers faded back into civilian life.

Canadian newspaper and magazine readers received a steady flow of dramatic and beautifully crafted journalism. Tuning into the CBC, they heard radio reports that were as good as anything made by the front-line correspondents of the big U.S. networks. Slogging through Italy, the CBC's radio reporters, supported by their shrapnel-perforated mobile recording studio, saw action at the vicious and bloody fights of Ortona and the Moro River, where correspondents watched and heard Canadians brawl in their night action against the famous 90th light division of the Panzer Grenadiers. Then they were transferred to northwest Europe, with several correspondents arriving soaked and shaken up because their transport had been sunk by a U-boat in the Mediterranean.

The war correspondents were weighed down by rules that protected the military (especially the reputation of the officer corps) but also helped ensure that a reporter who co-operated with censors would not be beaten by a correspondent who had eschewed co-operation. A dire instance of a reporter breaking from the pack occurred on the last day of the European war. Associated Press correspondent Edward Kennedy, who had been burned when he held back his story about Patton slapping two of his soldiers, scooped the world by witnessing the German surrender at Reims and breaking the army's embargo on the story. Kennedy believed the news had no military value: it was certainly no secret to the Germans, who had broadcast the news on what was left of their army radio network. The embargo had been ordered for political reasons, as a sop to Stalin. It was supposed to allow London, Washington, and Moscow to announce the news simultaneously after a second Soviet–German ceremony in Berlin. Kennedy's scoop was the lead story in most newspapers, including the next morning's *Toronto Star* and *New York Times*, touching off street parties in all of the Allied countries except the Soviet Union, where Stalin still sat on the news. The war correspondents in Eisenhower's headquarters shared Ike's rage and drummed Kennedy out of their ranks. Kennedy was stripped of his war-correspondent credentials, sent back to New York, and fired from AP soon afterwards. He spent the rest of his life working on small newspapers in California, angry and bitter about what had happened to him.

Sometimes, Canadian reporters crossed whatever was left of the line between correspondent and propagandist. During the big, secret movement of Canadian troops from Italy to northwest Europe in February and March 1945, the Canadian correspondents, who had already been sent to England, allowed their names to be used on stories written by army PROs and sent to Canadian newspapers from the "Italian" front. The army controlled the powerful press wireless station that was carted through the Sicilian/Italian campaigns and believed the Germans monitored the traffic of telegrams sent to newspapers and wire services—not only for the data in the stories, but also for the volume of traffic. A change in the pattern of the machines' use could signal a new Allied advance. Decoy stations were set up, with real journalists providing fake copy that would throw off German snoops.

But the troop movement would eventually be reported. Like Dieppe, it was too big to keep covered up forever. Censorship—both self-editing and official cuts—along with threats of disaccreditation, disgrace, and imprisonment kept the Canadian war corres-pond-ents in line. But so did the belief that the Nazis were going to wreck this world.

CHAPTER 9

The "Jap Pulitzer":
Censorship of the Japanese-Canadian Press

AT THE END OF THE GREAT DEPRESSION, Tommy Shoyama was ready for something big, something interesting. Bright, young, just out of the University of British Columbia with a stellar set of marks in economics and commerce, Shoyama wanted to make some money and change the country. As a Canadian-born ethnic Japanese, a *Nisei*, he hoped to wade as quickly as possible into the Canadian mainstream. Being a martyr was the last thing Shoyama would have chosen in the months after he earned his bachelor's degree, which, in those days, was still a ticket into the middle class for most Canadians. Still, in the short term, that was his fate. First, in 1939, he tried to join the ranks of B.C.'s chartered accountants, but they wouldn't let him or any other Asian write their exams. Then he volunteered for the air force and, for nearly two years, waited to hear back. Meanwhile, he needed a job. That's where martyrdom beckoned again.

Shoyama was born in Kamloops in 1916. His father ran a bakery on the town's main street. A friend of Shoyoma's father who lived in Vancouver agreed to let Shoyoma live with his family rent-free, but the young Shoyama had to pay for his own food. Shoyama earned his B.A. in economics at UBC, raised money for tuition, books, and food by working in a pulp mill and as a houseboy at a railway bunkhouse. Friends of Shoyama described him as a humorous, gentle, charismatic man, and a slight man who, according to someone who knew him much later in life—Senator Joyce Fairbairn—lit up a room when he walked in. He was also extraordinarily tough.

Shoyama and the rest of the *Nisei* had sat through school lessons on the "British" ideals of rule of law, liberty, and democracy. Their own experiences showed them a different reality. They had been subjected to dozens of political and social slights. Japanese Canadians could not vote, hold office, join many professions, or enlist in the armed forces. Those kind of snubs could be ignored, but how could a young, smart man like Shoyama put up with being shunted to the back of a movie theatre by a pimple-faced usher, told that he could not swim in a city pool except at very limited designated hours, or be hooted at by kids playing on the streets of white neighbourhoods? The *Nisei* fought so hard to be "Canadian," to the point of burning their bridges to their elders (most of them first-generation *Issei*), but in the face of unfair barriers erected by white Canada, many of the *Nisei* had to admit failure and fall back on their own communities for jobs.

Shoyama arrived at UBC at exactly the right time. The *Nisei* had just begun their fight for dominance in the Japanese-Canadian community and had embraced both politics and the media as the means of winning full political rights, including the vote. During his last year at UBC, Shoyama wrote articles on the world economy for the *New Canadian*, a fledgling Japanese-Canadian paper. The *New Canadian* was started as a free publication by the University Students' Club at UBC in 1938. Soon afterwards, it was taken over by Ed Ouchi, an insurance salesman. Its offices were rented in a print shop on the second floor of a boarding house in downtown Vancouver. Ouchi was general secretary of the Japanese Canadian Citizens' League. The *New Canadian* was published three times a week and sold through mail subscription and at newsstands.

Despite its early support for Japan's conquest of China, the paper was loyal to the Canadian war effort. It put very little emphasis on foreign affairs, as its main focus was on breaking down the racial barriers that barred Japanese Canadians from full civil and economic rights. In this spirit, it also advocated the movement of ethnic Japanese away from their traditional jobs in the fisheries dotting British Columbia's coast and it wanted Japanese Canadians to learn English and adopt the dominant culture. Ouchi and his tiny staff started

selling the paper in the traditional Asian neighbourhood around
Powell Street, then took it to Kitsilano and Fairview, New Westminster, the Fraser Valley, Vancouver Island, and the isolated fishing
hamlets along the Pacific Coast.

A sparkling personality and stellar grades in a difficult academic
program were not enough qualifications for a Japanese Canadian to
land a decent job in Vancouver in the early years of the war. Vancouver was slow to come out of the Depression, and part of the bigotry
of the local people can be traced to that decade of poverty and decay
(although anti-Asian hatred in the city had a long pedigree). So
Shoyama went into the bush for about five months and found a job
in a pulp mill. Ouchi asked him to come back to Vancouver in the
late fall of 1938 to become editor of the *New Canadian*. Very quickly,
Shoyama was pressured by Ouchi to invest the $300 he'd saved from
his mill job to keep the paper afloat.

Shoyama put up with missed paydays and bounced paycheques
because the *New Canadian* was the only paper in the country that
spoke for him. The older generation of Japanese immigrants saw
Nisei like Shoyama and his friends as weak, morally corrupted,
wasteful. These young people liked dance halls. They shunned
arranged marriages. They took jobs outside the fishery. The *Nisei*,
their elders believed, wanted to cut their valuable cultural bonds to
the Japanese homeland. The young people seemed to be trying to
out-Canadian the Canadians.

The war was both a trial for the Japanese Canadians and an
opportunity for the generation that was born in North America.
For the *Nisei*, here was a chance to prove their loyalty, to show that
they were "real" Canadians. The war's hardships could, they hoped,
be seen as a type of martyrdom, a trial in which they would emerge
as proven Canadians. Two days before Canada declared war on
Germany, the *New Canadian* had told its readers to "be prepared
to assume our burden and fulfill our part." Rallying to the colours
would be a "history-making commitment." The Canadian government was not, however, as eager to facilitate the patriotism of the
Nisei. It refused to enlist ethnic Japanese, including Shoyama, who,
as a university graduate, was entitled to a commission. Japanese-

Canadian organizations mailed unsolicited cash donations to the Department of National Defence, but Ottawa would not budge. Both Mackenzie King and British Columbia premier Duff Pattulla cringed at the idea of arming the *Nisei* while Japan loomed as a potential enemy.

Even before the attack on Pearl Harbor, racist politicians had targeted Canada's ethnic Japanese press. On February 25, 1941, Thomas Reid, a long-time municipal union leader and the MP for New Westminster, spoke in the House of Commons against extending the vote to naturalized and Canadian-born ethnic Japanese, calling them an "unassimilable race." Three days later, Shoyama's *New Canadian* published an editorial attacking Reid and Alan Neill, the MP for B.C.'s Comox–Alberni riding, who supported Reid's position. The newspaper invited Reid and his supporters "to an open debate to determine which proposition is the most valid: 'Once a Japanese, always a Japanese,' or 'Once an oriental-baiting polit-ician, always an oriental-baiting politician.'"

Reid didn't accept the invitation. Instead, he stood in the House of Commons to condemn the *New Canadian*'s "vilifying personal attack," which, he said, "comes with poor grace from a race of people who enjoyed, with the exception of the franchise, every phase of our economic and social life." Reid stopped short of saying he would like to roll back many of those rights. He also did not say he was eager to strip the Japanese Canadians of the lucrative salmon-fishing licences that they had sweated for over the previous half-century, but his later actions would prove this was, in fact, the goal of politicians who attacked the ethnic Japanese.

The Japanese government's decision to take on the Western powers in the Pacific gave Asian-baiters like Reid their opportunity. They were opposed by powerful people in Ottawa, including Mackenzie King advisor Norman Robertson and chief English press censor Wilfrid Eggleston. The Ottawa men saw the dangers of letting the Japanese Canadians be used as convenient targets for the impotent rage of Canadians who watched, day after day, hour after hour, the quick Japanese army and navy victories in the Pacific. Days after Pearl Harbor, as the Japanese juggernaut headed for

Manila, Singapore, and Hong Kong, the Directorate of Censorship sent out a memo asking editors to control themselves. The presence of the Japanese Canadians, many of whom were born in Canada, "creates a difficult situation." Gratuitous attacks on them broke up social cohesion and undermined the war effort. The censors told Canada's editors the vast majority of Japanese Canadians were loyal, and warned against publishing rumours and inflammatory statements that could cause them more trouble.

Some politicians and journalists were determined to cause as much trouble as possible. Vancouver alderman Halford Wilson was named in a Vancouver censorship memo as "a virulent anti-Jap" who was "tossing flame on the [white] fishermen's agitation to prevent the Federal Authorities from granting fishing licenses to any Japanese in 1942." Among other things, Wilson claimed Japanese saboteurs planned to poison Vancouver's water supply. Censor Lew Gordon pointed out to military officials that Alderman Wilson "as a rule tosses in anti-Jap bombs at meetings of the City Council or its committees, and it would be difficult to choke him off." Gordon, who called Wilson a "menace, nuisance and a pest," spent much of January 1942 debunking Wilson's false claims of Japanese sabotage in British Columbia and trying to keep Wilson's allegations out of the Vancouver papers.

In Ottawa, Undersecretary of State for External Affairs Norman Robertson, Mackenzie King's friend and confidant, asked Eggleston for advice on how to deal with Wilson's inflammatory statements. The censors suggested visiting the Vancouver newspapers to try to arrange a "fairly complete 'blackout' of the said alderman," a view with which Robertson concurred. Unfortunately for the ethnic Japanese on the Pacific Coast, the two major Vancouver newspapers found Wilson's quotes too tempting to ignore.

Wilson wasn't the only politician whipping up fear and prejudice in B.C. The province's minister of forests pushed the newspapers to run stories on his plan to hire fire wardens to put out incendiary bombs dropped by Japanese pilots on B.C. forests or set by Japan's agents in Canada. Gordon killed those stories, believing they would hurt civilian morale and discourage tourism. However, they made it into the papers in May when the province's chief forester told the Victoria Rotary Club he expected the worst fire season in history because of Japanese sabotage. Too many people heard the speech, so the censors let the story go, but Gordon said in a memo to Ottawa, "If the Japs fail to sprinkle incendiary bombs on the Coastal forests of British Columbia this summer the most disappointed man in the world will be Chief forester Orchard. No amount of persuasion has induced him to refrain from issuing invitations to the Japs to come over and do their worst."

Very few Japanese-Canadian journalists would have the opportunity to defend their community. The Vancouver censors were blindsided in January 1942 by the RCMP's closure of three of British Columbia's Japanese newspapers, *Tairiku Nippo*, *Minshu*, and the *Continental Daily News*. All of them, the censors argued, had a "good record" of loyalty to Canada. Only the *New Canadian* was allowed to stay open as a conduit of official news to the Japanese-Canadian community. The three papers that were shut down were dailies that published only in Japanese, while the *New Canadian* was published in English. Within days of the shelving of the three Japanese papers, a representative of the B.C. Security Commission came into Shoyama's office and asked him to print an ad in Japanese. The *New Canadian* did not have a set of Japanese type, so Shoyama used some of the Security Commission's money to buy the stock of one of the suppressed newspapers. The *New Canadian* was then able to publish in both English and Japanese for the rest of the war. Shoyama even wheedled a $100-a-month allowance from the Security Commission to cover the extra cost of publishing the Japanese-language material, although, in fact, it cost the *New Canadian* almost nothing.

Meanwhile, reports of the brutality of the Japanese armed forces at Hong Kong, Singapore, and Manila, carried by newspapers and broadcast across Canada in the first months of 1942, undercut the efforts of the censors to maintain domestic peace in British Columbia. On February 15, the Canadian Press carried a story about the appalling conditions of the Canadian soldiers captured at Hong Kong. The story told how the POWs were held in filthy, miserable conditions without decent food. The reporter described the sight of Canadian troops begging in vain for water as they were paraded by their captors through Kowloon. Censors had to allow the papers to publish the story because the facts, gathered by an Associated Press reporter in China, were accurate and the story did not break the Defence of Canada Regulations. The military and the Department of External Affairs subsequently pressured the censors to impose a blackout on all stories about the abuse of Canadian, U.S., and other Allied prisoners in Japanese hands, partly out of respect for the families of POWs but also to dampen down the reaction against Japanese Canadians. The military believed there were at least twenty-five Canadians interested in each Canadian internee and POW in Japanese hands, and, according to External Affairs' Norman Robertson, between 500,000 and 750,000 Canadians suffered anguish every time an atrocity story was published. Still, people knew the Japanese were rampaging through the Pacific, and they were angry and frightened.

War issues were especially prone to be twisted for partisan advantage in the first half of 1942: Arthur Meighen was trying to make his comeback as Tory leader, fighting to win a seat in Toronto's York South by-election of February 9, and publicity in the Conservative newspapers over the fall of Hong Kong would lead to the Duff inquiry and its fallout. In April 1942, the country voted on the question of conscription, and just days after the plebiscite, U-boats began sinking ships in the St. Lawrence River.

The British Columbia news media stoked local citizens' fears of a Japanese attack against Vancouver Island and the B.C. mainland, something that seemed like a real possibility in 1942. They also fed fears of sabotage. Art Layse, a *Vancouver Sun* reporter-photographer, rounded up some Japanese-Canadian men and convinced them to pose at power dams outside the city. Layse had also drawn a map showing any interested saboteurs the most effective places to plant bombs. The *Sun* planned to run Layse's work on February 15, 1942. Vancouver censor Lew Gordon killed the story and pictures, telling Ottawa with some disgust that his office would not approve "any pictures which diagram places susceptible to sabotage."

Meanwhile, the federal government was under pressure from provincial and municipal politicians in British Columbia to arrest and relocate the Japanese Canadians on Canada's West Coast. The Americans, locals pointed out, were already building concentration camps in the interior. Canadian politicians and bureaucrats quickly fell into line.

The Japanese Canadians were not eager to trade the West Coast for the winter bush camps of Lake Superior, the destination of the first group of expelled men. In early March 1942, some 100 Canadian-born Japanese men were ordered to report to Vancouver's Manning Pool for shipment east. Only thirteen men turned themselves in. Major Austin Taylor, chairman of the B.C. Security Commission, told Gordon to ban stories about this trouble, fearing the racist premier of Ontario, Mitchell Hepburn, would refuse to allow "fractious" internees into his province.

Eggleston refused, believing "we had to be very careful not to allow ourselves to be used by any government department to hide incompetency, cruelty, corruption or other ills." If, he said, "grousing" was a fundamental British right, the ethnic Japanese in Canada, unless openly pro-Axis, were entitled to complain. Eggleston said he would send out a circular only if the complaints of the Japanese Canadians generated a violent backlash among the majority population.

On February 24, five days after the Americans announced the internment of Japanese Americans, the Canadian government declared it would remove all ethnic Japanese people from the coast. Meanwhile, the government and censors were being pressured to shut down the *New Canadian*, which was still trying to find its feet as the main source of news for readers who were being uprooted and whose businesses were being shut down. Comox–Alberni MP Alan Neill told the House of Commons that the *New Canadian* was a menace. He demanded to know if the paper was published in "Japanese or Chinese characters" and if the person who censored the Asian text was "of other than Oriental birth." He was joined by New Westminster MP Thomas Reid, who was eager to settle his pre-war score with the *New Canadian*.

Meanwhile, some ethnic Japanese resistance continued on the West Coast. On May 13, 1942, men who had been locked up in the immigration shed on Powell Street broke windows, used a fire hose to soak a soldier and anyone else they could reach, and shouted slogans in Japanese, allegedly including "banzai." The RCMP asked the censors to keep stories of this small riot out of the papers. Gordon refused, saying he could see no obvious breach of the *Defence of Canada Regulations*, although he did tone down stories that were sent from the *Vancouver Sun* to papers in Seattle and Toronto.

Finally, after months of empty scare stories, a real bogeyman showed up in the northeast Pacific: Japanese carrier-based aircraft bombed the village of Dutch Harbor, Alaska. The attack is nearly forgotten now, but people along the West Coast believed the war had finally arrived on the Pacific Coast of North America. Newspaper reporters in Vancouver had the news before the censors and the minister of defence, who would not confirm the story when asked about it by Eggleston on the morning of June 3, 1942. That night was a tense one on the British Columbia coast. Prince Rupert and Victoria were blacked out, air-raid wardens were deployed in the cities, an air-raid warning was issued for southern British Columbia, and the region's commercial radio stations were shut down to prevent Japanese pilots from using them to find their way to targets. The *Vancouver Province* wanted to run a story the next day saying, "Wednesday night's air raid alert swept Pacific Coast broadcasting stations off the air, but radio entertainment via short wave sets was offered up as usual by the Japanese Broadcasting Corporation." The newspaper expected "readers who possessed short wave radios—and they number thousands on this Coast—would certainly sit right down tonight and do their best to get the Japs' short wave broadcasts." Rather than drum up ratings for Tokyo Rose, Gordon killed the story.

By the summer, the Japanese advance in the Pacific had been slowed and the fear level on the West Coast subsided, but on November 3, a mysterious explosion rocked the Vancouver courthouse. The *Vancouver News-Herald* wanted to suggest the blast was the work of the Black Dragon Society, a Japanese patriotic group, but

the censors warned the paper that sabotage—or suspicion of it—
could not be reported under the *Defence of Canada Regulations*. By
then, the 27,000 ethnic Japanese living along the coast were losing
their property and their rights. Most were people born in Canada
and posed no threat to the country. Still, supposedly out of fear that
their small fishing boats were secretly being used to chart the B.C.
coast for the Japanese navy, many of the Japanese-Canadian fishers
had been deprived of their livelihoods since January 1942. Later that
year, the RCMP began rounding up the boats. Companies and businesses fired their ethnic Japanese employees, and all military-aged
men were barred from a 160-kilometre strip along the B.C. coast.
On February 24, the federal government began using its powers
under the *War Measures Act* to intern all ethnic Japanese. Single
men and poorer people fared the worst. They were shipped to Eastern Canada and the interior of B.C. to toil as itinerant farm labourers or to work on roads. Japanese forced labour helped finally
bridge the gaps in the Trans-Canada Highway in northern Ontario
and British Columbia. People with more money and education
were interned in camps in the B.C. interior. Supposedly, they could
leave if they wished, but since they could not work or go to school
outside the camps, they were effectively imprisoned. They had to
come up with the money to pay their living expenses. This forced
them to agree to sell their property on the coast at fire-sale prices.

The *New Canadian* was one of the few institutions left to them.
Shoyama and later writers believed the government saw the *New
Canadian* as a means of getting news out to Japanese Canadians
wherever they were dispersed. The conduct of the censors, who
fought to keep the paper going and Shoyama out of jail, suggests
they, in fact, took up the *New Canadian* as their adopted cause and
saved it from being shut down. Part of their reason for doing so was
their respect as journalists for Shoyama. Lew Gordon, the long-time
city editor of the *Vancouver Province*, told Eggleston that Shoyama
was loyal, despite the pressures he was under. "I must say," Gordon
wrote, "that I would not expect a Canadian editor, cornered in Japan, to use as much common-sense and right-mindedness as is
here displayed by Shoyama. After all, vindictiveness is a trait com-

mon to many human beings, and yet I am unable to discern anything of a vindictive spirit in the Shoyama copy."

The *New Canadian* first made contact with the censors on January 16, 1942. A staff member, possibly Shoyama, called Gordon asking for advice on a minor story. At that point, the censors treated the
New Canadian the same as any other newspaper, expecting it to follow the voluntary censorship system and not requiring any pre-
censorship of its copy.

Within a month, however, the censors had assumed a tight grip
on the four-page newspaper. In March 1942, Ottawa censor Warren
Baldwin looked over the previous thirty issues of the *New Canadian*.
He decided Shoyama was a poor newspaperman whose attempts to
master North American journalese were "rather pathetic." Baldwin
didn't agree with Shoyama's very accurate prediction that the situation of ethnic Japanese in Canada and the United States would
become "more dire," and Shoyama's protestations of *Nisei* loyalty
were "rather wearisome." Still, the paper could be used as a propaganda organ if its editor was "taken in hand" by the newspapermen
who were censors on the West Coast. On March 10, Maurice Pope,
the director of censorship, wired the Vancouver office to instruct
Gordon and Graham to pre-censor all news and opinion articles
published in the *New Canadian*. Graham reported Shoyama "read-
ily agreed," even though the censors' demand had no basis in law
and no other Canadian publication had been forced to submit to
this type of supervision in this or previous wars.

Authorities maintained the *New Canadian* was censored to
prevent the position of the Japanese in Vancouver being misunder-
stood by any white readers of the paper. Censors, usually Gordon,
vetted the English material and gave the Japanese articles to a translator. Gordon noted that "during my long association with the press
I have done many queer things but the queerest of all is this job of
editing a Jap newspaper. Banzai!" By March 14, Gordon was describing himself as "ex-officio editor of Japanese bilingual newspaper 'New Canadian,'" and passed for publication an editorial that
attacked the *Vancouver Sun* for its inflammatory coverage of Japanese Canadians. Censors allowed members of the B.C Security

Commission to vet some of the newspaper's copy, such as a story related to the expulsion of *Nisei* to an isolated camp near Schreiber, on the north shore of Lake Superior, which B.C. Security Commission chair Austin Taylor shelved. Gordon believed Taylor did not want the story published because "he feared that at the last moment the Japs might refuse to entrain—in other words, he wanted the Japs in the bag before he would countenance the story." Gordon knew the story did not contain anything in breach of the *Defence of Canada Regulations* but he telephoned Shoyama to tell him "it would be diplomatic on his part to agree not to use the story in the issue of March 28th." Shoyama reminded Gordon the newspaper's production was running late, and that it would not be on the street until after the deportees left for Schreiber. The censors agreed with Shoyama and, for the first time, took his side of a dispute with the authorities.

By early April 1942, Gordon was referring to the *New Canadian* in memoranda as "my Japanese newspaper" and Shoyama as the "Jap Pulitzer." Gordon had very quickly developed an attachment and loyalty both to the newspaper and to its staff, noting he had "less trouble with my Japanese staff than I experience with any other Coast paper published by white men." Gordon began to worry about the *New Canadian* making its deadlines and sometimes stayed late to help get the paper out. The censor understood the deadening effects of the restrictions placed on Shoyama and sympathized with the editor, who was sometimes on the verge of quitting. Shoyama faced a multitude of obstacles, including the loss of the *New Canadian*'s Vancouver office space and an edict against Japanese Canadians using telephones. With the newspaper's reliance on freelancers who, in many instances, had recently been uprooted from their homes and dispatched to unfamiliar and isolated parts of the country, Shoyama was lucky to get the newspaper out at all.

Within a few weeks of assuming control of the *New Canadian*, Gordon's colleagues began chiding him as the "editor" and "advisory advisor" of the "Japalac" newspaper (so called because "it is Jap and it lacks news"). The censor drew the line when Shoyama suggested Japanese Canadians had some justification for resisting the

orders of the B.C. Security Commission, and when Shoyama wanted to print stories about Japanese Canadians who resisted the commission's orders. Caught between Shoyama's insistence on printing
the truth about the expulsions and the demands of the government
for secrecy, Gordon temporarily brought in Major A.H.L. Mellor of
the B.C. Security Commission to be "co-editor" of the *New Canadian*. This did not stop Shoyama's criticism of racist B.C. politicians
such as Alderman Wilson. Gordon warned the editor against an-
tagonizing the "pestiferous Alderman" but let him publish some
stories attacking him and other politicians who bashed the Japanese
Canadians.

By then, the censors were under pressure from Ian Mackenzie, a
distinguished law professor, Liberal MP for Vancouver Centre, and
minister of pensions and national health, to close the newspaper.
(Mackenzie would later campaign to have ethnic Japanese barred
from British Columbia forever.) Norman McLarty, the secretary of
state, who had jurisdiction over press censorship, went to Eggleston
and Charpentier's office to warn that the *New Canadian* had gone
"entirely too far" in its coverage of controversy surrounding the
expulsion. McLarty was insistent that the censors close the *New Canadian* and turn its assets over to the Custodian of Enemy Property.
Eggleston argued with McLarty, saying the *New Canadian*'s articles
on the expulsions were very similar to material carried by other
Vancouver papers. It would be difficult to justify legal action against
one and not the others. The minister then backed off.

McLarty was a stalking horse for Ian Mackenzie. For his part,
Eggleston represented the views of some of the most senior people
in the federal bureaucracy, including King's powerful deputy Norman Robertson. Robertson was from Vancouver and had grown up
among anti-Asian bigots. During the war, he received a steady
stream of letters from his own father, who wanted all of the ethnic
Japanese deported. Hugh Keenleyside, H.F. Angus, and Lester Pearson in Robertson's department had even less use for the British Columbia politicians and their racism. Through the war, they fought a
rearguard action against the attacks on the Japanese Canadians'
civil rights.

The officials at External Affairs were backed by the leaders of the army and navy. At the beginning of 1942, Maurice Pope was still chief censor and vice-chief of staff. He was one of the more vocal opponents of expulsion of the ethnic Japanese and the suppression of their civil rights. After losing control of censorship, Pope was a lieutenant general and Ottawa's liaison with Washington, and he continued to combat the overreaction against ethnic Japanese civilians.

Through that summer, the *New Canadian*'s coverage focused on the plight of the *Nisei*, who, unlike the first-generation Japanese internees, were not under the protection of the Geneva Convention. The convention spelled out the rights of foreign nationals held by a warring state, but the *Nisei* had no Japanese citizenship rights. They had to endure the loss of their jobs and businesses, along with endless humiliating slights and snubs. Many were serious, but some were mean and petty. In July, Shoyama ran an article on Vancouver's ban of ethnic Japanese children from east-end city swimming pools. Even that kind of story was considered inflammatory. Gordon refused to clear the story unless it was credited to its paper of origin, the *Vancouver News-Herald*, so readers would not think the *New Canadian* was tackling a controversial racial issue on its own.

In early August 1942, Gordon wanted to drop the Japanese-language stories in the *New Canadian* because he expected Shoyama and the paper to leave for the B.C. interior, where censoring the Japanese material would be "impractical." Eggleston insisted the Japanese material stay in the *New Canadian*, if Shoyama still wanted to print it. The editor was unlikely to do anything to alienate his readership, as the paper was barely breaking even with a circulation of 1,600.

In Vancouver, relations between Gordon and Shoyama were at one of their low points. Looking over galley proofs after the *New Canadian*'s issue of August 27 had already gone to press, Gordon found "certain objectionable material" in an article by W.R. McWilliams, former pastor of the New Westminster Japanese United Church. The piece had not been pre-cleared by censors, and Gordon accused Shoyama of "evasion." The editor believed the piece, written by a white former missionary to Japan, should not be subjected to prepublication censorship. However, Gordon considered McWil-liams's observations about the treatment of Japanese Canadians incendiary. He highlighted material such as the following:

> Canadians at heart, by choice and by intention, they see themselves debarred from army service in any form, from any necessary work unless perhaps it be as laborers on farms in some few scattered localities and this under conditions of rigorous supervision and inadequate pay. They are not treated as equals but as suspects, not as war prisoners or enemy nationals of other races, but as the white man has treated other coloured races in the past.

In his report to Ottawa, Gordon said McWilliams "is obviously pro-Jap" and "his propaganda, if given general press circulation, would boomerang on the Japs evacuated from the B.C. Coastal Area." Shoyama, Gordon told Ottawa, could not be trusted.

Despite Gordon's reluctance to let Shoyama out from under the thumb of the Vancouver censorship office, in late October 1942, Shoyama was ordered to leave Vancouver. He had been allowed to make a couple of scouting trips to the interior to look for a home for his newspaper and had decided on Kaslo, a ghost town in the remote Slocan Valley of the gorgeous Kootenay Mountains. The town had boomed fifty years earlier when silver had been found in the surrounding hills. Japanese Canadians had been moved into Kaslo in the spring of 1942 and had set to work repairing its abandoned houses and putting up new buildings. Kaslo was the only internment community that had already had a newspaper, the *Kaslo Kootenayan*, a long-established weekly that served the people of the other near-dead villages and old mining camps in the region. The Kaslo publisher, John Rouleau, was glad Shoyama showed up. The "kindly old fellow" made a deal with Shoyama that he would share his office with the *New Canadian*. In return for a small fee and some help around the shop, the Kaslo editor would print the four-page *New Canadian* and give it some office space and a mail room.

It was difficult to put out a newspaper when internment rules prevented Shoyama from possessing a camera and using a telephone. Mail censors read every letter between Shoyama and his network of writers. Many articles arrived in Kaslo full of holes where the mail censors had used their razor blades. The young editor still somehow managed to put out a newspaper and rebuild good relations with Gordon. In Kaslo, more and more articles were printed in Japanese because many of the new readers of the paper, who signed up for subscriptions after the Japanese-language papers were killed, were first-generation immigrants who couldn't read English. From their internment camps, the *Issei* sent sad stories about their treatment, often in the form of poetry.

On October 26, 1942, the *New Canadian* carried an editorial about leaving for Kaslo: "We will not say we go without regret or pain. Nevertheless, we go quite willingly. It is not hard to accept wartime evacuation, if in the opinion of our government and country it is a military necessity." Despite these protestations of loyalty, the federal government decided prepublication censorship would have to continue, Eggleston believing it protected the paper and was responsible for keeping Shoyama out of jail.

The young editor adapted, even thrived a bit, in his isolated imprisonment. Shoyama was a prolific letter writer with a wide circle of friends, especially young women. At least twice, he was given permission to visit his freelance contributors in Ontario. On one trip, he visited the Ottawa censors and was given a one-day membership in the Parliamentary Press Gallery so he could sit in its seats in the House of Commons and watch a debate. Because he saved money by sharing the print shop of the Kaslo paper, Shoyama was able to accumulate a $500 nest egg and several thousand shares of good-quality stock in resource companies by the time he left the *New Canadian* near the end of the war.

Shoyama was forced to work under humiliating rules, but he constantly tried to ease the mistrust of some of the people who held power over him. Once the paper moved to Kaslo, Dr. E.C. Hennigar, a member of the Post Office Censorship staff, vetted the Japanese copy. Almost immediately, Hennigar became a strict enforcer of what he felt were the censorship rules and, at least once, pressured the censors into ordering Shoyama to colour over an article that had already appeared in the paper. In February, Gordon cleared this poem for publication:

Today as before
Eating the tossed wheat.
When the straw is eaten
We cannot move
And we fall asleep.
When hunger calls again
We moo . . . moo aloud.
The life of a beast.

Hennigar said the poem was inflammatory. Gordon reversed his own decision, then axed a second poem because Hennigar said the title of the poem, "Chinook," was suggestive of a wind blowing from Japan across the Prairies. A few months earlier, Gordon told Shoyama not to print this poem, an attack on the tough curfews imposed on ethnic Japanese;

Cinderella
"Yeah, curfew! Mediaeval!
Yeh, laughed like the devil!
No loitering for Japs
After taps!
          Aw, nuts!

"Yea . . . someone being playful!
Must hurt him something awful!
To see yellow Japs
Loitering after taps!
          Aw, nuts!

     "What's that?
     Rata-a-tat . . . Rat-a-tat

SUNDOWN TO SUNRISE: CURFEW ON ALL JAPS!

"What the . . . !
    Ah, hell!
        Seven p.m. now!
Go home like good lil Canucks!
        Aw, nuts! . . .

I am Canadian born!
    Hell, we've a right!
    A damn good right!

Germans, Italians and Japs . . .
Kick 'em out and we'll go!

        Sure!
            Sure!
                Sure!
When the Italians and Germans, they go!

On December 28, 1942, Shoyama went to press with a story about the misery of Japanese-Canadian bush workers in Kapuskasing, Ontario. The article had not been cleared by the censors. Two lines, one saying they worked in minus-30-degrees-Celsius weather and the other about "the incessant howls of protest and discrimination which have hounded the *Nisei* since evacuation," were ordered blacked out of every copy of the 3,000-unit print run. Shoyama said he couldn't wait for the censors because the *Kaslo Koottenayan* needed to get the plates onto the press immediately. Gordon wrote to the editor, "Surely, Mr. Shoyama, your experience as an editor and publisher during the past year must have indicated to you that attempts to arouse racial passions and prejudices are deplorable even in normal times—today such actions cannot be sanctioned by this office."

Meanwhile, Shoyama was under pressure from other internees. Many of the Japanese Canadians who were interned became more defensive and radicalized as the months went by. People like Shoyama were called *inu* (dogs) for co-operating with authorities. *Issei* political leaders, many of them pro-Japanese, saw their influence increase as they railed against the *Nisei*. The cleavages in the Japanese-Canadian community were magnified. Some of the more radical *Issei* were packed off to isolated camps in northern Ontario, but the B.C. internees were, in the summer of 1943, seething with anger.

In March 1943, Ottawa decided Gordon was being too rough on Shoyama. Norman Robertson wrote to Warren Baldwin, saying the Japanese Canadians had every right to feel bitter about their treatment. The potential backlash of whites was not enough reason to strip the Japanese Canadians of their press rights: "You should not stop publication of harmless views because of the criminal acts that someone else may commit when he reads them," Robertson wrote March 12, after Gordon forwarded a *New Canadian* letter to the editor. "In a general way there is nothing in the proposed letter which the most exacting Canadian would not wish a Canadian of Japanese race to feel or to say." Gordon, however, believed Shoyama was doing less reporting and "more and more becoming a vehicle of propaganda to be assimilated by the Japanese evacuees who are subscribers to his sheet ..."

Gordon was not happy with Robertson's ruling. He told his superiors in Ottawa he would have clipped Shoyama's wings already. "My personal opinion is that there is a lot of potential trouble when the Japanese hit the propaganda trail, as Shoyama is now doing," Gordon wrote. Less than two months later, Warren Baldwin warned Gordon to give Shoyama some breathing room. If the *New Canadian* was too heavily censored, the Japanese-Canadian readers would soon decide that the newspaper itself was merely another example of persecution and it would become a constant thorn in their flesh.

Shoyama's colleagues in the Vancouver press were no help. In early April 1943, Japanese Canadians at Kaslo had appointed a committee to launch court action to fight the forced sale of their property on the coast. The *New Canadian* had supported the committee, saying, "In many cases this may well be the last straw which has mounted higher and higher, and heavier and heavier upon the backs of Japanese-Canadians since Pearl Harbor." With reservations, Gordon had cleared the editorial for publication on April 10. The *Vancouver Sun* struck back in an editorial on April 16, 1943, saying,

> Canada has treated her Japanese population with great decency and consideration. This "heavier and heavier" war burden they talk about is a pose, intended for propaganda purposes just as much as it is their care to disassociate themselves from racial responsibility for what happened at Pearl Harbor. But there is a curious and typical similarity between all that comes from Japanese sources, whether these emanate from Tokyo or the Kaslo camp. We dislike the tone of both of them.

At the same time, Graham killed a story on a decision by the navy to take over a boatyard seized from Japanese Canadians. He also suppressed a piece that, he said, likened the white people of Kelowna to the Ku Klux Klan. The *Kelowna Courier* had already printed a story about the Higuchi family, who were given twelve hours to get out of town by a self-styled commission of two members from the city council, two members of the Royal Canadian Legion, and two delegates from the Kelowna Board of Trade. The family had taken refuge in the local United Church mission after arriving in the city as labourers for a local fruit farmer, a Mr. Taneda. The locals were enraged that an ethnic Japanese farmer had been given a permit to bring in other Japanese Canadians. The frightened family loaded all their furniture onto the next ferry out of the city and left. Gordon believed publishing that article would "incite the anti-Japanese feeling in the Okanagan to further flare-ups."

From Ottawa, Baldwin laid out the principle that the Japanese were entitled to draw attention to what they considered to be abuses and to discuss them in "moderate terms." Of the Ku Klux Klan editorial, Baldwin said, "If the *New Canadian* had merely reported the incident or even commented on it moderately, it seems to me it would probably have been better to let them do so." But in this case, he maintained, the censors were justified in killing the story because the article would arouse unnecessary antipathy among the *New Canadian*'s readers. Still, Gordon had not been swayed toward the *Vancouver Sun*'s racist point of view. Gordon sent Baldwin an envelope of anti–Japanese Canadian editorials with a note saying, "Herewith a load of anti-Jap from the *Vancouver Sun*." But the *Sun* reflected the opinions of its readers in British Columbia and people across the country. For instance, the Royal City Orange Lodge in Guelph, Ontario, claimed the *New Canadian* "exercises a subversive influence and breeds dissatisfaction among the Japanese," and demanded the paper be suspended and Shoyama jailed.

Through the summer, the *New Canadian* kept up its attack on B.C. fruit farmers who exploited Japanese-Canadian labour. On November 12, Vancouver censor Lew Graham killed an article in which the writer, under the pseudonym "Hermitage," condemned "the cheap antics of that earnest body of business men who comprise the Nelson Board of Trade," which had earlier demanded the removal of Japanese-Canadians from the Kootenays but now wanted them back as cheap labour. In one section, the article stated, "The conclusion is inescapable that the Board of Trade is not influenced by a single commendable motive." In another part, it claimed that "British Columbia has given too many indications that it regards us simply as dumb beasts of burden."

In March 1944, Shoyama targeted his hometown, Kamloops, condemning the community for demanding the expulsion of local ethnic Japanese, even though Kamloops had no military installations other than "an adequately protected munitions dump." The censors ordered that phrase removed, saying it contravened the *Defence of Canada Regulations*, and requested it be replaced with the phrase "even though Kamloops assuredly has no greater need for military precautions than any other B.C. point." Graham ended the telegram with the word, "Sorry."

Graham did, on April 12, 1944, defend a tough *New Canadian* article protesting property seizures that was reprinted in the *Vancouver Sun* as an example of Shoyama's disloyalty. Along with it, the big Vancouver daily ran a vicious editorial of its own that claimed 1,600 Japanese Canadians were serving in Hirohito's armed forces.

Shoyama's article was strongly written, Graham said, but "the *New Canadian* was entitled to its day in court in view of the very vigorous anti-Japanese criticism which is voiced out there." Graham found public opinion on the issue of the treatment of ethnic Japanese people had split on political lines, with the Liberals and Conservatives in British Columbia supporting a tough policy against them and the CCF, especially provincial politician Agnes MacInnis, opposing "the anti-Japanese sentiments so often heard out here." As long as Shoyama stayed away from "subversive utterances," Graham would not tie his hands. "I am convinced that he is much too intelligent to take a chance like that as he knows he would be risking his neck," the censor wrote to his colleagues in Ottawa.

At that time, the censors were involved in one of their most embarrassing decisions. They axed a prize-winning essay by interned Japanese-Canadian elementary school student George Watanabe that was supposed to run in a forty-page booklet put out by the Tashme Correspondence Class. Watanabe's essay criticized the internment. The print run, 275 copies, was minimal. Graham had a week to agonize over his decision. He sent Watanabe's essay, "Our World Today," to Ottawa, where Baldwin read it and also expressed concern. The censors considered dropping the problem into the lap of the booklet's non-Japanese publisher, but he would not touch the project unless the censors stamped it. Writing to the school principal, Graham expressed his sadness for spiking Watanabe's essay but justified it by saying Japanese forces could use it as an excuse to mistreat Allied prisoners in their hands.

In a memorandum sent to Ottawa on April 22, 1944, Graham noted the anti-Japanese rhetoric in the West Coast papers was heating up and Graham expected Shoyama's replies to "become more and more outspoken." He believed the censors would be drawn in as referees parrying the views of the *New Canadian*, the West Coast anti–Japanese Canadian politicians, and the scaremongering newspapers that supported them. Graham's prediction was accurate. There would be no journalistic solidarity between Shoyama and his colleagues in the British Columbia press corps. On June 14, 1944, Graham received a call from Cliff MacKay, city hall reporter of the

Vancouver Sun, who complained about a brief item on the front page of the current edition which read, "No matter what the lyrics, Vancouver's Mayor blows a Nazi tune." In MacKay's view, the line was libellous and he criticized Graham for passing it for publication. Advice on libel, Graham responded, was not within the mandate of the censors.

Graham did not tell MacKay that Shoyama had slipped the line into the newspaper without vetting it with the censors. Graham called Shoyama, suffering through the usual difficulty of getting a line through to Kaslo. Shoyama could not remember whether he had stuck the comment in the envelope with the rest of the copy for that issue or just typed it as "filler," but he stood by it, arguing the intent of the sentence "was that the attitude of Vancouver's mayor in demanding repatriation of all Japanese was similar to that of the Nazis in their attitude toward Jews and other racial minorities." Graham resented being forced to choose either to defend something that he had no part in or to admit to the critics of the *New Canadian*—who also tended to be critics of censorship—that Shoyama had slipped something by him. Baldwin, after a short telephone conversation with Graham, agreed the item probably would have been passed, and accepted his advice that the censors should defend the statement. Again, rather than curtail the newspaper and leave its editor to the mercy of his critics, the Vancouver and Ottawa censors chose to protect it.

After receiving Graham's memorandum, Baldwin asked for a report on the *New Canadian* and its editor. Several days later, Graham spoke frankly and rather indiscreetly with George Collins, head of the B.C. Security Commission, about Shoyama, the *New Canadian*, and the problems that had arisen with Ottawa over the comment about the mayor. Collins passed the information on to the *Sun* and Graham found himself, on June 28, 1944, again having to defend censorship's position on the *New Canadian* to MacKay, the *Sun*'s beat reporter on Japanese-Canadian issues.

In the next issue of the *New Canadian*, Shoyama reported on a letter written by the Vancouver Consultative Council, a civil liberties group, to Prime Minister King objecting to demands for expulsion of all ethnic Japanese from Canada after the war. Nine prominent Vancouver clerics and business leaders signed the letter. One of them, N.E.E. Norman of St. George's United Church, was described as an "instructor in the Pacific Command Japanese Language School," the institution that was secretly training interpreters for the Pacific war. Graham wired Shoyama to remove any mention of the school. Shoyama was also asked to change an article written by an internee who had returned for a holiday in Kaslo after living in the East. The story was passed except for a paragraph which said that, when the writer first went east, he looked forward to nothing but hardship "and cruelty"; the reference to cruelty was taken out.

Pressure to shut the newspaper down continued to mount through that spring. At the beginning of June 1944, Shoyama submitted an editorial that attacked British Columbia politicians for advocating the permanent deportation and expulsion of the ethnic Japanese. This time, he noted the threat to the survival of the *New Canadian*, telling his readers a request, including a resolution from Vancouver-area Loyal Orange Lodges, had been made to the federal justice minister calling for suppression of the paper "for daring to criticize policies which by no stretch of the imagination can be called anything but Fascist in nature. It is well-known that a Fascist ideology, whether in Germany, Japan or elsewhere calls also for the suppression of a democratic Free Press as well as for racial intolerance."

Graham wanted to pass the editorial, as "this all sounded perfectly legitimate to me as far as DCR goes but in view of the touchy situation thought I had better consult with Ottawa to be sure they shared my views." Graham phoned Baldwin, who agreed the opinion piece should be cleared for publication.

Despite the attacks on Shoyama by the *Vancouver Sun*, one of its reporters called Kaslo on August 7 to ask Shoyama his opinion on the federal plan to disperse the ethnic Japanese across the country. Shoyama opposed the plan, but insisted if it did occur, the Japanese Canadians should have the same civil rights as other Canadians. The paper had published an editorial on July 18, 1944—"No Vote for Japs"—attacking Shoyama's paper, which, the editorial writers claimed, has been partly devoted to an arrogant display of demands of fulfillment of their "rights" as Canadians. . . . You might expect informed people who posed as Canadian Japanese citizens would have condemned Japan's savagery in the war, but this publicity is conspicuous by its absence. Instead, by inference, the paper has upheld the Japanese imperial cause. Our government would be wise to suppress this publication, which is a constant worry to Canadian censorship authorities.

The editorial ran directly under the newspaper's masthead slogan, which said, "The *Vancouver Sun*, owned and operated by Vancouver people, is a newspaper devoted to progress and democracy, tolerance and freedom of thought."

By then, the fear of a Japanese attack had died down along the coast. On September 22, 1944, censorship of the *New Canadian* was relaxed. Only material written by Shoyama's staff would be pre-screened. Anything clipped from papers and wire services could be run without censoring, even if translated into Japanese, because Post Office censors had always found the translations to be honest. Graham reported to Ottawa on Hallowe'en that he'd had very little trouble with Shoyama in the last few months. The Kaslo settlement was expected to be disbanded the following spring and Shoyama was planning to move east, along with many of the *Nisei*. In early 1945, Shoyama made an exploratory trip to Winnipeg—which was still in the West Coast censors' jurisdiction—and made an agreement with the owner of the Israelite Press to print the *New Canadian*. Shoyama's staff set up a print shop and office in Elmwood and crammed themselves into the rest of the house.

There were a few fights left. In February 1945, Shoyama took on J. Alex Paton, Conservative MLA for Vancouver–Point Grey and, according to Graham, "one of the second-string anti-Japanese orators on the Coast." Graham enjoyed Shoyama's "ironic" attack on Paton, and his mockery of the MLA's anti–Japanese Canadian letters to the Vancouver newspapers. Paton, Shoyama wrote, had "built a Japanese dragon and is now going to try to suffocate it with a petition against return of the Japs." A petition to deport all ethnic Japanese in Canada was "being woven out of the cloth of race hate and intolerance by the fishermen of the Fraser." With his petition, Shoyama said, Paton would "bestride the public platform, a 20th century Saint George the Deliverer. . . . It is related, is it not, that in much the same way Der Fuhrer bestrode a beer hall to deliver the German people." Graham was willing to pass the article because it did not compromise security in any way and he could not see any violation of the *Defence of Canada Regulations*. After telephoning Baldwin in Ottawa and receiving his support (although Baldwin told Graham "it was very unwise of Shoyama to stick his neck out by running such articles"), Graham approved the editorial.

As the Pacific War progressed, Britain and the United States realized the value of *Nisei* as translators of Japanese military radio traffic, which, at a local level at least, was usually sent without being encoded. The Canadian military refused to follow the lead of the other Allies and accept internees for service in the Pacific War or to follow the lead of the Americans, who raised Japanese-American fighting units that fought with great distinction in Europe. Here, Shoyama realized, was a chance to begin a debate on Canada's Japanese race policies, for the internees to prove their loyalty, and for publicity that might help put pressure on the authorities to give better treatment to those people who remained in custody.

In late January 1945, Graham and Baldwin finally pushed through a censorship ruling to allow the *New Canadian*, and mainstream publications in Canada, to report on the recruitment by American and British forces of ethnic Japanese soldiers and translators from among the internees, but Shoyama was warned not to mention their work as spies. In mid-January, Shoyama clipped a short article from *Newsweek* that reported "since the British Army recently started accepting some Canadian-born Japanese for Intelligence work in the Far East, the question of Canada's refusal to use her Japs in any military capacity is expected to come up in the Commons." Military intelligence had upheld the ban on reporting the recruitment of *Nisei* the previous September, when Graham had queried them in three requests to lift it. This time, because the item had been published abroad, Graham had little choice but to approve it for the *New Canadian*. He contacted Major Bray at the Vancouver office of army intelligence and told him about the break in *Newsweek*. The news "disturbed" Bray, and he told Graham some officers had been severely reprimanded for mentioning the subject. Graham informed Bray the matter was out of his hands because the subject had received wide circulation in *Newsweek*.

Five days later, Shoyama submitted a story about British officers recruiting *Nisei* in Canadian camps. This time, Graham received clearance from Baldwin to allow publication of any stories about *Nisei* service in the Pacific, except for articles that mentioned intelligence work behind Japanese lines. Shoyama followed up these stories in early March with a favourable editorial about the U.S. army's recruitment of ten thousand *Nisei* (though many were also in combat roles, where some *Nisei* units covered themselves in glory in the European theatre). Shoyama criticized the Canadian army's decision not to accept ethnic Japanese: "There is no question but that the majority of us are destined to remain and work out a future in Canada," he wrote. "Nothing can or will contribute greater security or happiness to that future for all of us, than the *Nisei* actively serving in uniform."

Not until the spring of 1945 did the Canadian army reverse its policy on the recruitment of *Nisei*. Shoyama was allowed to report on the rush of ethnic Japanese candidates who wished to join the military. Apart from the positive publicity that it gave to the ethnic Japanese, Shoyama had his own reasons for closely following the policy shift. In July 1945, Shoyama joined the army's intelligence corps. The *New Canadian* survived Shoyama's departure. Its new editor, a Mr. Oyama, edited the newspaper from Winnipeg and had no conflict with the censors.

Even after the war, however, the censors were not finished with the Japanese-Canadian internment issue. Eggleston was the first president of the Ottawa Civil Liberties Association (OCLA), which was founded in the spring of 1946 in large part to protest breaches of the civil rights of Japanese Canadians and people suspected of being Communist agents. In July 1946, Eggleston wrote to Prime

Minister King, "If we as citizens do not protest now against steps taken in so-called 'special' cases, we may find ourselves powerless to protest later on when the 'special' cases are found to extend to much wider fields."

Although the war in the Pacific ended about six weeks after Shoyama enlisted, he continued to work as a translator, rising to the rank of sergeant by the time he was discharged in 1946. Interviewed years later, Shoyama reflected on his wartime experiences, including his success in sustaining the *New Canadian*, by saying, "We had to tell people: Look, in spite of all these terrible things that happened to you, stand on your own feet. Look within yourself, to your own strength and self-respect and your own sense of dignity."

After his discharge from the army, Shoyama met a wartime friend, George Tamaki, in Regina. Tamaki was a senior bureaucrat in the two-year-old Co-operative Commonwealth Federation (CCF) government in Saskatchewan headed by Tommy Douglas. Tamaki took Shoyama to hear Douglas speak and Shoyama was so impressed with the young premier that he immediately applied for a job in the Saskatchewan provincial government. Shoyama's hiring was opposed by some CCF members, in both Saskatchewan and British Columbia, where the *Vancouver Sun* ran the headline "CCF Government Opens Posts to Japs" over a story reporting the hiring of Tamaki, Shoyama, and one other Japanese Canadian.

In 1950, Shoyama rose to the rank of secretary of the province's Economic Advisory and Planning Board, placing him on the top tier of the bureaucracy along with Treasury Board secretary Al Johnson, a civil servant with whom Shoyama would work for three more decades. Shoyama was an architect of Saskatchewan's Crown corporations and fine-tuned the province's medicare system, acting as right-hand man and chief political strategist for the CCF in Douglas's final years as premier.

When the CCF lost power in Saskatchewan in 1964, Lester Pearson lured Shoyama and seventy other Saskatchewan bureaucrats to Ottawa. Shoyama was hired as senior economist at the Economic Council of Canada, rising to assistant deputy minister by 1968. He prepared the federal position for the Western Economic Opportunities Conference after the 1972 election, and in 1974 began a five-year term as deputy finance minister under three ministers: John Turner, Donald Macdonald, and Jean Chrétien. Shoyama retired in 1980 after serving in the Privy Council as a special advisor to Prime Minister Pierre Trudeau on economic aspects of the repatriation of the Constitution.

For his work in public service, Shoyama was awarded the Order of Canada. After his retirement, he returned to British Columbia, where he volunteered to become a visiting professor in the School of Public Administration and the Department of Asian and Pacific Studies at the University of Victoria. He taught there until 1991, and stayed on at the university at a salary of $1 a year, supervising independent studies and graduate students, until 1998. Tommy Shoyama died in Victoria on December 22, 2006, aged ninety.

The censors, men of their time who called Japanese people "Japs," still understood how the ethnic Japanese of British Columbia were being targeted by racist politicians and worked to protect the single surviving Japanese-Canadian newspaper. By advocating on behalf of the *New Canadian*, working to keep its editor out of jail, and supporting his bid to enter the army, the censors not only often acted with integrity toward the Japanese Canadians but also helped launch the career of an outstanding public servant. They, much more than many of their colleagues in journalism, came out of the internment of ethnic Japanese with relatively clean hands.

CHAPTER 10

Balloon Bombs and Atomic Bombs

TECHNOLOGY—BOTH AXIS AND ALLIED—played a key role in the war, and, in the Pacific theatre, was instrumental in determining its outcome. Censoring news of technological advances was difficult, since none of the censors had scientific training, nor did the journalists who wrote about weaponry and tried to cover the overwhelming wartime changes to the economy. The press censors tried to compensate by learning as much as they could from the rather tight-lipped military experts and scientists at the National Research Council. By the end of the war, the Ottawa office developed massive files on military hardware and Eggleston had developed expertise and connections that he used later when he wrote a book about wartime science. The press censors knew more about the Manhattan Project than most generals and U.S. politicians: they were briefed on atomic secrets at least three months before Harry Truman, who learned of the bomb only after Franklin Roosevelt's death. By the beginning of 1945, top Canadian news editors were also let in on the atomic bomb secret.

The censors had a hard time pulling their technological information together. Weapons research was in the hands of C.D. Howe's Department of Munitions and Supply, and its press-relations department simply ignored most of the censors' requests for facts. Eventually, the department gave censorship officials "Secret Lists," and, by the war's end, the power relationship flipped, so much so that Howe's flacks relied on the Directorate of Censorship for advice about their press releases. Still, the censors were mostly left to react to coverage, and not forewarned. After years of dealing with the armed forces, the RCMP, and the rest of the government's security apparatus, this was nothing new for the press censors.

In March 1942, the British army helped out by issuing a list of "Stops and Releases," a sort of catalogue of military secrets, including a breakdown of "secret" and "most secret equipment" covering all weapons in use or under development by the British and Canadian forces. The censors asked the Canadian army for a similar list. It took eleven months, but one finally arrived in the censors' offices in February 1943. That September, the Royal Canadian Air Force came up with its own list of equipment used in Canada and on RCAF bases across the country. The censors needed more, so they turned to Britain's Air Ministry for advice on technical descriptions of new airplanes. At the end of 1943, an Allied list was issued to cover army equipment of British, Canadian, and U.S. design. Predictably, the Royal Canadian Navy's list of secret equipment did not arrive at the Directorate of Censorship until 1944, and the navy's material was vague and incomplete. Again, the Canadian press censors were often compelled to turn to the British, getting advice from the Admiralty Technical Mission in Ottawa, or even the British Admiralty in London.

The navy insisted that asdic—or sonar—was a secret that had to be kept from the Germans, although they already knew about it. Just before Pearl Harbor, the *Christian Science Monitor* published an article on underwater echo location technology; the *Ottawa Citizen* picked up the story. Navy brass demanded charges be laid against the *Citizen*, but Eggleston searched the scientific literature and back issues of magazines and newspapers to get ammunition to argue that sonar was already widely publicized. In July 1941, the Toronto censor passed an article for the *Toronto Telegram* based on interviews with Canadian sailors Alan Shedden and Eddie Badger, who named asdic as the device for spotting submarines "by means of an echo received by our earphones after sending out a sound wave." The director of naval intelligence demanded the seamen be immediately disciplined, a request that resulted in Shedden and Badger facing a court martial that ultimately sentenced them to a month in jail.

More serious, as far as Eggleston was concerned, the navy demanded the firing of Toronto censor Bert Perry. Eggleston went back to the library and ferreted out eight books published between 1920 and 1939, all of which gave far more extensive information than was published in the *Christian Science Monitor* or the *Toronto Telegram*. The pièce de résistance, however, was obtained from a volume published in Germany by Dr. Ludwig Bergman in 1938 giving full technical details of underwater echo technology. After receiving Eggleston's report, the navy stopped demanding censorship of asdic and Perry kept his job. Throughout the war, however, the censors and the navy continued to fight over control of information about echo location technology.

The "cat gear," a very useful and simple piece of technology, was kept out of the papers for the duration of the war, and was, perhaps, Canada's most valuable naval secret of the time. It was a cluster of short pieces of pipe chained together and towed behind ships to thwart acoustic torpedoes that homed in on the vibrations created by ship propellers. The cat stayed secret for more than three years, even remaining under wraps after Germany's surrender to keep the secret out of Soviet hands.

The censors were also responsible for killing all mention in Canada's press of Habbakuk, a bizarre plan supported by Admiral Lord Louis Mountbatten to install refrigeration tubes in a 2-million-ton block of ice and tow it to the coast of Europe. This giant iceberg would be used as an almost-indestructible, easily repaired airfield during the Allied invasion of mainland Europe. In 1943, National Research Council scientists conducted feasibility experiments at Patricia Lake in the Rockies. The concept was discussed by Roosevelt and Churchill at the 1943 Quebec Conference and quietly dropped.

Japanese balloon bombs were perhaps the strangest weapon launched against the Allies in World War Two. Made of paper and silk, the 12-metre balloons were filled with hydrogen and designed to catch the jet stream at 10,000 metres for a 220-kilometre-an-hour, four-day trip to North America. The bombs were fitted with altimeters and ballast weights to keep them in the stratosphere. Each night, as they cooled and dropped below the jet stream, the balloons automatically let go of enough sand bags to give them the buoyancy to drift back up to the jet stream. By the time they arrived on the Pacific Coast of Alaska, British Columbia, or the southern United States, all the ballast was used up. If things worked as planned, the balloon's cluster of five 4.5-kilogram fire bombs and one 15-kilogram high-explosive bomb took the place of the sand bags and were released one by one as the balloon drifted inland. Some made it across the Mississippi River as far as the suburbs of Detroit.

A Canadian military intelligence officer called the bombs "fiendishly clever but a military failure." They had the potential to damage and kill, but while the balloons were ingenious, there were two big flaws in the Japanese strategy: almost all of the fire bombs were launched during the Pacific Coast's rainy season, and the chance of one of the explosive bombs landing on anything other than a tree or a mountain were quite slim. Their one great symbolic coup, hitting the power line leading to a reactor that made plutonium for the Nagasaki bomb, was covered up by U.S. press censorship. While news of the balloon bombs spread by word of mouth, they inspired more curiosity than fear. Their single lethal attack was a public-relations disaster to the Japanese: a woman and five school-aged children were killed in an explosion when they explored the site of a downed balloon during a Sunday school picnic near Lakeland, Oregon, in May 1945.

The first wave of balloon bombs arrived in the fall of 1944. Early in the campaign, military and censorship authorities knew very little about them and the natural reaction was to stifle coverage. Journalists, like the general public, were left to speculate. Some Canadian newspapers got away with printing theories the balloons might carry biological weapons, but the censors cracked down on anything that discussed their numbers or flight paths. On November 13, 1944, the censors cut part of a *Vancouver Province* story saying only about one out of every forty balloons launched from Japan reached the coast of North America. A picture of one of the balloons drifting over Vancouver Island was allowed to run in the *Province*, but the caption was altered to remove the location. A Canadian Press story submitted to the Vancouver censors that evening was edited to remove a line saying six balloon bombs had made it to the Canadian Prairies.

A second wave of balloon bombs was launched by Japanese schoolchildren in early 1945. On January 5, 1945, Colonel B.R. Mullaly, head of operational intelligence at Pacific Command, contacted Graham to advise the censor that the United States had imposed a complete blackout on the bombs. Any news about them had to be approved by the U.S. press censors or the War Department. Mullaly asked his Canadian colleagues to follow the U.S. policy.

Canadian newspapers were fairly co-operative. The *Regina Leader-Post*'s editor did not quibble when Vancouver censor John Graham told him to spike a story about a balloon bomb landing south of Regina, near the U.S. border. Eyewitnesses told a *Leader-Post* correspondent the balloon was as high as a two-storey house and drifted along at treetop level. The bombs had dropped but had not exploded. Graham promised the *Leader-Post* first crack at the story once it was released and gave the information to military intelligence.

Canadian journalists followed the lead of their U.S. counterparts, who wrote in vague terms about the balloon bombs and datelined their stories "Somewhere West of the Mississippi." This embargo on locations and specific details held until the first week of June 1945.

Graham had expected weekly newspapers to sit on the balloon story, so he had not sent copies of his letters to them. George Murray who, with his wife "Ma" Murray, ran a newspaper in Fort St. John, in northwestern British Columbia, saw the balloon bombs as an opportunity. When one of the Japanese balloons drifted across the town and landed in northern Alberta, Murray sold stories on the sighting to several Canadian daily newspapers. Graham had to contact Murray's customers to kill the story and told Murray to check with him before sending out any more balloon bomb news. At the same time, a task force of military and forestry officials was established to create a workable province-wide balloon-detection organization. Since this type of news was interesting to small-town papers in B.C. forestry towns, the censors imposed a blackout on this group.

On April 3, Hal Slaight, the managing editor of the *Vancouver Sun*, demanded the censors end the blackout of balloon bomb stories. They were common knowledge in the province, Slaight said, especially among forest rangers and members of the militia. School-teachers in Vancouver warned their students about them. Censorship wouldn't keep the Japanese from learning about the damage done by the bombs: the Germans knew of the carnage the V-rockets had caused in the United Kingdom and Western Europe, despite the British government's news blackout on the attacks. The difference, replied Graham, was the Nazis' ability to send aerial reconnaissance flights over v1 and v2 target areas. The Japanese had no planes near B.C. If the newspapers printed stories about the balloon bombs, any Japanese agent in North America would get "the very information he was seeking." Graham concealed another reason for the news blackout: Canadian authorities knew the balloons carried explosive and incendiary bombs, but they still had not ruled out bacteriological warfare. Some of the bombs held a strange container that had no obvious purpose and might, intelligence officers believed, carry germs.

The week that Slaight and Graham argued about censorship, balloon bombs were landing all over western North America: one near Puyallup, Washington; two in rural Montana; and one in northern California. One bomb blew up at Pine Lake, Alberta, without causing any harm.

On April 23, Graham called Baldwin to report B.C. security officials' concerns over a current *Tim Tyler's Luck* syndicated U.S. comic strip, which had begun a series about Japanese balloons and carried the suggestion of bacteriological warfare. In "Man Eating Enemies," the intrepid Tim Tyler and his pals in a U.S. submarine see a balloon flying low over the water. The crew finds that the balloon has "Jap markings on it" and is "something like the balloons reported recently in the States." The balloon does not carry bombs, just a box containing something that looks like seeds. Home-front defence writers, knowing how many balloon bomb stories had been spiked, were shocked but saw this as an opportunity. Gordon Root, military reporter at the *Vancouver*

Province, called Gordon to ask for censorship's opinion on the strip. Root argued his paper should be allowed to print its large collection of suppressed balloon bomb stories since the comic strip gave them the defence of prepublication.

Very soon afterwards, Graham fielded complaints about the popular comic strip from senior military intelligence officers in Vancouver, who were also on the phone to Department of National Defence headquarters in Ottawa. The strip was distributed by the U.S.-based King Features syndication service, so Graham suggested Canadian censorship officials talk to their colleagues in Washington about having the rest of the storyline suppressed. Baldwin accepted this advice and sent a teletype to the U.S. censorship headquarters in Washington, which eventually effected storyline changes in the comic strip.

Soon after, balloon bomb censorship waned on both sides of the border. Radio commentator Walter Winchell broke the story of the Lakeland, Oregon, fatalities, leaving out details about the balloons and saying the children had been killed by "enemy action." On May 7, the Associated Press moved a story on the tragedy with an eyewitness account from Archie Mitchell, pastor of the Christian Alliance Church in Lakeview, the only living person who saw the explosion. The Canadian censors allowed the story into Canada but then tried to screw the censorship lid back on.

On May 22, 1945, the U.S. press censor released a short statement on the balloon bombs, allowing the press to print the basic details. The Toronto and Vancouver newspapers tried to use the American release as a lever on Canadian censors to allow the publication of balloon bomb stories. The *Toronto Star* was sitting on a stack of exclusive stories and pictures from across Western Canada, but Perry told the *Star* to stick with the U.S. press release carried on the Canadian Press news wire. Graham believed the balloon bombs were one of Canada's best-kept secrets. "Security people here are very disturbed. They feel, now the lid has been removed, it is going to be very hard to keep the situation under control. In addition, I think that the U.S. Censorship could quite easily have given us a few days advance notice on their decision to take the lid off, so we could have had a chance to fix a firm policy." Graham believed the news release was probably sparked by Winchell's broadcast. Canadian censors relented in early May. Stories about the civil- and air-defence measures taken to prevent bomb damage were allowed, but details of specific landings were still under the ban. Later, after the Washington censors put out a warning against reporting the shooting down of the balloons, the Canadian censors followed suit.

The confusion continued for another day as the censors, senior military officers in Ottawa, and West Coast reporters jockeyed to determine how much information on the balloon bombs could be released. Canadian Press and the *Vancouver Sun* believed they were free to describe the technology of the balloons. Graham and many of the military officers he contacted at National Defence Headquarters objected, believing news stories might give the Japanese the information they needed to fine-tune the ineffective balloons and their bombs. The balloons had been a worthless weapon due to their high loss rate over the ocean and, the damp climate of the West Coast, and because many of their bombs were duds.

On May 24, Baldwin received a call from Colonel Richard Malone, director of public information (army), saying National Defence was preparing a further official release on Japanese balloons which, when finally vetted in Ottawa and Washington, would likely be issued by the end of the month. The DND in Ottawa wanted the Canadian public to know more about the balloons so they could spot them and tell the difference between the bombs and weather balloons. The Americans held up the release of information for nearly a week while one faction in the U.S. army's press-relations department tried to shelve it. (Later, the censors speculated the Americans weren't trying to suppress the balloon bomb story, they just wanted U.S. journalists to have it first.) Still, Canadian censors released descriptions of the first balloon found in Montana on the basis of prior publication, as well as general references to aerial patrols and to organization of spotters, including the fact that occasional balloons were shot down, though with no time or location given.

The censors still buried details about the heights aircraft flew to shoot down the balloons, speculation about germ warfare, and anything about the time and location of balloon landings. The Canadians noted U.S. censors suppressed several facts the Japanese surely knew, namely that the balloons supposedly carried Japanese writing denouncing the U.S. air raids on Tokyo; that they had no steering apparatus; and that some bombs exploded when they hit the ground while others seemed to have timers. The censors also shelved stories of shoot-downs by U.S. fighters and speculation the balloons were launched from submarines.

Finally, on May 30, 1945, U.S. censors allowed the Associated Press to move a story revealing most of the balloons' secrets. The Canadian censors felt their U.S. colleagues had double-crossed Malone and the Canadian army's public-affairs department. The Vancouver papers jumped on the story and pressed censors for clearance to use some of their balloon pictures to illustrate the piece. The Canadians received permission, along with photographs from the army, which ran despite mild protest from the Americans. Some restrictions did remain: nothing could be published about the time or place of balloon sightings or groundings, the damage or casualties they caused, or counter-measures taken against them, nor was speculation permitted on disease or chemical warfare possibilities they posed.

The *Toronto Star* broke that embargo on May 31 by publishing a story saying a total of 190 balloons had been seen over B.C. and that at least one balloon carried a jelly that might contain germs. When the censors complained, the *Star* dropped those details from its later editions. The *Star*'s chief rival, the *Telegram*, scalped the story and carried the "190 balloon" detail, which was, Graham said, "the very information the Japs are looking for—the number of balloons reaching North America." Censors nixed stories that showed the balloons had crossed the Rockies, including pictures and text about a balloon that drifted in plain sight over Moose Jaw, Saskatchewan, in late June, but the *Lethbridge Herald* did publish a story on how the bombs worked.

Despite all these leaks, the Canadian and U.S. news blackout of the balloon bomb campaign is one of the few proven successes of the censorship system. In 1948, Brigadier General W.H. Wilbur, the wartime chief of staff of the U.S. West Coast Command, went to Japan to meet some of his old adversaries. Major General Sueyoshi Kusaba, who ran the balloon bomb campaign, was willing to talk to Wilbur. Kusaba told the American general that Tokyo had pulled the plug because Emperor Hirohito's generals believed few of the balloons were reaching North America. The Japanese High Command thought the newspapers of the U.S. and Canada should have been full of stories, not just the handful that Tokyo's agents had clipped.

The decision came in mid-April 1945. If the Japanese had waited a few more weeks, the forests would have dried out and the balloon bombs might have caused fires that did some serious damage.

By then, the Axis was on the ropes. The Germans were a few weeks away from complete collapse and, in secret labs, Allied scientists were putting the finishing touches on the weapon that would end the war against Japan. Arguably, the development of the atomic bomb was the biggest secret held by any of the belligerents of World War Two. Senior Canadian press censors were kept informed of the Manhattan Project, at least in a general way, by Leslie Thompson, an official of the Department of Munitions and Supply. Thompson was sometimes called upon to examine news stories to determine if there was leakage of important information on atomic research. He also vetted some of the coverage of the mining industry, looking for stories about uranium. Deputy Radio Censor Charles Shearer warned Canada's radio stations in January 1943 against mentioning the arrival of European scientists in Canada. This ruling was passed on to the press by Bert Perry, the Toronto press censor, on January 8. Yet it did not prevent stories on nuclear research from finding their way into the newspapers.

One notable breach of Manhattan Project secrecy occurred in April 1944. Dr. Joshua Haldimand, a Regina chiropractor, took the podium of the national Social Credit Party convention at Toronto's Royal York Hotel and spilled the entire story of the work on the atomic bomb to a crowd of about seven hundred people. Haldimand had picked up his very accurate facts from some of his patients who were working on the Eldorado uranium mine in northern

Saskatchewan. A physics buff, Haldimand had correlated the information from his chatty patients with studies he had read in U.S. science and technical journals. Amazingly, the *Toronto Star* and *Toronto Telegram* missed the implications of Haldimand's speech. The first inkling of trouble came when a reporter from the *Regina Leader-Post* called the Toronto censorship office asking for clearance of his story on Haldimand's speech. Perry called the *Star* and the *Telegram* and warned the papers to kill any mention of atomic research. Worried that a reporter for a weekly paper or a Social Credit publication might write a story, Perry tracked down Haldimand at the convention and asked him to make an announcement to the gathering warning delegates and reporters against spreading the information.

In mid-November 1944, the Montreal *Gazette* carried a story quoting Dr. F. Cyril James, the principal of McGill University, saying a cyclotron and radiation laboratory was being built at the school. Dr. James discussed the recent experiments in "atom smashing" and, according to Baldwin, "the story pin-pointed developments in Canada and to some extent indicated progress in one of the most secret of war projects. To make it worse, Dr. James mentioned the project undertaken by the Massachusetts Institute of Technology, a project which has been under a very strict veil of secrecy." Baldwin asked the Montreal censor, Eddie McMahon, to try to remove the story from later editions of the *Gazette*. McMahon found the Canadian Press had picked up most of the story, though it missed the MIT angle.

Enemy agents seeking information about Canadian participation in atomic development would have been wise to turn their attention to the business pages. There, a drama was being played out between the shareholders of the Eldorado Mining and Refining Company uranium mine and the Canadian government. The shareholders believed the government's expropriation of their property was illegal, or, at the very least, the government had paid too little for their mine. On April 30, 1944, the Associated Press wire carried a story about the U.S. State Department's refusal to come to the aid of the U.S. shareholders of Eldorado. The story described Eldorado as a "radium mine" and said the Canadian government had expropriated it "in order to use the mine for war purposes." The censors could not axe the story, since it had come from the States and was likely being carried in many of that country's newspapers. However, censorship authorities had already issued two directives about reporting on El-dorado, forbidding discussion of the mine's product.

Gil Purcell, general manager of the Canadian Press wire service, claims that one of the censors, likely Bert Perry or Warren Baldwin, tipped him off in late 1944 to the existence of the Manhattan Project. On July 10, 1945, Baldwin met with Purcell, Bert Buckland of the *Toronto Telegram*, and Ken Edey of the *Toronto Star* to explain to them why they should tread carefully in their coverage of the government-directed investigation into the Eldorado nationaliza-tion issue that had opened in Toronto that day. The investigation's hearings were closed to the press and public, but government offi-cials feared the U.S. shareholders who were angry with the terms of the expropriation might take their complaints to the press. Baldwin assured the journalists the government was not afraid of the polit-ical aspects of the dispute. It did, however, want suppression of all discussion of the potential uses of Eldorado's interesting product.

Another set of news stories gave snippets of information about Canadian participation in nuclear research. In 1944, the censors ordered a blackout of information on the expropriation of land at Chalk River and the development of Canada's first large nuclear re-actor. In August 1944, the *Ottawa Citizen* learned of the expropria-tion and speculated the land was to be used by Canadian Industries Limited for a munitions plant. Censor Jacques Girouard contacted the Parliamentary Press Gallery and warned its members not to make any mention of mysterious work at Chalk River.

Censorship of news that might have tipped the Axis to the exist-ence of the atomic bomb was crucial. The construction of the bomb relied on a huge secret industrial complex that was vulnerable to sabotage. Canada's journalists sat on the secret of the atomic bomb, the greatest technical secret of the war. When the secrets of the bomb were betrayed to Stalin's Russia, the treason was committed by scientists, not the press.

CHAPTER 11

Censorship and the Zombies

CANADA'S DECLARATION OF WAR against Germany in 1939 had been a political decision, carefully staged and crafted by a prime minister who wanted to make a statement to his country and the world that Canada was an independent power. Mackenzie King knew the major military decisions would be made in Whitehall, but he still created a cabinet war council. But the generals had their own agenda. Canada had gone into the war with a small, poorly equipped army, a skeleton of an air force, and a navy that could barely mount a coastal patrol. As the months went on, power shifted from the politicians to generals who were determined to establish a professional army complete with conscripted soldiers, separate from Canada's militia tradition, that would survive the war.

The military clique had little use for political oversight. The generals despised both the government's ineffective recruiting campaigns and King's weak *National Resources Mobilization Act* (NRMA) scheme and worked to undermine both. They were determined to build the army to such a size that the government was forced to turn to the conscripts if it was to have any hope of replacing casualties and giving leave to soldiers overseas, some of whom hadn't seen their families for five years. At the same time, the economy was white hot. For the first time in more than a decade, Canada's young men had a decent chance at well-paying jobs and were reluctant to enlist. The generals had strong support in the media, especially the Tory papers such as the *Globe and Mail*.

On June 21, 1940, the federal government began using the NRMA to draft young men into the army, force unemployed people to work in war industries, and seize property that was needed for the war effort. Soldiers drafted under the NRMA were assured they would not have to leave North America. After Pearl Harbor, NRMA soldiers were deployed to British Columbia to defend the coast against a Japanese invasion and, starting in February 1942, were sent north to guard the flank of what was believed to be the strategically vital Alaska Highway and Canol Pipeline. They had a relatively easy war. The draftees could wear the country's uniform without seriously worrying about enemy bullets. As the war dragged on and Canadian volunteers slogged through Sicily, the Italian mainland, and France, the soldiers in the regular forces developed a stronger loathing for the draftees, whom they labelled "Zombies." The public began to hate them too, and their contempt developed an ugly anti-Quebec edge because of French-Canadian opposition to conscription and, in places, to the war itself.

In a sense, the war against Japan gave Ottawa the chance to argue that the Zombies were actually real soldiers. According to Mackenzie King's calculations, a Zombie defending Vancouver was as much of a contribution to Allied victory as a U.S. soldier fighting panzers in North Africa. King's government could present Canada's people and the country's Allies with figures showing about five thousand combat and anti-aircraft soldiers working Canada's Pacific defences. In many ways, because fear of everything Japanese played into King's conscription game, the Japanese Canadians paid for King's fun with figures. NRMA draftees were among the five thousand Canadian troops sent to Kiska, in the Aleutian Islands of Alaska, in 1943 to take on the Japanese garrison that had been dispatched to the North Pacific during the Midway campaign. The Zombies were ready to fight, but Tokyo had pulled out its troops before the Canadians arrived.

Through the war, even after the 1942 referendum on conscription, the draftees clung to King's promise that they would not be sent to Europe or to the western Pacific. As the war went on, morale among the Zombies continued to sink. Many of the NRMA soldiers were draftees from Quebec who served under predominantly anglophone officers and felt discriminated against in their own country.

The ugly French–English split in the 1942 conscription campaign had radicalized many of the francophone NRMA soldiers. There were also anglophone Zombies who were equally unwilling to go overseas, mainly farm boys and unionized factory workers who believed they were needed at home. Portrayed in popular culture as cowards and shirkers, the NRMA soldiers were often taunted by teenage civilians and harassed by general service soldiers who believed their Zombie colleagues were unfit to wear the uniform. There was really nothing good about being a Zombie.

By the summer of 1944, the Canadian army was desperate for men to replace losses in Italy and northwest Europe. Normandy had become a meat grinder, with Allied casualty rates higher than those of the Germans and Russians on the Eastern Front. In July 1944, the British and Canadians were scrounging for replacement troops, feeding ill-trained infantrymen, former cooks and clerks and tradesmen into the front lines. Many of these recruits were quickly killed or wounded, became psychiatric casualties, inflicted wounds on themselves, or committed suicide. In the distance, it seemed at the time, loomed a full assault against Japan. King's government, along with the country, split on the issue of whether to use conscripts to make up for the manpower shortfall. A large block of English-Canadian politicians, especially Conservatives, wanted Canada to follow all of the other major countries involved in the war and send draftees to the fighting fronts. Most francophone political leaders, both in Quebec City and Ottawa, opposed the use of conscripts on the fighting lines. The English- and French-language presses generally mirrored the attitudes of the politicians. Each side worked the issue for its own partisan advantage.

By the crisis months of autumn 1944, NRMA soldiers' fears of conscription and deployment to the fighting theatres had already generated trouble among the West Coast conscripts, many—but, despite the common misconception at the time, not all—of whom were French Canadians. They were pitted against local civilians who despised them and general service volunteer soldiers. In mid-July 1943, about 250 draftees deserted from a base on Vancouver Island after a false rumour swept their camp that they were about to be sent overseas. Civilians on the island saw regular soldiers with Tommy guns rounding up the deserters. Islanders tipped off the *Vancouver Sun*, which was advised by the censors to spike its proposed article. On July 19, 1944, as Canadian soldiers struggled in Normandy, fighting erupted at Currie Barracks in Calgary when the draftees broke into a song, "It's Better to be a Zombie than a RS Man," during dinner in the mess hall. Regular army soldiers in the hall charged into the draftees, fists flying. Those NRMA men who could get away rushed to their huts, barricaded the doors, and armed themselves with rifles and bayonets. The regulars did likewise. Fortunately, everyone stayed where they were and no one was seriously hurt.

Media across the country jumped on anything negative about the Zombies. Two months before the November draftee protests, the *Cowichan Leader* of Duncan, British Columbia, carried an editorial about a Zombie attack on a 60-year-old man and his two soldier sons, who were in uniform. The father had to be hospitalized. The paper went on to criticize draftees in general for the trouble they caused in B.C. and for showing pride in the name Zombies (so much so that they had given the name to their camp's baseball team). Canadian Press editors considered picking up the editorial and sharing it with the agency's member newspapers, but decided at the last minute not to put it on the wire for fear of stirring up more resentment in the country.

The largest breakdown of military discipline in Canadian history occurred in November and December 1944 in British Columbia and Ontario. The British Columbia troubles, especially in Terrace (then a tiny community of four hundred people on the Skeena River, inland from Prince George), made their way into the history books, while the mass desertions in Ontario did not.

Through the summer and fall of 1944, Allied military manpower demands increased drastically, a situation that was quickly picked up by Opposition politicians who knew conscription could divide and perhaps topple the King government. Major Conn Smythe, principal owner of the Toronto Maple Leafs hockey club, had been badly wounded in Normandy. Like many other Canadian army officers, Smythe believed conscription was the only answer to the perceived manpower shortages of the units serving in France. By late August, Smythe was back in Toronto, fanning the draft debate in the city's newspapers. He was right about one thing: the replacements being sent to France were not as well trained as the men who had landed on D-Day and in the weeks afterwards. Many of them were tossed into the meat grinder and could not adapt physically and mentally. They were far more likely to be killed than their more seasoned colleagues, who, knowing the weakness of these soldiers, refused to try to form the bonds that were so important to their survival.

On October 5, 1944, George Drew, by then premier of Ontario, made a speech to the Canadian Corps Association saying there was no real shortage of reinforcements "while 80,000 men wearing the same uniform are kept here in Canada in the sixth year of the war, performing no real duty of any kind." The minister of defence, Colonel J.L. Ralston, Drew said, bore "the heaviest guilt for that situation," an allegation that stung the minister and would later be seen as ironic. Ralston, a World War One veteran and still honorary militia colonel who used the military designation, had tendered his resignation to King (who refused it) in the autumn of 1942 in response to Bill 80, which removed the geographic restriction to conscription but only if it was "necessary." In cabinet, Ralston remained the strongest proponent of conscription for overseas service.

In September and October 1944, Ralston, wanting to know if the Tories' accusations were true, was in Europe and England visiting Canadian soldiers. While there, Ralston grew more adamant than ever in his private conversations with King and members of cabinet that adequate reinforcements—which were essential to maintain units at required fighting strength—could be achieved only by drafting young men. King asked Ralston to reply publicly to Drew's attack, but Ralston told King from London that Drew was right: Canadian forces were badly overextended and many soldiers were in need of leave from the fighting. Ralston returned to Ottawa on October 18 armed with a memorandum from the army saying the manpower situation was dire. Ralston may not have realized the generals were playing their own game: there were actually enough men in England to fill the gaps, but the Allies still lacked the ports, railways, and roads in Western Europe to quickly move troops and supplies to the places they were needed and to bring tired men out of the lines.

The following day, Ralston, King, and the War Committee of cabinet held one of the most dramatic meetings in Canadian political history. Ralston shocked his colleagues with the claim that the infantry would be short fifteen thousand men by the beginning of 1945. Because of the time needed to ship these soldiers overseas, cabinet had to fix the situation immediately. The cabinet was split into two factions, one supporting the prime minister and willing to accept conscription only if Canada seriously risked losing the war, and another group, somewhat smaller, supporting Ralston and his generals.

King pondered firing Ralston and appointing newly retired general A.G.L. McNaughton, a Tory who did not hold a seat in Parliament, as minister of defence. King believed McNaughton did not prefer compulsory service. The prime minister stalled for time, knowing he already had Ralston's resignation, submitted during the dust-up two years before, in a desk drawer. King sent the ubiquitous Lieutenant General Maurice Pope to Washington to explain the situation to President Roosevelt.

King had pinned his hopes on scraping the country for volunteer soldiers still stationed in Canada—people like cooks, carpenters, and radio operators—and convincing NRMA draftees to volunteer for active service. The prime minister thought he was being realistic: some nine thousand Zombies had made the move to the regular army in the previous six months. The military, however, told the PM that the rest of the draftees were diehards who would not volunteer to go overseas. Conscription was the only reasonable solution to the shortage of front-line soldiers, the generals said.

A cabinet meeting on October 25 turned into a verbal brawl, with Prime Minister King blaming the army for the manpower problem and each minister staking out his own position. Cabinet met again the following day. The ministers talked about using cooks and truck drivers as fighting troops. They considered weakening some of Canada's tough medical rules for recruits and allowing men older than thirty-eight to enlist.

The controversy sent the prime minister into a deep bout of paranoia. He began to focus more closely on the hands of clocks, believing if they formed an upward V at the time of an event, psychic forces were working in his favour, while if they formed a downward V, the fates were against him. King came to believe the manpower shortage was part of a military plot to force him out of office after more than two decades as head of the Liberals and nearly twenty years as prime minister. In his mind, he was the target of a right-wing conspiracy that involved members of his own government, one aimed at destroying his plans for sweeping postwar social programs.

On November 1, the day after a cabinet meeting in which King mulled resigning and challenging his opponents to try to form a government, he pulled Ralston's resignation from his desk drawer and announced he was accepting it. McNaughton was given Ralston's job, along with a lecture from King that conscription for front-line fighting had to be a last resort. McNaughton agreed and recommended to King that the top generals should be fired in a shakeup of army headquarters. General Kenneth Stuart, chief of the defence staff and an architect of the crisis, was sacked but most of his colleagues, seething at the loss of Ralston and Stuart, stayed in their jobs. They did, however, hint that they might resign en masse, a threat that haunted King through the rest of the crisis.

The firing of Ralston simply added to the air of crisis. Nasty debates continued in Parliament, with the PM unsure of the support of senior members of his own cabinet. King believed McNaughton's rank and reputation would soothe the armchair conscriptionists, and that he would be able to drum up enough volunteers to avoid sending draftees into combat. He was wrong on both counts: McNaughton was booed when he spoke in Ottawa-area legion halls and the minister's pleas brought very few new overseas recruits from the NRMA ranks. Within his department, officers crunched the numbers and wrote that a minimum of sixteen thousand soldiers were needed and that, to achieve this, conscription was necessary. These were the same numbers and conclusions that had killed Ralston's career in cabinet.

By November 22, facing the resignation of six key cabinet

ministers—including finance minister J.L. Ilsley, munitions and supply minister C.D. Howe, and navy minister Angus Macdonald— King finally relented and committed his government to providing sixteen thousand conscripts from the ranks of the NRMA draftees. McNaughton had finally folded on the issue in the face of threats by the country's generals to walk away from their jobs. Quebec City– based air minister Charles "Chubby" Power, who had staked his po- litical career so many times on King's promise not to impose con- scription, quit the cabinet in protest of King's *volte-face*.

On November 23, 1944, the government announced its decision. Two days later, it introduced a bill in the House of Commons to allow the army to transfer sixteen thousand drafted soldiers to the Euro- pean theatre. The NRMA Fifteenth Infantry Brigade in British Co- lumbia, along with NRMA soldiers in southern Ontario and Valcar- tier, Quebec, were to be shipped overseas early in the new year. At the same time, the generals made it clear they weren't happy with just sixteen thousand men. Brigadier Robert MacFarlane resigned as head of Military District 10 (Manitoba, part of northwestern On- tario, and the District of Keewatin in what is now Nunavut). He is- sued a statement denouncing the government's position and de- manding unlimited conscription for overseas service.

The timing of the unrest—both by the Zombies and by the generals, and the threatened rebellion in cabinet—was terrible. In Quebec, political momentum was on the side of the anti-conscription movement: in August 1944, Maurice Duplessis had been returned to power, in part to resist this type of action by Ottawa. Quebec was embroiled in municipal elections that provided soapboxes for anti- conscription politicians. Camillien Houde, the corpulent Montreal mayor whose defiance of King in 1940 had fuelled one of the early disputes between censorship officials and the press, was out of jail and would soon be swept back into office. His re-election showed where voters' sympathies lay. Municipal governments had no power over the drafting of troops and their deployment, but that did not stop Quebec isolationists from holding mass rallies and parades against the conscription during the municipal election campaign.

Once the draftee mutinies started, the protesters were stoked by nationalists in Quebec and francophone radicals among the drafted soldiers, although most of the Zombies were English-speaking. Their anger did not come out of the blue. Any draftee who had read British Columbia's newspapers in the days leading up to the first round of anti-draft riots was bound to have some fear and bitterness. In British Columbia, like the rest of English Canada, the people and the press smelled victory on the Western Front. Like the Canadian army, they wanted to be in on the kill. The *Vancouver News-Herald* of November 20 carried a front-page, two-column headline reading, "Untrained Men Being Rushed to Line Is Claim— Cannon Fodder Say Troops." The writer claimed the army was trying to fill depleted overseas infantry ranks by taking non-commissioned officers and skilled tradesmen from British Columbia army bases to become "untrained cannon fodder," sent to Europe without proper training in weapons and battlefield tactics.

The reporter talked to carpenters, electricians, and plumbers who had been drafted and sent to camps in British Columbia. They said people running the military workshops in Canada did not want them around, especially as replacements for tradesmen fed into the fighting front. Volunteer soldiers would not work alongside them and the army cheated them out of the higher pay and the promotions to which they were entitled.

The policy of sending tradesmen overseas, many regular soldiers muttered, was a plot hatched in Quebec to have a Zombie home army left in Canada while all volunteers, no matter what their skills and training, were sent to the front. "Esprit de Corps is now a lot of hooey," one non-commissioned officer told a *Vancouver News-Herald* reporter. He said bitterly that volunteer units whose men had trained as teams in Canada were being broken up and their men fed piecemeal into the front lines. Zombies quoted in the story said they were in no better position to fight and needed many more months of weapons training before they would be ready to go overseas.

Many of the top officers of the army camps in British Columbia were at a meeting in Vancouver when radio stations began broadcasting news of the November 23 draft announcement. The next day, the first trouble broke out at Vernon, in the Okanagan Valley. According to reporters at the scene, about one thousand Zombies stationed near-by marched through the streets of the town on November 24 shouting, "Down with conscription" and "Conscript wealth and industry as well as manpower." The *Vancouver Province* reported that the draftees marched under the gaze of glaring regular army soldiers carrying machine guns. After listening to some speeches in the town park, the men went back to their barracks. One report filed by a freelancer in Vernon to the *Vancouver News-Herald* said an army captain had been punched when he ordered the marchers to disperse. The Canadian Press carried a story on the protest that moved on the wire after the Vancouver censors told CP to take out the names of the units involved.

When the disturbances grew into a mutiny and national press reaction split along linguistic lines, the government believed fighting might break out within the army itself. On the second day of the troubles, four units in Terrace refused to assemble for their daily parade. Le Premier Battalion Fusiliers du Saint-Laurent, the No. 19 Canadian Field Ambulance, the 15th Canadian Infantry Brigade, and the Prince Edward Island Highlanders, to varying degrees, mutinied against their officers. Some of the Fusiliers du Saint-Laurent broke into an armoury and took ammunition and grenades, an action that horrified regular army soldiers and many of the other draftees who feared lethal fighting would break out in the camp. The weapons were used to arm the Zombies who were stationed at blockades thrown across the roads going into the base.

By then, the troubles had spread across British Columbia. For once, the censors had a fairly good idea of what the real story was. The censors went into the 1944 conscription riots knowing the anxiety of the draftees was well founded. The first night of the protests, Major Bray of military intelligence showed Vancouver censor John Graham an order marked "SECRET" that confirmed the fears whipped up by the November 20 *News-Herald* front-page story. Fighting-age draftees working in B.C.-based anti-aircraft, signals, engineering, and trades units were to be taken out of their assignments and put into infantry units bound for Europe. Graham sent a memorandum on B.C.'s troubles and Bray's disclosure to the rest of the press censors.

The night of November 24, the telegraph censor called Graham with intercepts of two brief stories sent from Terrace to the *Prince Rupert News* and the *Vancouver Sun* describing protest marches at the local draftee camp. Gordon let the stories pass. However, army intelligence officers stationed in Terrace called the *Prince Rupert News* to say their story was wrong: there were no protests in Terrace. The newspaper knew the army was lying and printed a story, carried on the British United Press wire, saying the military had tried to censor their coverage.

The next day, a Sunday, Bray called Graham at home at 1:00 p.m. to say he was angry about "inaccuracies" in recent coverage of the conscripts' protests. For instance, Bray said, there had not been a thousand protesters at Vernon. At most, there were two hundred. And there had been no regular army troops brandishing machine guns, the intelligence officer insisted. Shows of force were to be used only as a last resort. Bray wanted the censors to straighten out the newspapers, but Graham said it was not his job to correct errors. He suggested Bray talk to the army's public-relations department. As well, Graham wanted to know about the army's meddling in coverage of the Terrace protest. Bray said he had spoken to his men in Terrace and warned them not to do it again.

Meanwhile, several hundred Zombies stationed in Chilliwack in the Fraser Valley took to the streets Saturday night, tried to burn an officer's car, and beat two regular army soldiers, breaking one man's kneecap. They went back to their barracks after regular army troops carrying rifles were deployed in the town's streets.

Pressure began building on censors in Ottawa. The Directorate received a letter from the general staff asking that censors discuss with the military any "doubtful" stories on the Zombie troubles. Ottawa censor Jacques Girouard agreed and put up a warning on a bulletin board in the Parliamentary Press Gallery's newsroom on the third floor of the Centre Block. Telegraph censors intercepted traffic between Alan Morley, the *Vancouver News-Herald*'s parliamentary correspondent, and his editor, Ken Drury. Morley believed the crisis "looks political from an Ottawa point of view." Censor John Graham in Vancouver also believed the issue was political, not military, and that journalists should have "a pretty free hand" in covering the unrest.

On November 27, King went on the radio to plead for national unity and an end to the protests. His speech was broadcast across the country and picked up in the draftee camps, where the Zombies listened attentively. "If there is anything to which I have devoted my political life, it is to try to promote unity. My friends can desert me, they can remove confidence in me, they can withdraw the trust they have placed in my hands, but I shall never deviate from that line of policy," King told the House of Commons and the Canadian people. "Whatever may be the consequences, whether loss of prestige, loss of popularity or loss of power, I feel I am in the right, and I know that a time will come when every man will render me full justice on that score."

King did not realize his speech had done a lot to calm the situation. Instead, Ottawa settled in for a long crisis. Baldwin and Girouard met two senior military intelligence officers in Ottawa to try to brace them for the news stories that the censors knew would come out in the next few days. The censors insisted they would recommend cuts to articles only if the stories were a threat to national security. The newspapers, Baldwin said, would co-operate with censorship if the censors could prove that soldiers' lives were at stake, but they would balk at any attempts at political censorship.

The following day, readers in British Columbia and across the country learned how close the Terrace troops came to fighting a pitched battle in their camp. Draftees had tried to stop the Prince Albert Volunteers, a Saskatchewan regiment, from entraining for Halifax. The Zombies warned the Saskatchewan soldiers they had guns and ammunition. The regular army soldiers reminded the Zombies they too were armed. Gordon Root, the *Vancouver Province*'s military reporter, had gone to Terrace with General George R. Pearkes and came across a scene "as ugly as any in the history of Canada's Militia."

Pearkes, like most senior officers, blamed the media for the crisis. The public agreed with him, particularly in English Canada. King knew which way public sentiment was breaking: he saw

Wartime Information Bureau polls that found Canadians believed the newspapers sensationalized the disturbances at the conscript camps and overplayed stories on the entire issue of conscription. This gave the government, which shared the data with the
censors, something of a mandate to use the full force of the *Defence
of Canada Regulations* against any media outlet that was judged to
have reported inappropriately on the disturbances.

During the entire crisis, King was seriously afraid that Brigadier
MacFarlane's high-profile resignation and his public protest was the
beginning of a mass defection of senior members of the army, one
that would be at least as dangerous as the split in cabinet. James
Mess, the brigadier general in charge of recruiting, quit on November 29. Through December, as the Germans launched their Ardennes offensive, the prime minister expected more brass would
follow Mess out the door, but few did.

Meanwhile, the *Province*'s Root had gathered more material on
the conflict between the Zombies and the Prince Albert Volunteers.
The draftees had backed down after officers said the Prairie soldiers
were being moved to another B.C. camp, not overseas. When a Vancouver radio station broadcast the truth, that all of the B.C. troops
were likely to be sent to Europe, Zombies surrounded the troop
train and refused to let it leave. They let it go at 1:00 p.m. on November 25, after holding it overnight and for most of a day.

CBR Radio, the Vancouver CBC station, inflamed the situation
by carrying a story, which reached the army camps in the noon
news broadcast, saying the mutineers were mostly French Canadians who demanded to be returned to Quebec. The phone at Vancouver's censorship office rang all day as reporters called to vet new
details coming from the B.C. interior. In the midst of dealing with
these stories, the Vancouver censors received a call from Frank
Turner of the Canadian Press. He said he had been phoned by Brigadier W.C. Hyde of Pacific Command, who was furious about the
"inaccurate and sensational" news and radio stories, which, he said,
were fanning the flames of the mutiny. Hyde demanded reporters
at British United Press, Canadian Press, and local radio stations
submit their stories to the army before they were published. If they

did not, he would order all soldiers under his command to refuse to talk to reporters.

Turner dug in his heels. He told Brigadier Hyde he would not deal with a dual censorship. The Canadian Press would talk only to the government's press censors. Hyde's threat to impose a news blackout was not a big problem for CP, Turner said, since most officers had been uncooperative anyway. One Canadian Press reporter had asked the officer in charge at Chilliwack for information and had been told to go to hell. The Vernon and Terrace officers had not been any more pleasant.

Turner called Purcell, Canadian Press's general manager, who then phoned censorship headquarters in Ottawa and the Army Press Service at National Defence's headquarters. Purcell wired back to Turner that censorship and the army press officers were opposed to Brigadier Hyde's suggestion. Therefore, Purcell said, CP would not submit to Hyde's proposal. If any attempt was made to interfere with the Canadian Press, Purcell would publish a complete report of the army's pressure tactics.

McNaughton was warned of Hyde's demands and Purcell's threat to expose the army's attempt at censorship. King had already decided "immediate steps should be taken to censor the press; also to see that the radio did not add fuel to the flames by making additional unnecessary sensational reports which had been the case up to the present . . ." The prime minister decided to take charge of the situation. He called in Eggleston and Augustin Frigon, general manager of the CBC. When they arrived at the cabinet meeting, King told them to stop the coverage of the mutiny. The PM wrote in his diary, "I made it clear to them this was not a matter of politics, it was a matter of patriotism . . . [O]nce shots were fired and blood began to flow, no one could say where the whole condition of things would end, and we as a Government were helpless in avoiding a situation without co-operation of the press and radio." King wanted the executives of the major media brought to Ottawa at once so the situation could be explained fully to them.

Eggleston was, for a moment, willing to let the military decide what was to be censored. King opted to maintain the voluntary system. McNaughton agreed, saying he would rein in the factions in the military that wanted to take control of censorship. They decided King would handle the political side, calling in the opposition leaders to get their support for an emergency evening debate in the House of Commons.

King believed the mutiny was the greatest crisis of Canada's war effort. He wrote in his diary that he was terrified "the conscriptionist people of this country would get control of the Government and would then be for all-out conscription." Behind all of this trouble "was the desire of the financial interests to destroy our social legislation" like family allowances.

Eggleston left the cabinet meeting and phoned Graham to tell him that the crisis was causing "a great deal of concern in high official circles in Ottawa." The army, he said, blamed the press for sensationalizing stories that fuelled the anger of the draftees. Eggleston told Graham the situation was so serious that a system of compulsory censorship might be imposed upon newspapers and radio stations.

After the night sitting of Parliament, the lights stayed on late in the East Block, where the prime minister and most of his senior aides had their offices. Mackenzie King, McNaughton, and Justice Minister Louis St. Laurent met to discuss the situation at Terrace. "I have seldom seen a look of greater concern on anyone's face than that which came over St. Laurent's face as he thought of the situation as it might develop," King wrote in his diary. "The gravity of the situation was apparent the moment McNaughton told us what he had said in . . . [cabinet] might happen." McNaughton offered to call out the militia to keep the peace but warned King that most of its men were employed in munitions factories and couldn't be spared from the production lines. The supply of bullets and shells for frontline soldiers could dry up.

The next day, King was horrified by a false report that General Pearkes had sent fighter planes to fly low over the Terrace camp in a show of force. In the meantime, a new story had surfaced to add to the censorship crisis. The Canadian Press had been sent a piece written by G.A. Hunter of the *Prince Rupert News*. Mutineers at Terrace told Hunter they would stay in their camp until they received discharge papers or, at least, were publicly promised by the federal government they would not be sent overseas. They would try to remain peaceful but would violently resist anyone, including their officers, who tried to move them. "We have 4,000 men with us and all the brigade armament," a corporal who had served in Jamaica told Hunter. The soldier said the troops would attack any trains sent to pick them up. Graham shelved that story.

Back in Terrace, General Pearkes had told the *Province*'s Gordon Root that the French-Canadian units would be sent back to Quebec. Pearkes was afraid to let the news out because he did not know how the English-speaking Zombies would react. The cable censors intercepted Root's telegram to his newsroom. Graham called the *Province* to make sure the paper did not use anything from Root's message.

That day, E.R. Bertram, the assistant censor in Montreal, visited some of the leading political activists in the city and the editors of all of the French- and English-language newspapers in Montreal, Trois-Rivières, and Sherbrooke to, in his words, "appeal for calm." Bertram spelled the situation out for them in stark terms: if the media did not do their part to defuse the crisis, there would be bloodshed. The French editors, including the censors' old adversary Léopold Richer at *Le Devoir*, agreed to help. The Montreal *Gazette* was the only holdout. Its editors demanded a "very specific and written document" ordering them to tone down their coverage. Bertram went over their heads to the newspaper's publisher, John Bassett, and got a promise that the paper would fall in line.

The night Bertram sent off an upbeat memo on the co-operative Quebec press, two hundred marchers took to Old Montreal's St. James Street to protest conscription. For three days, newspapers in the city had carried ads for the rally, which was sponsored by Le Bloc Populaire, an anti-conscriptionist political party that emerged from La Ligue pour la Défense du Canada and was led by André Laurendeau. Despite Richer's pledge of co-operation, *Le Devoir* and most of the anti-conscription press had advertised the meeting. The marchers listened to a speech by nationalist politician and journalist Laurendeau, who accused francophone Liberal politicians of betraying Quebec. Then some of the younger people in the crowd smashed the windows of the offices of the Liberal newspaper *Le Canada. Le Devoir* carried a story the next day denouncing the violence and blaming teenage troublemakers in the crowd.

On November 30, the army began investigations at the seven camps in B.C. where there had been trouble. The conscripts at Terrace sent a list of their grievances to Ottawa, where senior soldiers and government officials had already decided to move them out of the province. The army had set up a public-relations unit to deal with media inquiries and Baldwin in Vancouver met editors and radio-station managers.

"Everything seemed to be sweet and pretty when suddenly, at 1:15 p.m. the *Daily Province* dropped a bomb-shell into the office," Graham wrote to Ottawa. Gordon Root, the *Province*'s military reporter, was still in Terrace and wanted to file a story on the "mutiny" (the censors replaced that word with "disturbance") to remind his readers that about two hundred armed men were still refusing to follow orders. The story said, "A form of reprisal is now spreading [in] the camp . . . and a substantial number have volunteered to go Active to escape possible Court Martial." Graham cut out the phrase about reprisals. He also ordered the wording changed "to avoid any suggestion that a bargain was being made with the recalcitrants that they would be free from penalty by going GS." Indeed, one soldier was quoted as saying that "the boys are just beginning to realize what they have been doing and it worries them. In his outfit alone, close to a hundred have gone active since Monday."

When he talked to editors at the *Province* and *Sun*, Graham asked if the military had told the newspapers to call the army to check the facts in their stories. The editors said no, but if they had, they expected they would have been ignored. In fact, the army's public-relations officers were elusive that day. Graham could not even find them to confirm Root's figure of two hundred mutineers under arms. Graham decided to warn the *Province* to cut that number from Root's story, a demand that caused Syd Scott, the editor handling the piece, to accuse Graham of indulging in political censorship. Scott said he would make an issue of the cuts. Graham told him to take the matter up with Warren Baldwin, who was in the city holding meetings with editors and publishers at the Hotel Vancouver.

Through the next week, the censors had to deal with stories from papers across Western Canada as the draftees entrained at their B.C. camps and were shipped east. On December 4, the *Toronto Star* wanted to run a story from Fort Francis, a small town in northwestern Ontario, about a three-hour brawl between 150 Zombies and a large crowd of civilians, including army, navy, and air force men returned from Europe, and military cadets from the town's high school. Six people were hurt badly enough to need medical help, while many more nursed cuts and bruises.

Meanwhile, Baldwin sat down in the Hotel Vancouver and typed a memo blaming most of the censorship problem on the military. The army, and especially Hyde, had made it nearly impossible for the newspapers and radio stations to get accurate information. Hyde had overreacted to the news coverage. Baldwin believed the B.C. reporters had, in fact, pulled their punches on "one of the most important stories of the war in British Columbia." When asked by the censors, journalists had even removed factual material that might have stirred up resentment. "We believe there is very little ground for any complaint of sensationalism," Baldwin said. The media co-operated despite, not because of, the near-unanimous hostility shown to them by military officers during the mutiny. Still, King toyed with tougher censorship, including advanced vetting of military stories, something Eggleston fought until his last day on the job.

Trouble began brewing again among the NRMA men in mid-December, when the Fusiliers du St-Laurent, now at Valcartier, Quebec, went on a five-day strike, refusing to do anything but assemble for meals. On December 16, the anti-conscription activist MLA René Chaloult told a public meeting in Loretteville, just outside Quebec City, that Canada's constitution should be amended after the war to allow Quebec to decide its own foreign policy independently of other provinces. If Quebec did not get that power, he said it should leave Confederation. While the Terrace mutiny was more violent and involved a far larger number of soldiers, King believed the second wave of trouble was a potentially graver threat to his government, given its possible consequences for national unity and the stature of the federal Liberals in Quebec.

Eggleston's resignation, tendered months before when it appeared the war was almost over, took effect New Year's Day 1945. Charpentier took over as director of censorship and Baldwin remained as chief press censor. That day, National Research Council director Dr. C.J. Mackenzie visited the Rideau Club after the Governor General's Levee. There, he ran into King. He wrote that the prime minister said he expected to be "out of a job in a few hours" because of the Zombie crisis and "a general resignation of Army officers." King was showing signs of the physical and psychological decline that dogged him in his last years in office. After the 1944 Conscription Crisis, King was no longer the brilliant, driven tactician. He was a man who clung to power because his cabinet was too afraid to shake him off.

The New Year's crisis had started among draftees who set up camp in London, Ontario, on December 29, waiting to be transferred to Halifax and on to Europe. About five hundred draftees, mostly from southwestern Ontario, got into fights in the city. On December 30, most of these men left London, fleeing down the highways and rail lines out of town. The censors had been left in the dark by military intelligence. They first heard about the original troop-movement plan from a *London Free Press* reporter. The army immediately asked for very tough censorship of all details of the trouble. It also issued a statement saying there had been no problems in London. The censors were angry at this lie, but Charpentier, lacking Eggleston's grit and political skills, republished it in a special censorship directive that was sent to every paper in the country. Within three weeks, the lie came back to haunt and embarrass the censors.

During this round of NRMA troubles, the censors had a solid legal ground for killing stories on the mass desertion of troops from the London park and from other camps across Canada. They simply needed to point to the fact that the London soldiers were part of a major troop movement, so were automatically under a news blackout. This left the *London Free Press*'s editor, Arthur Ford, in a tricky situation. Everyone in his city knew of the disorders and the AWOL soldiers, he told Charpentier. He could not put out a paper that ignored the story or print the military's ludicrous press release. The censors, however, would do nothing to help him and they also nixed a story from Valcartier about deserter draftees there. The censors called the Canadian Press and the major Ontario papers and asked that they run no stories on the London troubles.

On January 18, the *Globe and Mail* ran an editorial disclosing the desertions from London and attacking the censors. The *London Free Press*'s Ford was furious at being beaten on his own turf on a story that he had on his desk, and he blamed Charpentier. Censors allowed other papers across Canada to report on the *Globe* article. Two days later, the defence minister made a frank statement about the second mutiny.

Editors across the country complained about the untrue press release and the initial clampdown on news from London. On January 23, Baldwin, Shearer, and Girouard tried to smooth things over with the country's media with a memorandum sent to all journalists explaining the rationale of the censors during the New Year's crisis.

After publishing an angry editorial in his newspaper, John Bird, the well-respected editor of the *Winnipeg Tribune*, wrote to Baldwin on January 25, 1945, asking, "How did it happen that the Censorship Directive, on January 2, relayed a flat statement by the Department of National Defence—'In point of fact there have been no disorders.'?" Baldwin denied the editorial's claim that the censorship had been politically manipulated by General McNaughton, claiming that "our only power is to determine what is not a violation of the *Defence of Canada Regulations*." Bird believed Baldwin was playing a game of semantics. "Maybe the directorate of censorship was not playing politics," the editor wrote, "but the entire information management system of the government was holding back information that was embarrassing to King's administration."

Whatever McNaughton's role in stifling news of the Zombie discontent, his political lifespan was short. On February 5, 1945, he lost the by-election in Grey North and could not win a seat in the general election on June 11. As for the Zombies, few of them saw serious fighting. The first draftees arrived at the front lines in February 1945, less than three months before the end of the war. Eventually, only about thirteen thousand would join infantry battalions. Very few of them were killed in action.

In the last weeks of the European war, as Canadian troops fought their way through Holland and Hitler went to ground in his bunker, General Pearkes became a Progressive Conservative candidate for Parliament, hoping to represent the riding of Nanaimo. Pearkes, a Victoria Cross winner, was still smarting from the King government's decision to accept his resignation and replace him as head of Pacific Command. Pearkes blamed the Zombie riots and King's conscription policies for what he saw as the collapse of his military career. And he took a direct shot at the censorship system. "Politics had a priority over the national interest," he told Conservatives in Duncan, British Columbia, on April 15, 1945. "After a fair trial, it became obvious that the policy of asking officers to appeal repeatedly to their soldiers to volunteer for active service has been disastrous. Discipline has been ruined and the authority of officers undermined by refusal of large numbers of men to accede to their officers' requests. . . . One is tempted to ask if the censorship regulations are being applied for military purposes or as a political blanket."

The Ottawa press censors clipped a story on the speech from the next day's Montreal *Gazette* and carefully filed it away. The federal government later named the building that houses the Department of National Defence's headquarters in Ottawa after General Pearkes, who was elected in 1945, served as defence minister under John Diefenbaker, and (notoriously) played a large role in the cancellation of the Canadian-manufactured Avro Arrow aircraft.

And the army, in its own way, got its revenge. Colonel C.P. Stacey, the military's best official historian, wrote just one political biography: *A Very Double Life: The Private World of Mackenzie King*, which, when it came out in 1976, reshaped King's reputation, changing him in the public's mind from a cautious, crafty politician to a superstitious neurotic.

The 1944 Conscription Crisis was the biggest threat faced by the voluntary censorship system. The government, faced with a break-down in military discipline among draftees and the threat of mass resignations of officers who supported conscription, gave serious consideration to amending Section 16 of the *Defence of Canada Regulations* to force newspapers and radio stations to submit before publication all military information. The minister of national defence (and soldiers appointed by him), the president of the Privy Council, and the censors of publications would have been given the authority to manage the country's news. Baldwin believed the idea wouldn't work. Journalists would not submit to mandatory pre-censorship. As well, he argued, so many different people would have been able to rule on stories with no real guidance or rules.

The King government spent the war walking on eggs on the conscription issue, trying to fend off pro-conscription forces in English Canada and reassuring Quebec that conscription would not be implemented. It was Mackenzie King's good fortune that the war evolved as it did, with the European invasion occurring so late in the conflict and Germany collapsing relatively quickly. Censorship's situation in the fall of 1944 resembled that of the Liberal government, an institution that needed some luck to survive unscathed. That luck almost ran out when the situation in Europe required the quick movement of Canadian reinforcements. The Conscription Crisis that ensued shook the government and caused it to call into question its news-management system. The army quickly blamed the press for the outbreaks and attempted to institute its own censorship apparatus. The voluntary censorship system survived, partly because of the stands taken by King and Eggleston, but also because of Germany's rapid collapse after the failure of the Ardennes offensive. Had Canadian troops been required for a summer 1945 campaign or in large numbers for the Pacific war, the censorship system might well not have been able to withstand the pressures that would have been placed on it by the government and the media.

Victory Day

EGGLESTON, CONVINCED IN THE FALL OF 1944 the major fighting was over, announced he was leaving the Directorate of Censorship, with his resignation taking effect at the end of the year. Even the setbacks of the German winter offensive in Belgium and the Zombie riots did not change his plans. Elsewhere, wheels were set in motion to wind down press censorship. On September 7, 1944, Byron Price, head of the U.S. press censorship system, delivered a letter to Eggleston outlining his country's plans for dismantling censorship at the war's end. Price wanted most media censorship to end as soon as Germany fell. Postal censorship was to last slightly longer. On September 11, Eggleston replied to Price, saying Canada agreed with a quick end to press censorship. However, news from British Columbia ports would need to be censored for the duration of the war against Japan. He told Price the top people in the Canadian intelligence and security services did not support a quick end to censorship, but they probably had no choice, he wrote, since Canadian policies had to fit with whatever developed in the United States.

Price called a meeting in Washington on January 24, 1945, to discuss the future of press censorship. It was still Washington's policy, Price told the Canadians, to quickly get rid of press, wireless, and mail censorship. Negotiations and discussions among Canadian, British, and U.S. officials to draw up a plan for censorship demobil-ization continued through the spring of 1945. Ottawa censorship officials received timely updates of U.S. press censorship's draft plans. The British wanted to continue censoring the press through what was expected to be a long war against Japan, and they wanted a complete censorship of news coming out of the parts of Germany occupied by the Western Allies. Charpentier, now heading the Directorate of Censorship, believed, as late as May 4, 1945, that the British would hang on to all press censorship powers for as long as politically possible. When an official of the Wartime Information Board sent Charpentier a clipping of a *Washington Times Herald* story, dated May 2, 1945, saying an immediate relaxation of British censorship would "come with V-Day in Europe but a security check will be kept on military, naval and air news leaving Britain until Japan is defeated," Charpentier wrote on the accompanying note, "This sounds like press censorship to me."

On May 5, Charpentier received a letter, dated April 27, from Byron Price, the director of United States censorship, concerning "X Plan," the schedule for the reduction of U.S. censorship. Price warned that President Truman wanted to cut $5 million of his department's $19 million budget. This, Price said, was Truman's clear signal that the great bulk of wartime censorship was to wrap up with the German surrender.

"X-Day" was defined as the day on which an armistice with Germany was signed or occupation of Germany became substantially complete, whichever came first. At X-Day, Price wrote, the director was to instruct all divisions and stations in the U.S. censorship system that no personnel, military or civilian, could be added to the staff without express approval of the director, and that "civil service promotions [were] to be made sparingly." The day after X-Day, the U.S. press censorship system was to effectively end. Within thirty-six days, virtually all offices of radio, print media, and film censorship were to be closed, and their staff discharged.

Despite Charpentier's misgivings about the sincerity of British plans to scale back censorship with the collapse of the Nazi regime, the Canadian censors worked on a schedule that was viewed as similar to those of its Allies. On VE day, about half of the censorship directives then in force were cancelled, and two weeks later the Directorate of Censorship sent out a booklet listing the new, modified restrictions that attempted to shift the full attention of press censorship to the campaign in the Pacific.

On August 15, 1945, the day following the surrender of Japan, the prime minister announced the lifting of all censorship restrictions. The chief censor of publications sent notices to Canadian editors and broadcasters to advise them formally that all directives were cancelled and to thank them for their co-operation throughout the war. A censorship official, speaking anonymously, told the *Ottawa Journal* it would be "useless" to continue censorship with the war over, but, in reality, censorship had not been a serious government priority since May 1945, when the last German U-boats surrendered. This was a marked contrast to World War One, when the government continued to use censorship to deal with the postwar "Red Scare," and, in fact, tightened the rules just before the armistice. This time, however, no one pressed for postwar censorship. It was anathema to King, the censors were a far different breed from their World War One counterparts, and the political press in Canada would not have tolerated censorship unless the government could identify a tangible threat to Canada.

Newspapers welcomed the end of censorship and were, in the main, kind to the censors and appreciative of their work. Quebec City's *L'Événement-Journal*, which had a few rough brushes with the censors when it had published its fake letters from Hitler, carried an editorial praising the censors' tact. The *Saint John Telegraph-Journal* noted most of the censors were "trained newspapermen and it must have irked them grievously when they had to suppress news. They were men whom the newspapers respected, even if there was not in all cases complete agreement." The *Windsor Star* said the success of the censorship system could be traced to the hiring of Walter Thompson, who "laid down a pattern followed throughout the war. . . . It continued under Wilfrid Eggleston, a good newspaperman with sound judgment, and latterly under Warren Baldwin, another good newspaperman." However, the *Globe and Mail*, the English-language paper that had been most vocally opposed to the censorship system, still had no kind words, simply announcing the end of restrictions in a brief story buried on page 10.

In the late summer of 1945, a draft history of the censorship system, probably written by Baldwin and Charpentier, was completed. Its authors devoted several pages to ideas about running a censorship system during a major war. To function successfully, they argued, a censorship system needed

1. the ability to define the true line of security in any given situation.
2. the authority and ability to make independent decisions.
3. the machinery to give adequate and willing service to press and radio at any hour of the day or night.
4. the respect and trust of publishers.
5. the confidence of the government authorities, and particularly the military services.

Publishers would, the censors wrote, willingly suppress information that hampered the war effort if the censors earned the trust of "every individual publisher." That trust would be earned if publishers came to believe that the censors' rules were devised solely for the purposes of winning the war, and not to protect people in the government and the military. It was also said that supporting the censors must not place a publisher at a commercial disadvantage. Publishers who co-operated with censors should not be "scooped" by publishers who did not, but Baldwin and Charpentier had no advice on how to solve this problem, which had vexed the Canadian censors so many times during the war. There were, of course, no objective criteria to measure the value of information to an enemy and its importance to the Canadian public. "It would take a superman to define this line accurately at all times," Charpentier wrote.

By the end of 1945, the Directorate of Censorship was closed and its leadership scattered. Eggleston had been given the Order of the British Empire for his wartime work. He spent almost two years as a Parliament Hill freelancer but, in 1947, left full-time journalism to be the first director of Carleton University's journalism school. When he died in 1985, his old navy sparring partner, Lieutenant

Commander C.H. Little, gave a eulogy. Charpentier returned to Parliament Hill as head of the French-language journals section of the Senate, eventually accepting a diplomatic post as ambassador to several small former French colonies in West Africa. He returned to political journalism in the 1960s and wrote a federal politics column for Ottawa's *Le Droit* until his death in 2001 at the age of 103. Except for his stints in government service, Charpentier was a member of the Parliamentary Press Gallery for nearly eighty years, a record that is unlikely to be broken.

After his release from the Directorate of Censorship, Warren Baldwin joined the staff of the *Globe and Mail*, the newspaper that was so critical of his wartime work, and was posted to the Parliamentary Press Gallery. Oliver Mowat Biggar, once he recovered from his heart attack, did some volunteer wartime work before returning to Smart & Biggar. Maurice Pope stayed in the army until his retirement, then wrote his memoires. Of the regional censors who could be traced, Toronto's Bert Perry retired after the war and Bruce Jefferson took a position with the Nova Scotia provincial government, running its publications department until his retirement in the 1950s. Just before his death in 1970, he founded a short-lived weekly newspaper in New Brunswick. Crotchety to the last, his final journalistic act was to write a letter to the editor of the *Halifax Herald* claiming the students gunned down at Kent State in Ohio were the cause of their own misfortune. Lew Gordon retired and became a mink rancher in Langley. John Graham went to the *Vancouver Sun*.

In 1948, as part of Cold War planning, army headquarters launched its own study of censorship. The soldiers wanted to develop a system to deal effectively with information management in any future crisis. They toyed with a British contingency plan but, in the end, decided not to make plans for press censorship in wartime. If an alternative press-censorship plan exists, it appears that senior military intelligence officers and military public-affairs people have not heard of it. In the October Crisis of 1970, when Pierre Trudeau had no qualms about jailing people under the *War Measures Act* without trial and suspending other civil rights, there was no attempt to censor the media. It's an irony that Trudeau, whose name adorns the copies of the *Charter of Rights and Freedoms* that are handed out by the federal government, had seventeen journalists arrested and carted off to jail. King, in six years of war, never did that.

These days, the Canadian federal government, like most governments, has chosen to choke off news at the source and to rely on public-affairs officers to shape much of the coverage of military activities. Espionage, conspiracy, and subversion laws cover much of the rest of the censors' mandate. Still, the *War Measures Act* has been replaced with legislation that could, in times of war or insurrection, give the government the power to impose some kind of news control, and the *Charter of Rights and Freedoms* does not have the teeth to prevent the imposition of wartime censorship.

In World War Two, the Canadian government tried to control news coverage as part of an effort to prevent the country's media from being used as sources of information by the Axis powers, prevent enemy propaganda from finding its way into Canadian publications and onto the country's airwaves, and prevent the publishing of news that would ruin public morale to the point that young men would not enlist to fight. This was a daunting task, one that might have been easier if the government had simply assumed editorial control of the country's media. Instead, it instituted a voluntary, advisory censorship system, one in which journalists could choose to submit their articles for vetting by censors but were not obliged to do so. Had the Canadian media functioned as an adversarial "Fourth Estate," the federal government would not have been able to censor the press and radio with the tiny staff and meagre resources dedicated to media censorship.

While there is some evidence of political interference in censorship at several junctures during the war, the censors were, for the most part, defensive of their independence. Eggleston addressed the issue in his autobiography: "The gravest charge made against us by the press (which by and large supported us and at the end of the war praised us) was that on occasion we made political decisions, even that we were guilty of playing party politics." He insisted that "usually" the censorship authorities were "left alone by the government to make our own decisions." Still, he admitted, as "war-time civil servants," they were "responsible to the cabinet, which in turn was responsible to Parliament and the Canadian people." If "ordered to do something he regards as unwise, unethical, illegal," that civil servant has a choice. "He can try to persuade his minister that the request should not be pursued, or he can resign." Eggleston had fended off several ill-advised requests "by persuading my minister that they were unsound; and at least once I was prepared to turn in my resignation if my protest was unacceptable." It helped that the censors were men who were liberal and federalist, with political views that tended to mesh with those of official Ottawa. They also shared many of those political views with the most important journalists in the country.

Still, the censorship system could not avoid appearing arbitrary. There was no way for the authors of the *Defence of Canada Regulations* and the various directives sent out by the censors to anticipate every scenario that might arise. The censorship system was made up of a small group of men operating over wide distances at a time when long-distance telephone, the only practical way to communicate in real time, was very expensive and undependable. The staff communicated through mailed memoranda and, in times of crisis or emergency, by telegraph. There was very little opportunity for face-to-face meetings. But it took very little to rattle this system. During the crises over the Houde statement, the Drew letter, and the Terrace "mutiny," the censorship system was barely able to function effectively in the face of a hostile press. It's doubtful the system would have survived a prolonged stalemate on the Western Front that would have generated stronger demands for conscripts.

Fortunately for the censors, the press was rarely rebellious. In fact, as the war progressed, the press's submissive attitude began to distress Wilfrid Eggleston, a man given to deep philosophical thought about journalism. After the war, Eggleston wrote, "In its anxiety to cooperate to the fullest extent in the successful prosecution of the war, the press of Canada as a whole leaned backward in carrying out censorship directives and in 'suffering in silence' government policies of secrecy in military matters. While this compliance was highly commendable in some respects, there was, in my opinion a duty for the press to discharge even in wartime in criticizing and opposing any policies of secrecy which could be demonstrated to go beyond what was necessary and desirable. . . ." It is not surprising, then, that Eggleston went on to try to change journalism by developing a professional school at Carleton University for the education of reporters and editors.

Fulgence Charpentier and Warren Baldwin had advice for anyone who might someday hold the job of press censor. From the beginning, they wrote in their final report, censors and journalists needed to develop "mutual confidence and understanding." The press and radio of Canada "must feel that Censorship is being administered in a manner which, while it takes adequate account of security, is not unduly or unnecessarily restrictive, and does not worship suppression as an end rather than a means." Censorship needed to be clear of any sign of "political taint," and censors had to give advice that was seen by journalists as "honest and realistic." Governments had to avoid the temptation to listen to their military leaders and push the press around. As such, they advocated any future press censorship should be placed under a Ministry of Information that could fight the inevitable pressures from the Department of National Defence.

Was censorship worth all the trouble? Even now, more than sixty years after the end of World War Two, it is extremely difficult to determine the effectiveness of the domestic press censorship system. We have one tantalizing clue that the Japanese stopped their fire balloon campaign at the beginning of the 1945 forest-fire season because there were few stories about the balloon bombs in North American newspapers. There is even less proof that the censors succeeded in thwarting German and Vichy spying, primarily because of a lack of research on German intelligence gathering in Canada, coupled with the dispersal and destruction of German records in the mayhem of the collapse of the Third Reich. Perhaps some lucky or diligent researcher will find a cache of material in Germany, Russia, or one of the Western Allies' capitals that will shed light on this aspect of the war, even if it's just a file full of *Halifax Herald* and *Globe and Mail* clippings in the Abwehr records.

Without that information, it is still safe to assume that censorship did serve some useful purpose. The Germans knew about U-boat successes off the Canadian coast and especially in the Gulf of St. Lawrence soon after their attacks, but did not succeed in sinking any of the big Cunard Line troop transports after they left Halifax. They did not learn about the "cat," the simple, homemade device used to thwart acoustic torpedoes. As well, censorship and counter-intelligence in North America appears to have hidden the secret of the Manhattan Project—at least from the Axis, if not from the Soviets.

Domestically, the press-censorship system was fraught with problems. Perhaps these problems were inevitable in a liberal democracy where there was still media competition. The most important political newspapers in the country, the *Globe and Mail* and *Le Devoir*, came out against censorship. They both accused the federal government of using censorship for its own ends, a charge that must have stung conscientious censors such as Wilfrid Eggleston very deeply, and partly because the charge had some element of truth. The *Globe* and *Le Devoir* were the exceptions, and perhaps Eggleston and Baldwin were right to conclude censorship had the very unexpected result of making many of the country's newspapers timid and incurious.

The system failed in Quebec and in several crises in English Canada. Still, it was an improvement on World War One's nasty, politically motivated censorship system. The World War Two censors had a healthy respect for liberty, one that showed in their treatment of Tommy Shoyama and in their six-year defence of the voluntary censorship system. Their insistence on fairness and their fight for freedom of the press reflected well on them and on Canada at a time when liberty faced its greatest modern challenge.

Acknowledgments

This book would not exist without the help of the late Fulgence Charpentier, Canada's last director of censorship. He encouraged this project, and, equally important, carefully packed the voluminous records of the Directorate of Censorship in 1946 and tucked them away in Canada's National Archives. Then, in 1998, he told me about them and hinted about the best parts. At the time, he was over 100 years old.

A few—very few—of the people involved in this story were still alive when I began the project. Most of the time, I was chasing echoes, talking to people who had known Eggleston, Shoyama, Richer, and Laurendeau. As the years went by, I realized how small Canada really is, how few the degrees of separation between people. Had I enrolled at Carleton's School of Journalism as a 19-year-old undergrad, I would have known Wilfrid Eggleston. Instead, I went to Ryerson and took a course in economics from Harry Pope, the son of Lieutenant General Maurice Pope, who had been Eggleston's boss in the early war years. As a master's student at Carleton, I saw Eggleston's Order of the British Empire on display, but, of course, no one on the faculty knew the full details of his war services. Still later, I came to realize how much the founding of Carleton was linked to the cluster of bright lights attracted to Ottawa in the war years, including the people who worked in both the censorship and propaganda systems. Early in my thirty-odd years in journalism, I had crossed paths with some of the people mentioned in censorship memoranda, but I regret never having had a long conversation with

Eric Dennis and some of the other reporters and editors who had so vexed the censors and the government.

Still, I have been blessed with amazing luck since starting work on *The Fog of War*. For instance, my friend Denis Gratton at Ottawa's *Le Droit* helped arrange my first conversation with Fulgence Charpentier. Major James McKillip of the Department of National Defence's Historical Section, a lifelong friend, helped me with research and introduced me to my thesis supervisor, Dr. Jeffrey Keshen of the University of Ottawa, who read this work several times with varying degrees of frustration, especially when it was considerably longer. Professor Keshen is the author of the definitive history of Canada's World War One censorship and propaganda system. He is a skilled editor and university administrator whose patience and encouragement saved me from my own rather low tolerance for bureaucratic stupidity and frustration with mediocrity.

My good fortune continued when I found myself sitting across a National Archives desk from Dr. Roger Sarty, one of the country's foremost naval historians, at a time when I was researching the censorship of stories about U-boat attacks in the St. Lawrence. Dr. Sarty was asked to be external advisor on the thesis and contributed very productive and constructive edits to it.

Both G. Stuart Adam and Joe Scanlon of Carleton University gave me valuable insight into the personality of Wilfrid Eggleston, who had taught both of these distinguished professors when they were undergraduates. Senator Joyce Fairbairn was also helpful with insights on Eggleston, who was one of her professors at Carleton, and on Tommy Shoyama, whom she knew through her years working in Pierre Trudeau's Prime Minister's Office. Ned Franks of Queen's University also offered valuable insights on Shoyama and gave advice on the chapter of the book that deals with the Japanese-Canadian editor. Lawrence Cannon, Canada's minister of foreign affairs at the time of writing, gave me useful information on his uncle, Francis Power, who was captured at Hong Kong.

Dan Conlin at the Nova Scotia Archives found Bruce Jefferson's picture of the French monitor submarine *Surcouf*, while naval historian Pete Johnson gave me several pictures of this bizarre vessel that helped me understand how a submarine could capture St. Pierre and Miquelon. Marjorie Roberts at Smart & Biggar LLP provided a picture of Oliver Mowat Biggar and kindly directed me to material about Mr. Biggar and his firm. Sgt. Ryan T. Davidson, Department of National Defense, helped find balloon bomb pictures.

When this manuscript was a thesis, it was, in parts, greatly improved by the internal examiners at the University of Ottawa. I am especially indebted to Professor Eda Kranakis for her very positive remarks and Serge Durflinger for his editing. I'd also like to give a big thanks to Nichole St.-Onge for her kindness and friendship. Nic Clarke, a fellow Ph.D. student who is quickly emerging as one of the country's best young military historians, provided valuable help on the historiography of war correspondents and the military's Directorate of History. John Maker, another University of Ottawa doctoral student, gave me valuable insight on the Normandy campaign. Sarah Cozzi was always extremely supportive and enthusiastic.

Friends in the media were also extremely helpful. Steve Maher of the *Halifax Chronicle Herald* lent me material on the history of his newspaper and contacted the Dennis family, owners of the paper, to ask for information on Eric Dennis, the journalist who dominated coverage of the Battle of the Atlantic. Terry Guillon of the Parliamentary Press Gallery was very helpful with information on the workings of that organization and supplied me with booklets issued to press gallery members and guest journalists in the 1930s. Parliament Hill journalist E. Kaye Fulton was a constant support and worked hard to track down information on the Vancouver censors.

This project was encouraged by my wife, Marion Van de Wetering. She and our children took up the slack in our household while I was chained to the keyboard, and I appreciate their patience. Marion caught many typos in the original manuscript, giving me all the more reason to love her.

I had valuable help from Library and Archives Canada and the Library of Parliament. Staff at both institutions tracked down books and files with a level of skill and determination that was impressive.

Dr. Lloyd K. Keane of Carleton University's archive and research collection kindly helped me locate photographs and information on Wilfrid Eggleston.

At Key Porter, I'd like to thank Linda Pruessen for quarter-backing this project through the approval process and for her support and friendship. Michael Mouland, who edited this book, was always supportive and extremely helpful. Joe Zingrone, the book's copy editor, cleared up many typos that had made it past so many other sets of eyes. Any mistakes that survive are mine.

I am also very grateful to the University of Ottawa for the generous financial assistance provided to me during my years as a doctoral student.

APPENDIX A

Canadian Newspapers Banned by the Secretary of State under the *Defence of Canada Regulation 15*

The Clarion, English-language Marxist weekly published in Toronto. It was banned November 21, 1939, for its opposition to the war effort.

La Clarté, French-language weekly published in Montreal. It was banned October 4, 1939, for its opposition to the war effort.

Hlas L'Udu, Slovak-language paper, published twice weekly in Toronto. It was banned June 28, 1940, for its opposition to the war effort.

Jiskra, Czech-language weekly published in Toronto. It was banned July 31, 1940, because of its Communist Party–friendly policies and its attacks on the Allies.

Glos Pracy, Polish-language weekly published in Toronto. It was banned August 17, 1940, because of Communist Party–friendly policies. The paper was denounced to Ernest Lapointe, the federal justice minister, as disloyal by the Polish Army Veterans Association of Winnipeg on May 27, 1940.

Der Veg, Yiddish-language weekly published in Toronto. It was banned August 17, 1940, because of Communist Party–friendly policies.

Pravda, Serbian-language weekly published in Toronto. It was banned August 17, 1940, because of its Communist Party–friendly policies.

Slobodna Misao, Croatian-language paper published three times a week in Toronto. It was banned August 17, 1940, because of its pro-Nazi attitude.

Kanadsky Gudok, Russian-language paper published three times a week in Winnipeg. It was banned March 29, 1940, because of its pro-Nazi attitude.

La Voix du Peuple, French-language weekly published in Montreal. It was banned June 23, 1941, because of its Communist Party–friendly policies.

La Droite, a magazine published monthly in Quebec City. It was banned April 30, 1941, for disseminating fascist propaganda and opposing the war effort.

The Canadian Tribune, published weekly in Toronto, was suspended for three weeks, beginning with the February 28, 1941, issue, as it disseminated Communist Party–friendly propaganda and opposed the war effort.

APPENDIX B

Letter from Wilfrid Eggleston, press censor for Canada, to T.A. Stone, acting chairman, Censorship Co-ordination Committee, August 13, 1941

Ottawa, August 13 1941.
T.A. Stone, Esq., Acting Chairman,
Censorship Co-ordination Committee,
Ottawa, Canada.

Dear Mr. Stone:

Since our meeting on Monday I have been giving some thought to a couple of aspects of press censorship which were thrown up in a somewhat challenging way in the course of our discussions. As I believe there is a good deal to be gained by frank and thorough examination of our mutual problems, I hope you will bear with me while I comment as briefly as I can on these two angles.

1. I was much struck by the reference to the instructions to Nazi Intelligence Agents which are believed to have been intercepted, and the remark that practically all the information they were asked to get could be found either in the press of Canada or in *Hansard*. This may be true, and if it is, it is a highly disturbing thought, although I believe too much should not be made of the apparent implications of it. In this connection I came across what I regard as an illuminating passage in an article on press censorship which appeared in the magazine "Fortune" for June 1941. I quote three paragraphs:

"As may have been gathered by now, censorship is no fourth-grade subject. Stated at its simplest the problem is to keep from the enemy information of value. The first area of confusion centers about what is valuable. Now, all information is of value to the enemy. The population of a country, its government, the location of rivers, cities, ports, its resources, its ethnic and linguistic composition, are all of value to the enemy. These, of course, the enemy already possesses. Plants and facilities can be located from standard reference works. Naval and aircraft registers, army organization manuals, officer rosters, Congressional hearings contain 95 per cent of the material that the military considers secret, confidential, or restricted—or will when hostilities begin."

"Beyond true secrets and army and naval movements and dispositions lies endless disputed territory. Secrets may be deduced from isolated bits of apparently innocent information. (Navy's deductive classic is their cracking the dark secret of Japanese naval guns by checking the export of a special kind of steel from a small middle-western steel plant.) Disclosures of production lags may tip off the enemy to vital weaknesses. But it may also be more important that the people at home should know the weakness than that the enemy should not know. There is in all censorship a strong unconscious tendency to cut off the nose to spite the face. On technical grounds of secrecy the army, say, may show good reason to conceal the failures of a new tank, though such censorship may lead to false optimism with consequent reaction of despair. A German deputy after the last war declared before the Reichstag that military censorship had done more harm—militarily—than all the papers in Germany could have if the censorship had been lifted entirely."

"The press in a democracy is still the fourth estate; it is almost a fourth branch of government. It is not, as in Germany or the U.S.S.R., a branch of the government, but a part of our constitutional system. There is the legislative, the executive, and the judicial branch—and there is the press. It is impossible to imagine governmental processes in the U.S. without a press. Its first function is to inform, its second to criticize. Censorship is a direct threat to both functions and hence a direct threat to effective democracy. Without information there is no basis for criticism and without criticism there is, as the saying goes, tyranny."

Exactly the same problem crops up in connection with Canada's manpower. Our public census figures are, of course, accessible to the enemy, but the press has gone considerably further. For example, Grant Dexter, in the Winnipeg "Free Press," has made a careful analysis of the manpower available for the services, based on 1931 figures and on estimates of 1941 figures. This is precisely the sort of thing that an enemy agent might be expected to compile and forward. Another item of keen interest to the enemy is the state of Canada's morale, our unity or disunity on major issues, the political strength or weakness of the Government. Yet all this is published and a very strong case can be made out for continuing to publish it.

How can conscription vs. voluntary enlistment be discussed and settled by democratic means if the press is not free to inform the public? Or, how can our leaders cope with disunity if every sign of it is suppressed? They may never even hear of it.

11.   This brings me to the other challenging remark. Are the Press Censors "in the middle," i.e., between the interest of security and the interests of morale? Perhaps "in the middle" is an awkward phrasing of it, because it may suggest that we have only a detached academic interest in security which is certainly not the case. Would it not perhaps be more accurate to say that it is our duty to interpret certain phrases of the Defence of Canada Regulations, such as "information of value to the enemy"? Suppose we interpret that phrase solely from the viewpoint of security. Then, by the principles outlined above, we should have to regard vast categories of information now freely published as "information of value to the enemy," and suppress them. For example, to be thorough, we should have to urge *Hansard* be not circulated, certainly not with its wide peace-time distribution, that Munitions and Supply cease publishing informa-

tion about contracts, that the Bureau of Statistics pretty well close up its printing plant, that the Bank of Canada and others stop estimating the national income, etc.

This, of course, is the absurd extreme. The Press Censor has to "draw the line." That is really what I mean by being "in the middle." But "drawing the line" involves weighing considerations. Practically everything printed has some small theoretical value to the enemy. This value must be weighed against the value to Canada and to the war effort of allowing it to be published. In other words, the Press Censors in making any ruling must attempt to weigh security against other intangibles. Sometimes there is not the least doubt as to what ought to be done. Any value for the Canadian people of knowing when a convoy sails is completely and overwhelmingly off-set by its value to the enemy. When you come to a ruling like that of the Arvida strike, you run into a much more puzzling and complex weighing of values. On the one hand it is of comfort and value to the enemy to know about this loss of vital war material. Publicity, if sabotage is involved, may help the enemy to develop the sabotage or may enable the saboteurs to get away when they know they are suspected. Publicity may fan the controversy between the affected parties and make it more difficult to settle the dispute. But there are weighty considerations on the other side. If at the root of the dispute there was ignorance, indifference, lack of consideration, lack of adequate governmental or labour leadership, perhaps it is better, on balance, to give the episode the most thorough airing.

If Canada adopted a press censorship which in its zeal for security impaired the democratic method, cut off from the Canadian public information vital to a proper contribution to the successful prosecution of the war, the responsibility must lie on the Press Censors' shoulders. They have been given the job of interpreting the Defence of Canada Regulations in respect to press censorship. If they insist on security at all costs, they may do serious damage one way. If they are too much impressed by the importance of public enlightenment and morale, they may do irreparable damage the other way. That is what is in my mind. When I talk about Press Censors being "in the middle," press censorship would be very simple if we had to think only of security. In that case we could afford to be drastic and sweeping and hew to the line, letting the chips fall where they would.

In practice the whole thing boils down to a sensitive weighing of pluses and minuses. Our question must always be: On balance, will the publication of this item aid or impede Canada's war effort? Since we have to act quickly and under pressure and cannot possibly be in complete possession of all the relevant facts, we do not pretend that we always draw the line in exactly the right place. And wherever we draw the line those interested in security are likely to think that we went too far one way and those interested in publicity think we went too far the other way.

Pray pardon the length of this essay which got somewhat out of hand. We find it useful to analyse our problems occasionally and will appreciate any light we can get from any quarter.

Sincerely your,
(W. Eggleston)

Press Censor for Canada

APPENDIX C

Defence of Canada Regulations Relating to Press Censorship (pursuant to the *War Measures Act*)

15.(1)The Secretary of State of Canada may make provision by order for preventing or restricting the publication in Canada of matters as to which he is satisfied that the publication, or, as the case may be, the unrestricted publication thereof would or might, be prejudicial to the safety of the State or the efficient prosecution of the war, and an order under this paragraph may contain such incidental and supplementary provisions as may appear to the Secretary of State to be necessary or expedient for the purposes of the order including provisions for securing that documents, pictorial representations, photographs or cinematograph films shall, before publication, be submitted or exhibited to such authority or personas may be specified in such order.

(2) In this Regulation—

(a) the expression "cinematograph film" includes a sound track and any other article on which sounds have been recorded for the purpose of their being reproduced in connection with the exhibition of such a film;

(b) the expression "publication" means, in relation to a cinematograph film, the exhibition of the film to the public, and includes the mechanical or electrical reproduction of any sounds, in connection with the exhibition of the film as aforesaid.

16. No person shall, in any manner likely to prejudice the safety of the State or the efficient prosecution of the war, obtain, record, communicate to any other person, publish, or have in his possession any document or other record whatsoever containing, or conveying any information being, or purporting to be, information with respect to any of the following matters, that is to say:

(a) the number, description, armament, equipment, disposition, movement or condition of any of His Majesty's forces, vessels or aircraft;

(b) any operations or projected operations of any of His Majesty's forces, vessels or aircraft;

(c) any measures for the defence or fortification of any place on behalf of His Majesty;

(d) the number, description or location of any prisoners of war;

(e) munitions of war;

(f) any other matter whatsoever information as to which would or might be directly or indirectly of use to the enemy.

17. No person shall communicate or associate with any other person if he has reasonable cause to believe that such other person is engaged in assisting the enemy:

Provided that in any proceedings taken by virtue of this Regulation in respect of any particular communication or association, it shall be a defence to prove that communication or association was not prejudicial to the public safety or the safety of the State.

18. (1) Subject to any exemption for which provision may be made by order of a competent authority, no person shall, except under the authority of a written permit granted by or on behalf of a competent authority make or publish any photograph, sketch, plan or other representation—

(a) of a protected place, or of any part of or object in a protected place, or of an object, of any such description as may be specified by order of a competent authority, or

(b) of, or of any part of or object in, any area in Canada as may be specified by order of a competent authority, being an area in relation to which the restriction of photography appears to that competent authority to be expedient in the interests of the safety of the State.

(2) A competent authority may make such orders, and any person acting on behalf of a competent authority may give such special directions, as the said authority or person thinks necessary for securing that photographs, sketches, plans or other representations made under the authority of a permit granted in pursuance of paragraph (1) of this Regulation, shall not be published unless and until they have been submitted to, and approved by, such authority or person as may be specified in the order or directions, as the case

may be; and a competent authority, or any person acting on its behalf, may, if that authority or person thinks it necessary in the interests of the safety of the State so to do, retain or destroy or otherwise dispose of, anything submitted as aforesaid.

(3) For the purposes of this Regulation, "a competent authority" shall mean the Minister of Justice or the Minister of National Defence.

---

39. No person shall

(a) spread reports or make statements intended or likely to cause disaffection to His Majesty or to interfere with the success of His Majesty's forces or of the forces of any allied or associated Powers or to prejudice His Majesty's relations with foreign Powers;

(b) spread reports or make statements intended or likely to prejudice the recruiting, training, discipline, or administration of any of His Majesty's forces; or

(c) spread reports or make statements intended or likely to be prejudicial to the safety of the State or the efficient prosecution of the war.

39A. No person shall print, make, publish, issue, circulate or distribute any book, newspaper, periodical, pamphlet, picture, paper, circular, card, letter, writing, print, publication or document of any kind containing any material, report or statement

(a) intended or likely to cause disaffection to His Majesty or to interfere with the success of His Majesty's forces or of the forces of any allied or associated Powers, or to prejudice His Majesty's relations with foreign Powers;

(b) intended or likely to prejudice the recruiting, training, discipline or administration of any of His Majesty's forces; or

(c) intended or likely to be prejudicial to the safety of the State or the efficient prosecution of the war.

39B. (1) A prosecution for an offence against either Regulation 39 or 39A of these Regulations shall not be instituted except by, or with the consent of, counsel representing the Attorney-General of Canada or of the Province.

(2) It shall be a defence to any prosecution for an offence against Regulations 39 or 39A to prove that the person accused acted in good faith merely to criticize or to point out error, or defects in, the Government of Canada, or any province thereof, or in either House of Parliament of Canada or in any legislature, or in the administration of justice.

63. (1) Every person who contravenes or fails to comply with any of these Regulations, or any order, rule, by-law, or direction, made or given under any of these Regulations, shall be guilty of an offence against that Regulation.

(2) Where no specific penalty is provided, such person shall be liable on Summary Conviction to a fine not exceeding five hundred dollars, or to imprisonment for a term not exceeding twelve months, or to both fine and imprisonment; but such person may, at the election of the Attorney-General of Canada or of the Province, be prosecuted upon indictment, and if convicted shall be liable to a fine not exceeding five thousand dollars, or to imprisonment for a term not exceeding five years, or to both fine and imprisonment.

NOTES

Prelude

p. 21   The best study of Canada's World War One censorship system is Keshen, *Censorship and Propaganda during Canada's Great War*;

p. 21   Censorship planning with British at Halifax, Nanaimo: *Report of the First Meeting of the Interdepartmental Committee on Censorship*, Feb. 17, 1928, LAC RDC, Vol. 5945, File 1-A-3;

p. 21   Meetings re: censorship in August 1914, and the drawing up of rules: *Report of the Chief Censor* (WWI), LAC RDC, Vol. 5439, File 1-A-3;

p. 22   Order-in-council re: troop movement reporting: P.C. 2358, Sept. 12, 1914;

p. 22   Ban on publishing material "not in accordance with the facts": P.C. 94, Oct. 8, 1914;

p. 23   Films, plays censored: P.C. 146, Jan. 17, 1917;

p. 23   Records censored: P.C. 1241, May 21, 1918. The censors discuss their examination of catalogues and record store inventories in the *Report of the Chief Censor* (WWI), LAC RDC, Vol. 5945, File 1-A-3;

p. 23   Foreign (Central Powers) language news ban: P.C. 2381, Sept. 25, 1918;

p. 23   Post-Armistice censorship: P.C. 2786, Nov. 13, 1918;

p. 23   Papers that were punished: *Report of the Chief Censor* (WWI), LAC RDC, Vol. 5939, File 1-A-3;

p. 23   Marxist, foreign papers closed: Keshen, *Censorship and Propaganda during Canada's Great War*, xiv and 79;

p. 26   "casualty lists, etc.": *Report of the Chief Censor* (WWI), LAC RDC, Vol. 5939, File 1-A-3;

p. 27   For a discussion of Beaverbrook's and Northcliffe's roles in wartime propaganda, see Knightley, *The First Casualty*.

Chapter 1: A Good Fishing Trip Ruined: The Genesis of the World War Two Censorship System

p. 29 Thompson was fishing and did not know he was picked for chief censor: Purcell thesis, chap. 1;

p. 29 Thompson job at CNR: Keshen, *Saints, Sinners and Soldiers*, 15;

p. 30 *Globe and Mail* welcomes Thompson: "The Man for The Job," *Globe and Mail*, Sept. 8, 1936, 6;

p. 30 "friend of all newspapermen," in "Capital Pauses and All Mourn Roger Lipsett," *Globe and Mail*, Oct. 3, 1939, 11;

p. 30 Eggleston high school dropout, found by Weber: Tribute at Eggleston's death, Wilfrid Kesterton Files, Carleton University Archives, LoA-122-09;

p. 31 Eggleston background, career, recruitment for censor: Eggleston, *While I Still Remember*;

p. 32 Censors' lack of resources: *Final Report*;
Thompson's threat to Chalmers, Gibson, and Robertson: *Ottawa at War: The Grant Dexter Memoranda: 1939–1945*, 16;

p. 33 Editors became disenchanted with Thompson: Nicholls, *The Story of* CP, 252;

p. 33 King cut Thompson loose: Gibson and Robertson, *Ottawa at War: The Grant Dexter Memoranda: 1939–1945*, 33;

p. 34 Press gallery rules: Kennedy Crone, *The Press Gallery, Ottawa, 1937–1938*, 20–21;

p. 34 Eggleston found secrets a burden: Eggleston, "Press Censorship," *Queen's Quarterly*, XLIII, No. 4, 556;

p. 34 For a good analysis of the culture of Canada's political reporters in this period, see Patrick Brennan, *Reporting the Nation's Business: Press–Government Relations in the Liberal Years 1935 to 1957*;

p. 35 Dexter's memorandums are held at the Queen's University Library in Kingston, Ontario. Many of the wartime memos are reprinted in Gibson and Robertson, *Ottawa at War: The Grant Dexter Memoranda: 1939–1945*;

p. 35 Social life of Ottawa reporters: Seymour to Ure, "The Parliamentary Press Gallery," 25, and Charles Lynch, *You Can't Print That*, 129;

p 35   King took office as papers shed political funding: see Minko
        Sotiron, *From Politics to Profits: The Commercialization of
        Canadian Daily Newspapers, 1890–1920*;

p. 36   King's newspaper work: Allan Levine, *Scrum Wars: the prime min-
        isters and the media*, 126;

p. 36   King and the Ludlow Massacre: Kirk Hallahan, "W.L. Mackenzie
        King: Rockefeller's 'Other' Public Relations Counselor in
        Colorado," *Public Relations Review*, 29 (2003), 401–414;

p. 37   Bowman and King: Charles Bowman, *Ottawa Editor*, 62;

p. 38   King's relationship with Atkinson is briefly detailed in Ross
        Harkness's *Atkinson of the Star*. The prime minister detailed each
        one of his visits in his diaries, which are searchable on the Library
        and Archives Canada website at www.collectionscanada.gc.ca/
        king/index-e.html;

p. 38   King's prediction of Japanese aggression in the Pacific in the early
        days of December 1942 is documented in Gibson and Robertson,
        Ottawa at War: The Grant Dexter Memoranda: 1939–1945, 19;

p. 39   King relationship with the *Gazette*, including gagged clam quote:
        Levine, *Scrum Wars*, 124;

p. 39   King and McCullagh's relationship: Mackenzie King Diary Jan. 6,
        Jan. 9, and Mar. 27, 1937. See also Brian J. Young, "C. George
        McCullagh and the Leadership League," *Canadian Historical
        Review*, September 1966, 201–226. There is, as yet, no full-length
        biography of McCullagh, which speaks volumes about the oppor-
        tunities still available in Canadian media scholarship;

p. 39   King's offer of Senate seat to Atkinson: Harkness, *Atkinson of the
        Star*, 151;

p. 39   Mrs. Atkinson put wreath on King's mother's grave: King diary
        Oct. 23, 1935;

p. 39   *Star* pages at King's disposal: King Diary, Oct. 24, 1936;

p. 39   King's list of bedside phone numbers: personal observation,
        Laurier House, Dec. 2009;

p. 40   Hutchison's secret missions: Bruce Hutchison, *The Far Side of the
        Street*, 145–152;

p. 41   All of the censorship directives can be found in LAC RDC, Vol.
        5944;

p. 41 Poll results re: public attitudes to the press: Jeff Keshen, *Saints, Sinners and Soldiers*, 18;

CP meeting in Moncton: Nicholls, *The Story of* CP, 252;

"bordering on hysteria": Eggleston, *While I Still Remember*, 255;

p. 42 Eggleston's view of the censor's role: Eggleston to Ephraim Weber, Dec. 26, 1939, LAC, MG2-382, Wilfrid Eggleston Papers, Container 30, File 2;

p. 42 For a list of papers closed with *Clarion*, see Appendix A of this book;

p. 43 *Scribners*: Mackenzie King correspondence, LAC, MG 26, J3, Microfilm C-4860;

p. 43 Censorship attitudes toward the U.S. press, including the "three walled house" quote: Eggleston, *While I Still Remember*, chap. 15;

p. 43 The fight with the *Chicago Tribune*: Memorandum, Eggleston, May 30, 1940, LAC, MG 26, J3, Microfilm C-4567, under cover letter of June 11, 1940. The issue was also raised several times in the House of Commons. Not all Canadian papers joined in the campaign. On August 2, 1940, the Montreal *Gazette* ran an editorial supporting the *Tribune*, saying it agreed with a pamphlet put out by the *Tribune*'s subsidiary, the Ontario Paper Company, that the *Tribune* had been unfairly attacked and was, in fact, pro-Allies. See also Carl Wiegman, *Trees to News: A Chronicle of the Ontario Paper Company's Origin and Development*, chap. 15;

p. 43 *Globe* criticizes McCormick: "Col. McCormick's Latest," *Globe and Mail*, Oct. 8, 1942, 6;

p. 43 Change in relationship with the U.S. press after Pearl Harbor: *Final Report of the Directorate of Censorship*, and Eggleston, *While I Still Remember*, chap. 15;

p. 43 For examinations of the U.S. role in Canada's North in World War Two, see Bob Hesketh, ed., *Three Northern Wartime Projects: Alaska Highway, Northwest Staging Route, Canol*; and Kenneth Coates, ed., *The Alaska Highway: Papers of the 40th Anniversary Symposium*;

p. 43 Canadian censorship's problems with U.S. officers in the North are described in *Final Report of the Directorate of Censorship*;

p. 44   Biggar's background: *Saturday Night*, Dec. 23, 1944;

p. 46   Race issue at Sault Ste. Marie: Ruling, R.W. Baldwin and W. Eggleston, March 4, 1942, LAC RDC, Vol. 5954, File I-B-2, Composition of Army and Ruling, J. Girouard, Aug. 25, 1942, LAC RDC, Vol. 5954, File I-B-2 Composition of Army–Military;

p. 47   Newspapers used censorship as excuse to reduce quality of their journalism: Purcell, "Wartime Press Censorship in Canada," preface;

p. 47   Details of the prosecutions can be found in the *Final Report of the Directorate of Censorship*;

p. 49   Mason reprimand: memorandum, Vancouver, Aug. 18, 1941, LAC RDC, Vol. 5948, File 1-D3-10;

p. 49   Reprimand of the *Globe* for reporting Banting research: Eggleston and Charpentier to Capt. T.S. Stone, acting chairman of the Censorship Co-ordination Committee, March 5, 1941, LAC RDC, Vol. 5982, File 29;

p. 49   Cranston dispute: Eggleston to Cranston, Nov. 15, 1940, LAC RDC, Vol. 5946, File 4. Cranston to Eggleston, Nov. 12, 1940, LAC RDC, Vol. 5946, File 4;

p. 50   *The Happy Gang: Memorandum*, H.B. Jefferson, June 10, 1944, LAC RDC, Vol. 5953, File 1-A-5, Marine Miscellaneous;

p. 50   Radio censorship: Memorandum, CBC, History of the Evolution of Canadian Broadcasting Policies in respect to Political Broadcasting with some reference to the application for time on the Canadian Broadcasting Corporation National Network by the Progressive Conservative Party for the Honourable John Bracken, Ottawa, Dec. 11, 1943, Library and Archives Canada, Microfilm MG 26, J3, Microfilm C-7052 under cover letter Dec. 13, 1943;

p. 50   "CBC had no news reporters": Statements by Dr. James Thomson, general manager, and Dr. Augustin Frigon, assistant general manager, CBC, before the House of Commons Special Committee on Radio Broadcasting, June–July 1942 (CBC handout), p. 4;

p. 51   Movies, newsreels and NFB shorts: *Final Report of the Directorate of Censorship*.

Chapter 2: Censorship and Military Intelligence

p. 52 Military intelligence's analysis of the press: Draft Memorandum for submission to the Chiefs of Staff Committee, on Co-operation of the Press with the Defence Forces in the Interests of National Security, Jan. 22, 1941, In LAC RDC, Vol. 5945, File 1-A-3, Advisory Committee on Publication of Military Information;

p. 54 Charpentier on talkative naval officers: interview, Feb. 1998, published in "100-year-old journalist still writes weekly column," *Toronto Star*, March 29, 1998, E1;

p. 54 Records of the directorate's advisory committees, including those dealing with intelligence, are in LAC RDC, Vol. 5945;

p. 55 Eggleston's memo to Stone is in LAC RDC, Vol. 5945, File Advisory Committee on Intelligence and Security;

p. 56 The records of the Advisory Committee on Publication of Military Information are in LAC RDC, Vol. 5945;

p. 56 Fight over sub attack coverage: LAC RDC Minutes of the Advisory Committee on the Publication of Military Information, Oct. 21, 1943, Vol. 5945, File 1-A-3;

p. 56 Discussions about Munro's Dieppe coverage: Memo re: Directive 4A. Minutes of the Censorship Co-ordination Subcommittee Intelligence, Sept. 25, 1942, LAC RDC, Vol. 5945, File 1-A-3, Advisory Committee Intelligence and Security;

p. 56 Stone's complaint about *Winnipeg Free Press*'s German bomb damage coverage: Stone Memorandum, April 22, 1944, LAC RDC, Vol. 5982, File 2A-G (External Affairs);

p. 57 For a discussion of the activities of enemy and neutral fascist diplomats in Canada, see: Graeme Mount, *Canada's Enemies: Spies in the Peaceable Kingdom*, 66;

p. 58 Ristelhueber and his staff's activities, and the Canadian government's monitoring of Vichy diplomats: see Mount, chap. 6;

p. 59 For a discussion of the cold war between Vichy and Britain, see: Colin Smith, *England's Last War Against France: Fighting Vichy 1940–1942*;

p. 59 Background on St. Pierre: Douglas Anglin, *The Free French Invasion: The St. Pierre and Miquelon Affaire of 1941*, chap. 1;

p. 60   RCMP assessment of Vichy threat of St. Pierre: Wood to Norman Robertson, Aug. 4, 1941, Library and Archives Canada, RG25 (Records of the Department of External Affairs), Vol. 8, 836–837;

p. 60   King's reaction to External's plans: Hilliker, *Canada's Department of External Affairs: The Early Years 1909–1946* (Vol. I), 255;

p. 60   Re: the *Surcouf*: The censors' reaction to the invasion was complex. Since the censors did not know the Free French had gained control of the monitor submarine, they were reluctant to pass stories mentioning its presence on the expedition. On the night of Jan. 8, 1942, some two weeks after the seizure of the islands, they needed to "dig someone of the Navy out of bed" in Halifax or wake Brand in Ottawa, "which I [Baldwin] did not relish," to ask who owned the vessel. If it was Free French, rather than Canadian or British, the censors would let the press say anything they wanted about it. See *Memo Ottawa*, Jan. 8, 1942, LAC RDC, Vol. 5952, File: St. Pierre and Miquelon;

p. 61   Muselier seized the town: De Bournat was promoted within the Legion of Honor and awarded the Francisque medal by Pétain on Dec. 29, 1941. He was repatriated to France in March 1942 but returned to St. Pierre in 1945 in a doomed bid to run for the National Assembly. After the war, de Gaulle sent him to Madagascar to head up construction projects. Anglin, *The Free French Invasion: The St. Pierre and Miquelon Affaire of 1941*, 180;

p. 61   Sir Desmond Morton's opinion of the transmitter's use: Mount, *Canada's Enemies: Spies in the Peaceable Kingdom*, 82;

p. 61   For memos about the news coverage of the St. Pierre takeover, see LAC RDC, Vol. 5952, File: St. Pierre and Miquelon;

p. 61   Censors were blindsided by the takeover: Memo Jefferson Halifax Dec. 27–28, 1941, LAC RDC, Vol. 5952, File: St. Pierre and Miquelon;

p. 62   Girouard's fight with Brand: Memorandum, Jacques Girouard, LAC RDC, Vol. 5950, File 1-A '3' 2. *Action-Marine*. See also LAC RDC, Vol. 5962, File: Internment and Prisoners of War. For a memorandum detailing an incident with specifics and evidence, see Memorandum, Lew Gordon, July 22, 1943, LAC RDC, Vol. 5962, File: Internment-Miscellaneous;

p. 63   Francophone journalists approached for intelligence work: Memorandum June 11, 1942, LAC RDC, Vol. 5965, File: general-2;

p. 64   Censors kill story on David Niven spying: Memorandum, B.B.
         Perry, Jan. 21, 1945, LAC RDC, Vol. 5967, File: general-1;

p. 65   Censors help Zhivaynov file: Memorandum, J. Girouard, Sept. 24,
         1942, LAC RDC, Vol. 5965, File: general-1.

Chapter 3: Spy Games in the Maritimes

p. 65   Military's belief in the benefit of stories about East Coast defence:
         Memorandum, Dominion Military Operations and Planning to
         Department of Military Intelligence, June 3, 1943. National
         Defence (Canada) Historical Section file, 112 3M2 D77 (Censor-
         ship);

p 66   Spy articles in the media before von Janowski's arrest: Memo-
         randa, H.B.J. Halifax (H. Bruce Jefferson), Aug. 12 and 19, 1942,
         LAC RDC, Vol. 5961, File: Sabotage;

p. 66   For the most complete account of von Janowski's sojourn in
         Canada, see Dean Beeby, *Cargo of Lies: The True Story of a Nazi
         Double Agent in Canada*;

p. 67   Von Janowski's smooth handling of the police who arrested him
         is detailed in Douglas, Sarty, Whitby, et al., *No Higher Purpose:
         The Official Operational History of the Royal Canadian Navy in
         the Second World War, 1939–1943* (Vol. II, Part 1), 467;

p. 68   Biggar's tip-off and the early coverage are detailed in a memo by
         H.B. Jefferson, Nov. 10, 1942, LAC RDC, Vol. 5965, File: general-4.
         Other useful material on this incident can be found in LAC RDC,
         Vol. 5983 Correspondence—Memoranda—Re: Gaspé Spy Story
         10/11/42–09/08/45;

p. 68   Detroit police had spy story: Memo, R.W. Baldwin, Nov. 10, 1942,
         LAC RDC, Vol. 5965, File: general-4;

p. 69   New York State Police had spy story on news wire, Toronto
         papers knew: Memo, R.W. Baldwin, Nov. 10, 1942. LAC RDC, Vol.
         5965, File: general-4;

p. 70   Memoranda on spreading media knowledge of von Janowski's ar-
         rest: McMahon and Perry, Nov. 10, 1942, LAC RDC, Vol. 5965,
         File: general-4, and H.B. Jefferson, Nov. 10, 1942, LAC RDG, Vol.
         5965, File: general-4, McMahon, Nov. 13, 1942, LAC RDC, Vol.
         5965, File: general-4;

p. 70   *Newsweek* story: The magazine said its information came from a "high political leader in Ottawa." See Memo, R.W. Baldwin, Nov. 20, 1942, LAC RDC, Vol. 5965, File: general-4;

p. 70   British skeptical: Beeby's *Cargo of Lies'* central argument is that von Janowski conned the RCMP and that few people in on the secret, other than the Mounties, took von Janowski's supposed "turn" seriously;

p. 70   "Double cross" agents fool Germany over V2 accuracy: Beevor, *D-Day: The Battle for Normandy*, 227–228;

p. 71   Louis St. Laurent kept House of Commons debate out of the papers: Memo, R.W. Baldwin, March 17, 1943, LAC RDC, Vol. 5965, File: general-4;

p. 71   *Fredericton Gleaner* carries big von Janowski story: Memo, R.W. Baldwin, April 28, 1943, LAC RDC, Vol. 5952, File: general-4;

p. 71   Spy story leaked at Quebec police convention: Memo, McMahon, July 29, 1943, LAC RDC, Vol. 5952, File 1-A '2' 4. Marine Experiences—Marine;

p. 72   For discussion on post–VE day publication of von Janowski double-agent story, see Beeby, *Cargo of Lies*;

p. 73   Germans paid von Janowski: Hadley speculates the Germans may have trusted von Janowski until the end of the war, using information sent by his handlers in the U.K. to determine submarine deployments in the spring of 1945. See Hadley, *U-Boats Against Canada*, 289;

p. 73   For a good analysis of Operation Pastorius and the U.S. military commission trials, see Pierce O'Donnell, *In Time of War: Hitler's Terrorist Attack on America*;

p. 74   Material on Langbein primarily comes from the records of the naval intelligence debriefing of Langbein, Library and Archives Canada RG 24 83-84/167, Vol. 305 S-1487-H-1, and from Dean Beeby's *Cargo of Lies*;

p. 73   Von Janowski's payment: von Janowski file, enemy aliens' property records, Library and Archives Canada.

Chapter 4: The Silent Service: Naval War Censorship

p. 81   "upon sealed lips": Greenfield, *Battle of the St. Lawrence*, 180;

p. 81   The "Queens" were used as troop transports during the war and
        were prime targets for the U-boats, which hunted them relent-
        lessly but without success. Bryden, *Canada's Secret War*, 123,
        quotes a March 9, 1942, Canadian intercept of a message from an
        Abwehr spy in Brazil who believed he had located the *Queen
        Mary* for his handlers in Germany: "With QUEEN MARY falls
        Churchill. Therefore, good luck."

p. 82   "Old Mary–Little Mary," *Gazette* (Montreal), May 9, 1945;

p. 82   Navy tries to kill coverage of *Graf Spee*: Eggleston, *While I Still
        Remember*, 264;

p. 82   Censors blindsided: This happened, for example, in the sinking
        of the liner *Lady Drake* in early 1942. The *Lady Drake* was one of
        the ill-fated "Lady" ships of the Canadian National Steamship
        Line. Four of the five liners were sunk during the war, but one
        was refloated and converted to a hospital ship. The *Lady Drake*
        was sunk May 8, 1942, while returning from Bermuda to Halifax.
        The 260 survivors of the sinking were brought to Halifax.
        Because the liner sank slowly, only 12 people were lost in the
        attack. See Censorship Ruling, May 11, 1942, LAC DRC, Vol. 5950,
        File 2. For an interesting article on the "Lady Boats," see *Legion*
        magazine, January/February 2007;

p. 82   "if Capt. Brand had not been so mysterious": Censorship Ruling,
        May 11, 1942, LAC DRC, Vol. 5950, File 2;

p. 83   Allied attitudes toward publicity: Memorandum, Ottawa, Feb. 20,
        1943, LAC RDC, Vol. 5950, File: Action-Marine. In October 1943,
        British and U.S. naval authorities agreed to issue monthly reports
        on sinkings. See Memorandum, Ottawa, Oct. 14, 1943, LAC RDC,
        Vol. 5950, File: Action-Marine;

p. 83   Censors worried news suppression would lead to public compla-
        cency: *Final Report of the Directorate of Censorship*;

p. 84   For a description of Jefferson, see Kimber, *Sailors, Slackers and
        Blind Pigs*, 29–35. For a description of Macdonald's role in
        government during the war and his advocacy on behalf of the
        navy, see T. Stephen Henderson, *Angus L. Macdonald: A Provin-
        cial Liberal*, especially chap. 3;

p. 85   Newspaper wartime coverage, circulation in Halifax: March, *Red Line: The Chronicle-Herald and the Mail-Star*, 333;

p. 85   Jefferson believed the *Herald* deliberately provoked him: Censorship Ruling, Halifax, July 4, 1941, LAC RDC, Vol. 5948, File 1-D3-10;

p. 85   Jefferson's fight with Rankin: Censorship Ruling, Halifax, Sept. 17, 1941, and Memorandum, Ottawa, Sept. 22, 1941, LAC RDC, Vol. 5948, File 1-D3-11;

p. 86   For *Western Prince* sinking details, see C.D. Roberts, *The Life and Times of C.D. Howe*, 96–97, and censorship recommendation to charge the *Citizen*, Eggleston and Charpentier to Secretary of State P.F. Casgrain, Dec. 16, 1940, LAC DRC, Vol. 5982, File 29;

p. 87   Eggleston cut quote about Britain losing Battle of the Atlantic, let pictures of *Margaree* survivors run: Memorandum, Wilfrid Eggleston, April 29, 1941, LAC RDC, Vol. 5953, File: Marine-Miscellaneous and Censorship Ruling; B.B. Perry, Toronto, Nov. 9, 1940, LAC RDC, Vol. 5946, File: Part 4;

p. 87   Censors opposed publishing of tanker fire stories: Rulings re: *Halifax Star*, Feb. 23, 1942, and *Halifax Herald*, Feb. 24, 1942, LAC RDC, Vol. 5950, File: Action-Marine;

p. 88   Censors allowed schooner–U-boat fraternization stories: Ruling, Dec. 16, 1940, LAC RDC, Vol. 5953, File: Marine-Miscellaneous;

p. 88   Jefferson sometimes helped his friends: In a memo dated Jan. 21, 1941, Jefferson wrote about how he had helped a writer of a *Maclean's* magazine piece get favoured access to Halifax naval authorities. LAC RDC, Vol. 5953, File: Marine-Miscellaneous;

p. 88   Jefferson thwarts Fayne: Censorship Ruling, Halifax, Feb. 12, 1942, with appendices. Library and Archives Canada, RG2, Privy Council Office (Records of the Directorate of Censorship), Vol. 5950, File: Action-Marine;

p. 88   June Callwood "sob sister": LAC RDC, Vol. 5953, File: Marine-Miscellaneous;

p. 89   "bleats": Memo, H.B. Jefferson, Feb. 24, 1943, LAC RDC, Vol. 5953, File: Marine-Miscellaneous;

p. 89   Papers glad to use navy releases: Memorandum, H.B. Jefferson, Jan. 14, 1945, LAC RDC, Vol. 5953, File: Marine-Miscellaneous;

p. 89   Jefferson's opinion of *Star*, Lytle: Memorandum, Halifax, July 14, 1941, LAC RDC, Vol. 5948, File 1-D3-10;

p. 89   Dealings with Newfoundland: Memorandum, Halifax, June 16, 1941, LAC RDC, Vol. 5953, File: Marine-Miscellaneous. The August 1942 handbook can be found in LAC RDC, Vol. 5944;

p. 90   Rules about East Coast location terms: Memorandum, H.B. Jefferson, Jan. 27, 1942, LAC RDC, Vol. 5950, File: Action-Marine;

p. 90   For very detailed accounts of the submarine campaigns in the St. Lawrence, see Douglas, Sarty, Whitby, *No Higher Purpose: The Official Operational History of the Royal Canadian Navy in the Second World War, 1939–1943, Vol. II, Part 1*; Greenfield, *The Battle of the St. Lawrence: The Second World War in Canada*; and Hadley, *U-Boats Against Canada*;

p. 91   King's attitude to the first St. Lawrence U-boat foray: Mackenzie King Diary, May 12, 1942;

p. 91   Government press release and King's attitude analyzed in Douglas et al., *No Higher Purpose: The Official Operational History of the Royal Canadian Navy in the Second World War, 1939–1943, Vol. II, Part 1*, 431;

p. 92   First call for news blackout and censorship of early sinkings: Montreal (McMahon), May 12, 1942, LAC RDC, Vol. 5950, File: Action-Marine;

p. 92   Censorship of May 11–12 attacks: Memorandum, Eggleston, May 15, 1942, LAC DRC, Vol. 5950, File: Action-Marine;

p. 93   German coverage: Hadley, *U-Boats Against Canada*, 88–89;

          coffin picture killed: Ruling, Toronto (Perry), May 14, 1942, LAC RDC, Vol. 5950, File: Action-Marine;

p. 94   Brand–Eggleston dispute over coverage: Memorandum, Eggleston, May 15, 1942, LAC RDC, Vol. 5950, File: Action-Marine;

p. 95   Censorship of coverage of U-132 attacks: Memorandum, Jefferson, Halifax, July 8, 1942, LAC RDC, Vol. 5950, File: Marine-Action;

p. 95   Attack on the *Prince Edward Island*: Memorandum, Jefferson, Halifax, July 8, 1942, LAC RDC, Vol. 5950, File: Action-Marine;

p. 95   Censorship response to Roy's statement: Memorandum, Jefferson, July 10, 1942, LAC RDC, Vol. 5950, File: Action-Marine; and Memorandum, Baldwin, July 10, 1942, LAC RDC, Vol. 5950, File: Action-Marine;

p. 96   Little tried to kill stories: Memorandum, Ottawa, July 14, 1942,
         LAC RDC, Vol. 5950, File: Action-Marine;

p. 96   Jefferson tried to "fuzzy up" minister's statement: Memorandum,
         Ottawa, July 14, 1942, LAC RDC, Vol. 5950, File: Action-Marine;

p. 96   McMahon "eviscerates" Capreol story: Memorandum, Montreal,
         July 14, 1942, LAC RDC, Vol. 5950, File: Action-Marine;

p. 97   August 1942 sinkings: Douglas et al., *No Higher Purpose: The
         Official Operational History of the Royal Canadian Navy in the
         Second World War, 1939–1943, Vol. II, Part I*, 444–446;

p. 97   *Chatham* sinking: Memorandum, Ottawa, Sept. 6, 1942, LAC
         RDC, Vol. 5950, File: Action-Marine;

p. 97   Censorship of *Raccoon*, other ship losses: Memorandum,
         Montreal (McMahon), Sept. 8, 1942, LAC RDG, Vol. 5950, File:
         Action-Marine;

p. 97   Blackout of houses, reporters taken to Metis Beach but stories
         cut: Ruling, Montreal, Oct. 13, 1942, LAC RDC, Vol. 5950, File:
         Action-Marine;

p. 97   Censorship of *Caribou* sinking: Memorandum, Halifax, Oct. 15,
         1942, LAC RDC, Vol. 5950, File: Action-Marine;

p. 100   Godbout's opinion of *L'Action catholique* series: Greenfield, *The
         Battle of the St. Lawrence*, 178;

p. 100   L'Heureux's opinion: L'Heureux to Charpentier, Oct. 14, 1942,
         LAC RDC, Vol. 5972, File: *L'Action catholique*;

p. 100   Ottawa leak and German coverage: Greenfield, *The Battle of the
         St. Lawrence*, 178;

p. 101   Attempts to kill rumour of U-boat crews welcome in Quebec: See
         memo Dec. 7, 1942, LAC RDC, Vol. 5952, File: Marine;

         Trudeau heard rumour: Trudeau, *Memoirs*, 27;

p. 102   Roy and Gagnon statements, reaction: Halifax, July 23, 1942, LAC
         RDC, Vol. 5950, File: Marine-Action; Memorandum, Toronto
         (Perry), March 15, 1943, LAC RDC, Vol. 5952, File: Marine;

p. 102   1943 Wabana raid coverage: Rulings, Ottawa, Feb. 19 and 20, 1943,
         LAC RDC, Vol. 5960, File: Miscellaneous-Production;

p. 102   Possible 1943 U-boat Arctic foray: Ruling, Perry, Toronto, Aug. 17,
         1943, Library and Archives Canada RG2, Privy Council Office
         (Records of the Directorate of Censorship), Vol. 5953, File:
         Marine-Miscellaneous;

p. 103   *Le Soleil* fined for *Cornwallis* coverage: Minutes of the Advisory
Committee on Intelligence and Security meeting of Dec. 20, 1944,
LAC RDC, Vol. 5945, File 1-A-3;

p. 103   *Herald* sitting on stories: Memorandum, H.B. Jefferson, Halifax,
Jan. 4, 1945, LAC RDC, Vol. 5951, File 2-Action;

p. 104   Jefferson makes *Herald* hold *Esquimalt* sinking stories: Memorandum, H.B. Jefferson, May 5, 1945, LAC RDC, Vol. 5967, File 1-G-7;

p. 104   Jefferson predicts Halifax riot: Memorandum, H.B. Jefferson,
Sept. 10, 1944, LAC RDC, Vol. 5953, File: Marine-Miscellaneous;

p. 104   Halifax riot: Jefferson wrote a very detailed memorandum on the
Halifax Riot. It was sent to Ottawa and to the regional offices
because Jefferson believed his account was far more complete
and unbiased than the coverage in the Halifax newspapers. See
Memorandum, H.B. Jefferson, May 10, 1945, LAC RDC, Vol. 5967,
File 1-G-7;

p. 105   *Empress of Asia*: Ruling, Vancouver, LAC RDC, Vol. 5950, File:
Action-Marine. Those survivors fortunate enough to evade
capture by the Japanese at the fall of Singapore landed in Halifax
April 18 and some arrived by train in Vancouver May 8, 1942.
Vancouver press censor Lew Gordon was besieged with requests
by the local press for permission to publish interviews. Gordon
would not agree, saying stories would provide too many hints
that the lost ship was the *Empress of Asia*. These requests are in
the same Library and Archives Canada file;

p. 106   Siberian bear: Memorandum, Vancouver, March 9, 1942, LAC
RDC, Vol. 5950, File: Action-Marine;

p. 106   Estevan Point shelling: Ruling, Vancouver, July 3, 1945, LAC RDC,
Vol. 5953, File: Marine-Miscellaneous;

p. 107   Rush–Bagot: Censorship Ruling, B.B.P. (Bert Perry), Toronto,
Nov. 6, 1940, LAC RDC, Vol. 5946, File: Part 4, Press Rulings.

Chapter 5: "These Little Treacheries": Censorship and the Quebec Media

p. 109   Papers shut in World War One, *Le Devoir* and press censorship in
World War One: Keshen, *Censorship and Propaganda in Canada's
Great War*, 76–78;

p. 110   Melançon's diplomacy: Activity Report, March 1942, LAC RDC,
Vol. 5940, File: Minutes of Various Censorship Advisory Committee Meetings Vol. 1;

p. 111   Censorship in Montreal before declaration of war: Telegram, Pelletier to Thompson, Sept. 6, 1939, LAC RDC, Vol. 5974, File: *Le Devoir*1; and Memorandum re: Anti-War Participation Meeting—Montreal, Sept. 7, 1939, RDC LAC, Vol. 5974, File: *Le Devoir*1;

p. 111   Editorial: "Ottawa and Paul Gouin," *Gazette* (Montreal), Sept. 6, 1939;

p. 111   "England never fought for Quebec," editorial and reaction: The English text is from the Government Translation Office. Memorandum for Walter Thompson, esq. chief censor, Re: Editorial signed by Georges Pelletier, Sept. 16, 1939, LAC RDC, Vol. 5974, File: *Le Devoir*1;

p. 111   Federal role in Quebec election: John MacFarlane gives almost all the credit for the provincial Liberal victory in the 1939 Quebec election to Ernest Lapointe. See MacFarlane, *Ernest Lapointe and Quebec's Influence on Canadian Foreign Policy*, chap. 9;

p. 112   *Le Devoir* predicts censorship will be issue: Memorandum, Sept. 28, 1939, LAC RDC, Vol. 6968, File 2A/E-35;

p. 112   *L'Événement-Journal* reaction: Memorandum, Sept. 28, 1939, LAC RDC, Vol. 6968, File 2A/E-35;

p. 112   The "letters" from Adolf Hitler to his sister: the translations are in LAC RDC, Vol. 6968, File 2A/E-35;

p. 113   Allegations men fired to starve them into joining the army: LAC RDC, Vol. 6968, File 2A/E-35;

p. 113   *Le Devoir* re: Lindbergh: Memorandum, Montreal, Oct. 23, 1940, LAC RDC, Vol. 6968, File: 2A/E-35;

p. 114   *L'Événement-Journal* attacks Lapointe over $200 million for Britain: Censorship Memorandum, Oct. 24, 1939, LAC RDC, Vol. 6968, File 2A/E-35;

p. 115   Station manager pulled the plug: Censorship memorandum, Oct. 8, 1939, LAC RDC, Vol. 6968, File 2A/E-35;

p. 115   CBF announces it is censoring because of orders from Ottawa: Memorandum, Oct. 13, 1939, LAC RDC, Vol. 6968, File 2A/E-35;

p. 116   *Le Devoir* and French argue over press releases: De Dampierre to Thompson, Nov. 16, 1939, LAC RDC, Vol. 5974, File: *Le Devoir*1;

p. 117   Melançon discusses *Le Devoir* with Department of Justice: Melançon to MacNeill, Feb. 12, 1940, and MacNeill to Melançon, undated, LAC RDC, Vol. 5974, File: *Le Devoir*1;

p. 118   Pelletier attacks critics of *Le Devoir* in English-language press: Memorandum, Pelletier to Charpentier, July 6, 1940, LAC RDC, Vol. 5974, File: *Le Devoir*1;

p. 118   *Le Devoir* threatened with pre-censorship: Charpentier to J.W. Pickersgill, Sept. 11, 1940, LAC RDC, Vol. 5974, File: *Le Devoir*1;

p. 119   "These little treacheries": Chevalier to Eggleston, Dec. 12, 1949, LAC RDC, Vol. 5974, File: *Le Devoir*1;

p. 119   Thompson at special cabinet meeting: Malone, *Portrait of War*, 89;

p. 119   Houde's statement: *Gazette*, Aug. 3, 1941, 1;

p. 120   Censors send warning re: national unity: Nicholls, *The Story of CP*, 253. Nicholls does confuse the chronology of the Houde incident.

p. 120   Censors' conduct on Houde statement based on legal opinion: *Final Report of the Directorate of Censorship*;

p. 120   Opposition complains about the Houde statement censorship: *Hansard*, Aug. 3, 1940, 1194;

p. 121   *Gazette* explains its actions: *Gazette* (Montreal) editorial, Aug. 6, 1940;

p. 121   *Globe* criticizes Houde censorship: *Globe and Mail* editorial, Aug. 7, 1940, 6;

p. 121   *Ottawa Citizen* criticizes censors: *Ottawa Citizen* editorial, Aug. 9, 1940, 1;

p. 122   Paper allowed to run fundraising ad: LAC RDC, Minutes of the Directorate of Censorship Advisory Committee on Intelligence and Security, April 21, 1943, Vol. 5945, File 1-A-3. For another analysis of the Houde incident, see George D. Kerr, "Skirting the Minefield: Press Censorship, Politics and French Canada, 1940," *Canadian Journal of Communication*, Vol. 8, No. 2 (1982), 46–59;

p. 122   *Le Devoir* wise enough not to overstep: Charpentier to Pickersgill, Sept. 11, 1940, Mackenzie King Correspondence, Library and Archives Canada, MG 26, J3, Microfilm C-4867;

p. 122   For an analysis of Britain's sometimes hot war against Vichy, see Colin Smith, *England's Last War Against France: Fighting Vichy, 1940–1942*;

p. 123   For background on Ottawa's unique relationship with Vichy, see Paul Couture, "The Vichy–Free French Propaganda War in Quebec, 1940–1942," *Canadian Historical Association Papers*, 1978: 200–216;

p. 123   For an interesting analysis of how the Quebec nationalist elite's attitudes toward Vichy affected Pierre Trudeau, see Max Nemni and Monique Nemni (translated by William Johnson), *Young Trudeau, 1919–1944*;

p. 123   Lapointe defends Vichy in cabinet: Cabinet War Committee minutes, Sept. 17, 1940. Cited in MacFarlane, *Ernest Lapointe and Quebec's Influence on Canadian Foreign Policy*, 161;

p. 123   Papers published in Vichy circulate in Quebec: Memorandum, Eggleston and Charpentier, Nov. 7, 1940, Mackenzie King Correspondence, Library and Archives Canada, MG 26, J3, Microfilm C-4868;

p. 123   Father Gravel's speech: Memorandum, Charpentier, April 17, 1941, LAC RDC, Vol. 5979, File: *L'Action catholique*;

p. 124   Dexter's comments about Vichy: Gibson and Robertson, *Ottawa at War*, 304–305;

p. 125   Peghaire article about Vichy schools: Charpentier to Norman Robertson, undersecretary of state for external affairs, Dec. 3, 1941, Mackenzie King Correspondence, Library and Archives Canada, MG 26, J3, Microfilm C-4861;

p. 125   RCMP and censors kill Ritz-Carleton meeting: Charpentier to McMahon, LAC RDC, Vol. 5974, File: *Le Devoir*1;

p. 126   *Le Devoir* vitamin pill accusation and censor recommendation to close *Le Devoir*: Charpentier and Eggleston to Casgrain, Nov. 6, 1941, LAC RDC, Vol. 5974, File: *Le Devoir*2;

p. 126   Montreal RCMP recommends action against *Le Devoir*: Insp. C. Batch to Superintendent of the RCMP, Dec. 4, 1941, LAC RDG, Vol. 5974, File: *Le Devoir*2;

p. 126   Chevalier says *Le Devoir* pro-German: Chevalier to Charpentier and Girouard, Feb. 6, 1941, LAC RDC, Vol. 5974, File: *Le Devoir*1;

p. 127   Eggleston recommends one-week suspension: Memorandum, Chevalier, March 15, 1941, LAC RDC, Vol. 5974, File: *Le Devoir*1;

p. 127   Pelletier defends *Le Devoir*: Memorandum, May 26 and July 6, 1941, LAC RDC, Vol. 5974, File: *Le Devoir*1;

p. 128   Censors recommend *Le Devoir* be shut down: Memorandum, July 6, 1941, LAC RDC, Vol. 5974, File: *Le Devoir*1;

p. 128   *Le Devoir* accepted copy from Vichy "news service": Mount, *Canada's Enemies*, 84;

p. 128 Article advocates tuning in Vichy radio: Col. R.B. Gibson, Director of Military Operations and Intelligence, to Eggleston, Nov. 4, 1941, LAC RDC, Vol. 5974, File: *Le Devoir*1;

p. 128 *Le Devoir* would stop supporting Vichy if Canada broke relations: Pelletier to Charpentier, Dec. 1, 1941, LAC RDC, Vol. 5974, File: *Le Devoir*1;

p. 129 St. Laurent targets *L'Oeil*: Louis St. Laurent to Charpentier, June 6, 1942, LAC RDG, Vol. 5969, File 2A/O-1a;

p. 130 Livinson's complaint about *L'Oeil*: Livinson to Charpentier, April 15, 1945, LAC RDC, Vol. 5969, File 2A/O-1a;

p. 130 *Vers Demain*: Memorandum, Charpentier, May 15, 1941, LAC RDC, Vol. 5969, File 2A/V3. The paper also portrayed women's war work as the government's attempt to destroy the French-Canadian family. On May 5, Louis Even and M.J.R. Bédard, the paper's printer, were jailed for refusing to pay a $10 fine for circulating a publication that did not contain the name of its printer. (Reported in *La Presse*, May 12, 1943, 3, and *Journal de Québec*, April 12, 1943, 3.) The paper continued publishing through the war, often running anti-Semitic rants and cartoons;

p. 131 *Le Devoir* "less objectionable": The Press Censors, Confidential memo on *Le Devoir*, Feb. 11, 1942, LAC RDC, Vol. 5974, File: *Le Devoir*1;

p. 131 *Le Devoir* could be blamed for violence in Quebec: Charpentier to Louis St. Laurent, Feb. 18, 1942, LAC RDC, Vol. 5979, File: *Le Devoir*2;

p. 131 Heureux warned not to promote Vichy radio: Charpentier to *L'Action catholique*, May 6, 1942, LAC RDC, Vol. 5972, File: *L'Action catholique*;

p. 132 "Judeo-Anglo Saxon": Memorandum, Charpentier, Dec. 17, 1942, LAC RDC, Vol. 5978, File: *Le Devoir*2;

p. 132 "comfortable plutocrats": Charpentier to Duhamel, Jan. 19, 1943, LAC RDC, Vol. 5978, File: *Le Devoir*2;

p. 133 Reaction to Bourassa speech: Varcoe to Charpentier, Feb. 5, 1943, LAC RDC, Vol. 5978, File: *Le Devoir*;

p. 133 Reaction to *Le Devoir* praise of Japanese at Hong Kong: St. Laurent to Laflèche, Feb. 17, 1943, LAC RDC, Vol. 5978, File: *Le Devoir*2;

p. 133   Radio Paris quotes *Le Devoir*: Girouard to M.E. Whittal, Press
Cable Censor, Feb. 24, 1944, LAC RDC, Vol. 5978, File: *Le Devoir* 2.

Chapter 6: The Hong Kong Cover-up

p. 137   For an example of the *Globe*'s strange waffling on censorship, see
the following editorials: "Newspapers and the War," *Globe and
Mail*, Dec. 11, 1939, 6, and "Sensible Censorship Wanted," *Globe
and Mail*, Dec. 12, 1939, 6. See also political columnist J.V.
McAree's column "Press Censorship in Capable Hands," *Globe
and Mail*, Dec. 13, 1939, 6;

p. 137   Robinson was one of the first women to win a National Newspaper Award. She was fired from the *Globe* in 1941, supposedly
because of a witty comeback she made during an editorial board
meeting. McCullagh told the writers he could easily talk Franklin
Roosevelt into bringing the United States into the war, to which
Robinson answered, "On whose side?" The story was told by
Robert Fulford in "George McCullagh," *Globe and Mail*, April 15,
1998, 7. She later went on to a distinguished career as a political
writer at the *Toronto Telegram*;

p. 137   "attack on constituted authority": Memorandum, Bert Perry, Dec.
8, 1939, LAC RDC, Vol. 5968, File: *Globe and Mail*;

p. 138   The *Globe*'s attacks on censorship in the 1940 federal election can
be found in "Between Mr. King and Quebec," *Globe and Mail*, Feb.
9, 1940, 13; "Recalling a Bequest to Youth," *Globe and Mail*, Feb. 13,
1940, 13; "Radio Censorship a Joke," *Globe and Mail*, Feb. 23, 1940,
6; "Drew Holds Free Speech Threatened," *Globe and Mail*, March 1,
1940, 1; "Drew Charges Censoring Here Just Like Nazis," *Globe and
Mail*, March 2, 1940, 1; "Manion Says Censorship of Radio Talks
Carried to 'Ridiculous Heights,'" *Globe and Mail*, March 2, 1940, 4;
"Manion Calls Vote For King Liberty Peril," *Globe and Mail*, March
4, 1940, 1; "Non-Partisan Rule is Urged," *Globe and Mail*, March 4,
1940, 3; "Frank Speaker Faces Arrest," *Globe and Mail*, March 6,
1940, 3; "Climaxing Censorship Comedy," *Globe and Mail*, March
6, 1940, 13; "Curb on Speech is Embittering to Roy Brown," *Globe
and Mail*, March 12, 1940, 1. Brown ran unsuccessfully as a Liberal
in the 1943 provincial election. See *Globe and Mail*, July 22, 1943, 6;
"Distrust Spread by Opponents, Rogers Says," *Globe and Mail*,
March 12, 1940, 9; "Censorship is Attacked," *Globe and Mail*,
March 15, 1940, 10; "King Charges Trickery is Used Upon Censors,"

Globe and Mail, March 19, 1940, 1; "Drew Charges Secret Accord For Gun Order," *Globe and Mail*, March 21, 1940, 8; "Blames Defeat on Censorship," *Globe and Mail*, March 30, 1940, 5; "Press Freedom is Held Vital to Democracy," *Globe and Mail*, April 12, 1941, 5; and "Full Discussion of all Issues is Urged by Drew," *Globe and Mail*, April 21, 1941, 4;

p. 140   The RCMP investigation into Robinson and Oakley Dalgleish was exposed in the House of Commons by Conservative opposition MPs. See *Hansard*, March 12, 1942, 1539, and March 22, 1942, 1570–1571;

p. 140   For descriptions and analysis of the Battle of Hong Kong and the problems with the Canadian contingent, see Greenhous, *C Force to Hong Kong: A Canadian Tragedy*, and Vincent, *No Reason Why: The Canadian Hong Kong Tragedy—an examination*. MacArthur's *Surviving the Sword: Prisoners of the Japanese, 1942–1945*, records the vile treatment of Allied POWs taken in the Japanese rampage in the Pacific, Indonesia, and Southeast Asia. For information on the fate of Canadian POWs, see Dancocks, *In Enemy Hands: Canadian Prisoners of War, 1939–1945*. For a good overview of Duff's life, with a chapter on Duff's conduct during the Hong Kong controversy, see Williams, *Duff: A Life in the Law*;

p. 143   King works on statement re: Hong Kong on his way to Montreal: Mackenzie King Diary, Nov. 17, 1941;

p. 143   Timing of deployment: Drew letter quoting the U.S.'s Roberts report on Pearl Harbor. The Drew letter is found in LAC MG 32 C3, Vol. 166, File 17. It and other Drew correspondence can be accessed on LAC microfilm M-9040 and M-9041;

p. 144   King's reaction to the Drew letter and the cabinet meeting: Mackenzie King Diary, July 1, 1942;

p. 144   Crerar looks for vindication in raid, begins negotiating Dieppe: Dickson, *A Thoroughly Canadian General: A Biography of General H.D.G. Crerar*, 200–201;

p. 145   Details re: Duff–King relationship and conversations during the Hong Kong inquiry and subsequent controversy come from the Mackenzie King Diary and from Williams, *Duff: A Life in the Law*, chap. 16;

p. 145   The material about cable censor Murray dogging Robertson with warnings about the Japanese can be found in the Drew papers (on LAC microfilm M-9041).

p. 147   The censors' decisions in the first days of the Drew letter controversy can be found in Memorandum, Jacques Girouard, Ottawa, July 14, 1942, LAC RDC, Vol. 5960, File: Drew Letter; Memorandum, Eggleston, Ottawa, July 15, 1942; Ruling, Lew Gordon, Vancouver, July 15, 1942; Ruling, B.B. Perry, Toronto, July 16, 1942; Ruling, W. Eggleston, Ottawa, July 16, 1942, LAC RDC, Vol. 5960, File: Drew Letter;

p. 151   *Globe* editor reveals facts of Drew controversy but not the contents of the letter: "Reveal All the Facts," *Globe and Mail*, July 18, 1942, 6;

p. 151   *Vancouver Province* editorial on Drew letter: *Vancouver Province*, July 18, 1942, 8;

p. 151   Eggleston kills second Drew letter: Ruling, W. Eggleston, Ottawa, July 19, 1942, LAC RDC, Vol. 5960, File: Drew Letter;

p. 152   Cable censors had tried to disrupt communication between newspapers: Memorandum, J. Girouard, Ottawa, July 17, 1942, LAC RDC, Vol. 5960, File: Drew Letter;

p. 152   Eggleston hints to Carnegie that charges might not be laid if the letter is published: Ruling, W. Eggleston, Ottawa, July 18, 1942, LAC RDC, Vol. 5960, File: Drew Letter;

p. 153   Blair Fraser "fishing": Memorandum, E. McMahon, July 21, 1942, LAC RDC, Vol. 5960, File: Drew Letter;

p. 153   McCullagh seemed unafraid of charges: Memorandum, B.B. Perry, July 21, 1942, LAC RDC, Vol. 5960, File: Drew Letter;

p. 153   The editorials opposing the censors' decision were published under the headline "Gagging Process of Censorship Draws Protests across Canada," *Globe and Mail*, July 24, 1942, 6;

p. 154   Biggar and Eggleston meet Hill reporters: Memorandum, Eggleston, July 22, 1942, LAC RDC, Vol. 5945, File: 1-A-3, Memorandums Re: Meetings of Various Committees;

p. 155   Drew claims phone bugged: "Mail Opened, Phone Tapped, Drew Claims," *Globe and Mail*, Nov. 14, 1942, 13;

p. 155   King shocked by condition of Hong Kong vets: Mackenzie King Diary, Sept. 22, 1945;

p. 166   Drew continues to push to have his letter put on the record, draws support from vets, families, and whistle-blowers: Drew Correspondence, LAC microfilm M-9041.

Chapter 7: The Battle of Bowmanville

p. 158   Rules about reporting on POWs held in Canada: Radio Broadcasting Censorship handbook, Consolidation of Directives, April 1941, p. 13. In LAC RDC, Vol. 5942;

p. 159   For a thorough analysis of Canada's role in the shackling controversy, see Jonathan F. Vance, "Men in Manacles: The Shackling of Prisoners of War, 1942–1943," *The Journal of Military History*, 39 (July 1995), 483–504;

p. 160   Munro tells Forum crowd of killing of POWs: *Gazette* (Montreal), Sept. 5, 1942, 13 (second section, front page). Simon Fraser became the 17th Baron Lovat and 25th chief of Clan Fraser in 1933. He was commissioned in the Scots Guards in 1932, and, in the fall of 1939, joined the Lovat Scouts, a commando unit originally raised in 1899 by his father for service in the Boer War. Most of the men in the unit were gamekeepers on large estates in the United Kingdom. Lord Lovat saw action with No. 4 Commando in the Lofoten Islands off the Norwegian coast in 1941. As a lieutenant colonel, he commanded No. 4 Commando on the Dieppe raid. Lovat was awarded the Distinguished Service Order for his actions at Dieppe and promoted to brigadier soon after the raid. At the Normandy landing, Lovat commanded the 1st Special Service Brigade. He was severely wounded and evacuated to England, June 12, 1944. He served very briefly as undersecretary of state for foreign affairs after the war. Cable and press censors dissuaded Canadian Press and British United Press from carrying the quote. Munro told Canadian Press general manager Gillis Purcell on Sept. 5, 1942, that he did not remember saying Lovat killed surrendering Germans. Purcell passed that information to the censors. See Memorandums LAC RDC, Vol. 5954, Montreal (McMahon), Sept. 7 and 8, 1942;

p. 160   British High Command reacts to quote: National Defence Historical Section Folder 112.3M2 D77;

p. 161   Prisoners in Canada are shackled over objections of German POW officers: Melady, *Escape from Canada*, 63;

p. 162   Kretschmer taken to Toronto officers' club: The censors allowed an account of that party to be printed in the *Toronto Star* (Jan. 20, 1942). Perry, who had been held in miserable conditions and forced to work in a coal mine by the Germans in World War One, hoped to embarrass Kretschmer's guards, because "I have always thought that a good many of the escapes from Canadian internment camps have been accomplished through connivance with or bribery of guards, having had some experience with that as a prisoner of war in Germany. When guards are so brash as to take a prisoner of war into a public place, which is certainly not in their line of duty, my personal opinion is that they should be taught a lesson, and publication of the story should bring the desired result." See Ruling, Bert Perry, LAC RDC, Vol. 5952, Internment Miscellaneous;

p. 162   Details of the riot are from Melady, *Escape from Canada*, 62–71, and Martin, *The Battle of Bowmanville*;

p. 164   Censor places blackout on Bowmanville riot coverage, kills *Globe* coverage: Memorandum, Perry to Baldwin, Oct. 11, 1942, LAC RDC, Vol. 5983, Bowmanville Incident;

p. 165   *Star* coverage killed: Memorandum, Perry to Baldwin, Oct. 13, 1942, LAC RDC, Vol. 5983, Bowmanville Incident;

p. 165   Even after VE day, Perry opposed publication of the *Star*'s Bowmanville riot coverage. On May 9, 1945, the *Star* asked the Directorate of Censorship to rescind its news blackout. Perry examined the *Star*'s material and refused to pass it. In his ruling, he called the article "graphic and mostly inaccurate," citing its description of "violent and bloody hand-to-hand fighting between Veteran Guards and the defiant Nazi officers when an attempt was made to put shackles on the Nazis in retaliation for the shackling by the Germans of the Canadian prisoners captured at Dieppe." After a discussion with R.W. Baldwin, then chief censor of English publications, Perry reversed his decision. Censorship ruling, Toronto, May 9, 1945, Bert Perry, LAC RDC, Vol. 5952, File 4 Marine Experiences;

p. 166   King's reaction to *Time* story: Mackenzie King Diary, Oct. 22, 1942;

Government clamps down on coverage of *Time* article: Memorandum, Baldwin to Biggar, Oct. 22, 1942, LAC RDC, Vol. 5983, Bowmanville Incident;

p. 166   RCMP assigned to find author: Memorandum, Eggleston and Charpentier to Cadiz, Oct. 22, 1942;

p. 167   Perry confronts Phelan, hunts for leak, and kills coverage: Perry to Eggleston, Oct. 23, 1942, LAC RDC, Vol. 5983, Bowmanville Incident;

p. 169   Lester Pearson tried to get name of author: Memorandums, Pearson to Hull, Oct. 24, 1942; Pearson to Robertson, Oct. 22, 1942, LAC RDC, Vol. 5983, Bowmanville Incident;

p. 170   Censors consider ban of *Time*: Charpentier and Eggleston to Biggar, Oct. 24, 1942, LAC RDC, Vol. 5983, Bowmanville Incident;

p. 170   The correspondence between the censors and the *Whig-Standard* and press clippings with comments about Richardson can be found in LAC RDC, Vol. 5983, Bowmanville Incident;

p. 171   Bowmanville story sent by mail: The Bowmanville riot controversy caused the postal censors to begin watching for news copy in mails destined for Allied and neutral countries. This practice, at least as far as mail destined for Allied countries, was discontinued in the fall of 1943. See Minutes of the Advisory Committee on Intelligence and Security, Oct. 27, 1943, LAC RDC, Vol. 5945;

p. 172   Rohrbough was *Star* stringer: To add to the *Toronto Star*'s insults and injuries, the paper was asked by the *Chicago Tribune* to file 250 words on the Rohrbough arrest. Presumably, the author of that story was to have been paid for his efforts. The request was intercepted by Canadian signals intelligence agents, who sent a note to Perry. Memorandum, Perry to Eggleston, Nov. 11, 1942, LAC RDC, Vol. 5983, Bowmanville Incident;

p. 172   Details about Rohrbough and RCMP recommendation not to lay charges: F.P. Varcoe to O.M. Biggar, Nov. 9, 1942, LAC RDC, Vol. 5983, Bowmanville Incident;

p. 173   Censors did not know in advance that Rohrbough would be charged: Memorandum, Bert Perry, Nov. 12, 1942, LAC RDC, Vol. 5962, Internment-Miscellaneous;

p. 173   Rohrbough pleaded guilty: *Globe and Mail*, Nov. 26, 1942. Rohrbough continued to work as a *Toronto Star* stringer after his conviction, reporting on military matters such as events at CFB Borden and POWs. He was, in fact, one of the reporters who covered a POW breakout in Washago, Ontario, just north of Orillia, in December 1942. On Dec. 12, 1942, Perry heaped fulsome praise on Rohrbough's article "How to Find a Nazi," a detailed magazine article submitted for censorship scrutiny by the *Star Weekly*. In Perry's 600-word memorandum, there is no mention of Rohrbough's involvement in the Bowmanville coverage controversy. Ruling, Toronto (Perry), Dec. 12, 1942, LAC RDC, Vol. 5962, File: Escapes of Prisoners;

p. 174   For the Cross incident, see LAC RDC Correspondence Memorandums re: Quebec Conference, Aug. 8 to Dec. 6, 1943.

Chapter 8: Censoring News from the Front Lines

p. 178   Ralph Allen, "How Do You Cover a War?" *Globe and Mail*, Jan. 17,
1944, 4;

p. 178   For the best overview of modern war correspondents, see
Knightley's *The First Casualty*. Keshen's *Saints, Sinners and
Soldiers* has a lot of material on the impact of war coverage on
Canadian society. For a good examination of the Canadian
Press's coverage, see Nicholls, *The Story of* CP, chap. XL. Ross
Munro's adventures are recounted in *Gauntlet to Overlord*. A.E.
Powley's *Broadcasting from the Front* is a comprehensive exami-
nation of the CBC's team in Europe;

p. 179   At the time of writing, Timothy John Balizer's "The Information
Front: The Canadian Army, Public Relations, and War News
during the Second World War" (Ph.D.: University of Victoria,
2008) was still available only as a thesis. It is an outstanding piece
of scholarship for anyone interested in Canadian correspondents
during World War Two;

p.183   Reporters' filing challenges: Malone, *Missing from the Record*, 176;

For a detailed account of radio correspondents and their work, see
Powley, *Broadcasting from the Front*. Halton's use of battle sound
effects is briefly described in Keshen, *Saints, Sinners and Soldiers*, 16;

p. 183   *Toronto Star* headline claiming Caen fell on D-Day ran June 7,
1944, on page 1. The paper claimed Heinrich Himmler was dead
on the front page of its Aug. 22, 1944, edition. Rudolf Hess's
"suicide" and the supposed unsinkability of the *Prince of Wales*
were reported in the *Toronto Telegram*'s May 12, 1941, edition.

p. 184   For information on the Canadian military's official historians, see
Cook, *Clio's Warriors: Canadian Historians and the Writing of the
World Wars*;

p. 184   Soldiers in Normandy did not know about V1 attacks: Powley,
Broadcasting from the Front, 95;

p. 185   Malone's two books on his wartime service are *Missing from the
Record* and *Portrait of War*;

p. 186   Munro wrote of his Dieppe adventures in *From Gauntlet to Overlord*, chap. XIII;

p. 186   PROs annoyance at journalistic mistakes: Malone, *Missing from the Record*, 161;

p. 187   Army Film Unit crew scoops world press at D-Day: Munro, *Gauntlet to Overlord*, 80;

p. 187   Halton in Paris, misses Market Garden but files story that parrots Montgomery: Powley, *Broadcasting from the Front*, 125–128;

p. 187   Maxted in Oosterbeek: Powley, *Broadcasting from the Front*, 125–128;

p. 188   Stursberg gets captain's cabin, relieved of liquor: Powley, *Broadcasting from the Front*, 117;

p. 188   "I was committed to the war . . .": Knightley, *The First Casualty*, 319;

p. 188   "It was crap . . .": Knightley, *The First Casualty*, 332–333;

p. 188   ". . . disaccreditation, disgrace, even imprisonment": Stursberg, *The Sound of War*, 57;

p. 184   ". . . he was himself part of the show": Malone, *Missing from the Record*, 164;

p. 190   Edward Kennedy's leak re: VE day: Knightley, *The First Casualty*, 331–332.

Chapter 9: The "Jap Pulitzer": Censorship of the Japanese-Canadian Press

p. 195   Shoyama's early life, systemic discrimination: Obituary of Tommy Shoyama, *Regina Leader-Post*, Jan. 24, 2007, 3, and Adachi, *The Enemy that Never Was*;

p. 194   Background on the *New Canadian*: Adachi, *The Enemy That Never Was*, 159–169, 177, 360, and 362; and Barry Broadfoot, *Years of Sorrow, Years of Shame*, Toronto: Paperjacks, 1975, 43. One of the great failings of this book, a collection of oral histories of the evacuation and internment of the Japanese Canadians, is that its sources are not named. However, this piece could only be an interview with Shoyama. The four-page account deals mainly with his difficulties finding typesetting and printing facilities during the war;

p. 195   *Issei–Nisei* relationship: Adachi, *The Enemy That Never Was*, 160–161. Adachi discusses the ramifications of the generational differences throughout his book;

p. 195   "... be prepared to assume our burden": *New Canadian*, Sept. 4, 1939;

p. 196   Censors send out directive asking for restraint from media: Directive No. 25, LAC RDC, Vol. 5942;

p. 196   "unassimilable race" and Reid's anti-Japanese comments: *Hansard*, March 14, 1941, 1526–1537 and 1563;

p. 197   Robertson opposed oppression of Japanese Canadians: Granatstein, *A Man of Influence*, 81–82;

p. 197   Gordon's assessment of Wilson: Memorandum, Ottawa, Dec. 9, 1941, LAC RDC, Vol. 5960, File: 1-E-1, Japanese;

p. 197   Eggleston and Robertson discuss ways of dampening Wilson's remarks: Memorandum, W. Eggleston, Jan. 23, 1942, LAC RDC, Vol. 5960, File 1-E-1, Japanese;

p. 197   Censors try to dampen stories on forest fire sabotage threat: Ruling, Ottawa (Charpentier), Jan. 29, 1942, LAC RDC, Vol. 5960, File 1-E-1, Japanese;

p. 198   Censors blindsided by closure of Japanese-language dailies, say they are loyal: Memorandum, Ottawa, Dec. 9, 1941, LAC RDC, Vol. 5960, File 1-E-1, Japanese;

p. 198   Mistreatment of Canadians captured at Hong Kong suppressed: Memorandum, W. Eggleston, Ottawa, April 23, 1942, LAC RDC, Vol. 5960, File 1-E-1, Japanese. Eggleston had misgivings about the ban, which was instigated at the time of the fall of Corregidor and the subsequent Bataan Death March: "I drew to Colonel Clarke's attention, as I had to Colonel Ralston's, the difficulty of persuading Canadian editors that they should suppress items freely carried in the United States press and over U.S. radio stations. I also raised the question as to whether the general public was not entitled to know what was going on, on the other side of the world, even if this caused some incidental distress to a group of our own citizens," he wrote in this memo;

p. 199   Layse of *Vancouver Sun* stages Japanese sabotage pictures: Memorandum, Lew Gordon, Feb. 15, 1942, LAC RDC, Vol. 5960, File 1-E-1, Japanese;

p. 200   Eggleston refuses to kill stories about Japanese-Canadian opposition to expulsion to northern Ontario: Memorandum, Vancouver, March 16, 1942;

p. 200   Reid and Neill ask for crackdown: *Hansard*, March 14, 1941, 1526–1537 and 1563;

p. 201   Gordon refuses to ban stories on Powell Street fight: Memo, Gordon, May 13, 1942, LAC RDC, Vol. 5960, File 1-E-1, Japanese;

p. 201   Reaction to Dutch Harbor raid: Ruling, Lew Gordon, June 3, 1942, LAC RDC, Vol. 5960, File 1-E-1, Japanese; and Ruling, Lew Gordon, June 4, 1942, LAC RDC, Vol. 5960, File 1-E-1, Japanese;

p. 201   Vancouver courthouse explosion: The dynamite blast, at 9:40 p.m., Nov. 3, 1942, smashed several windows and broke two ornamental lions outside the building. Police believed a "crackpot" or "vandal" was responsible. The *News-Herald*'s editor also wanted to publish a rumour that the Black Dragon Society had infiltrated the B.C. Security Commission and was extorting money from Vancouver's Japanese Canadians in return for better treatment. Memorandum, J. Graham, Nov. 4, 1942, LAC RDC, Vol. 5961, File: Sabotage–Possible;

p. 203   Baldwin assessment of *New Canadian*: Memorandum, Baldwin, March 12, 1942, LAC RDC, Vol. 5976, File: *New Canadian*;

p. 204   Censor helps produce *New Canadian*: Memorandum by Lew Graham to Censorship Headquarters and Regional Offices, March 2, 1942, LAC RDC, Vol. 5965, File: General-1;

p. 204   Taylor allowed to censor *New Canadian* to remove material about opposition to internment: Memorandum by Lew Graham to Censorship Headquarters and Regional Offices, March 28, 1942, LAC RDC, Vol. 5965, File: General-1;

p. 204   "my Japanese newspaper" and the "Jap Pulitzer": Memorandum by Lew Graham to Censorship Headquarters and Regional Offices, March 12, 1942, LAC RDC, Vol. 5965, File: General-1;

p. 204   Shoyama loses office space, has other troubles in Vancouver: Memorandum by Lew Graham to Censorship Headquarters and Regional Offices, March 20, 1942, LAC RDC, Vol. 5965, File: General-1;

p. 204   "Japalac": Memorandum by Lew Graham to Censorship Headquarters and Regional Offices, April 1, 1942, LAC RDC, Vol. 5965, File: General-1;

p. 205 Eggleston convinces McLarty not to close *New Canadian*: Memorandum, Eggleston, April 23, 1942, LAC RDC, Vol. 5965, File: General-1;

p. 205 Senior bureaucrats try to mitigate Japanese-Canadian mistreatment: Ann Gomer Sunahara, *The Politics of Racism*, chap. 3;

p. 206 Gordon objects to pastor's article: Memorandum, Lew Gordon to Censorship Headquarters, Aug. 27, 1942, LAC RDC, Vol. 5965, File: General-2;

p. 207 Shoyama's wartime correspondence can be found at LAC R10881-0-7-E, *New Canadian* files;

p. 208 Translator Hennigar interferes: Memorandum, Lew Gordon to Censorship Headquarters, Jan. 5, 1943, LAC RDC, Vol. 5965, File: Miscellaneous;

p. 209 Gordon clears one poem, kills another: Memorandum, Lew Gordon, Feb. 15, 1943, LAC RDC, Vol. 5965, File: Miscellaneous;

p. 210 Reaction to bushworker story: Memorandum, Dec. 28, 1942, LAC RDC, Vol. 5965, File: Miscellaneous;

p 211 *Inu*: Adachi, *The Enemy That Never Was*, 237–238; Robertson to Eggleston, March 12, 1943, LAC RDC, Vol. 5976: *New Canadian*;

p. 211 Kaslo Japanese Canadians form committee: *New Canadian*, April 6, 1943, and memo, Gordon, April 2, 1943, LAC RDC, Vol. 5976, File: *New Canadian*;

p. 212 Graham kills criticism of navy, Kelowna racists: Memorandum, Lew Gordon to Censorship Headquarters, April 29, 1943, LAC RDC, Vol. 5965, File I-O-1, General;

p. 212 Gordon kills "Hermitage" article on Nelson Board of Trade: Memorandum, Lew Gordon to Censorship Headquarters, Nov. 20, 1943, LAC RDC, Vol. 5965, File I-O-1, General;

p. 213 Graham cuts Shoyama criticism of Kamloops: Memorandum, Vancouver Censorship Office to Censorship Directorate, Ottawa, March 31, 1944, LAC RDC, Vol. 5960, File: Japanese;

p. 213 Graham defends Shoyama against *Sun*: Memorandum, John Graham, April 12, 1944, LAC RDC, Vol. 5960, File: Japanese;

p. 214 Censors kill kid's essay: Memorandum, John Graham to Ottawa Headquarters of the Directorate of Censorship, May 22, 1944, LAC RDC, Vol. 5967, File general-1;

p. 214 Anti-Japanese rhetoric heating up: Memorandum, John Graham, April 22, 1944, LAC RDC, Vol. 5960, File: Japanese;

p. 215 "Nazi tune": Memorandum, John Graham (Vancouver) to Ottawa Headquarters of the Directorate of Censorship, June 14, 1944, LAC RDC, Vol. 5960, File: Japanese. Shoyama told interviewer Barry Broadfoot this was his "only one real awkward moment" with English-language press censors during the war. Broadfoot, *Years of Sorrow, Years of Shame*, 45;

p. 215 Graham's troubles after talking about mayor quip: Memorandum, John Graham (Vancouver) to Censorship Headquarters, Ottawa, June 28, 1944, LAC RDC, Vol. 5960, File: Japanese;

p. 216 Reference to cruelty taken out: Memorandum, John Graham (Vancouver) to Censorship Headquarters, Ottawa, June 30, 1944, LAC RDC, Vol. 5960, File: Japanese;

p. 216 Censors support Shoyama editorial attacking pro-deportation B.C. politicians: Memorandum, John Graham (Vancouver) to Censorship Headquarters, Ottawa, July 2, 1944, LAC RDC, Vol. 5960, File: Japanese;

p. 217 No trouble in fall 1944: Memorandum, John Graham, Oct. 31, 1944, LAC RDC, Vol. 5976, File: *New Canadian*;

p. 217 Censor supports Shoyama attack on Paton: Memorandum, Lew Gordon to Censorship Headquarters, Ottawa, Aug. 5, 1944, LAC RDC, Vol. 5960, File: Japanese;

p. 218 Censors push to release stories on ethnic Japanese enlistment: Memorandum, Lew Gordon to Censorship Headquarters, Ottawa, Feb. 3, 1945, LAC RDC, Vol. 5960, File: Japanese;

p. 219 Eggleston fights for Japanese Canadians in 1946: Eggleston to King, July 8, 1956. Mackenzie King Correspondence, Library and Archives Canada, MG 26, J3 Microfilm Reel C-9169;

p. 220 Details of Shoyama's later life: Obituary of Tommy Shoyama, *Globe and Mail*, Dec. 30, 2006, S.9.

Chapter 10: Balloon Bombs and Atomic Bombs

p. 222 Censors got "secrets list" and British issue "stops and releases," navy slow with information: *Final Report of the Directorate of Censorship*, Library and Archives;

p. 223   Asdic controversy: Memorandum, Eggleston, Aug. 21, 1941, LAC RDC, Vol. 5952, File 1-A-6 Marine Equipment. See also Eggleston, *While I Still Remember*, 264;

p. 224   Navy tries to get Perry fired over asdic coverage: *Final Report of the Directorate of Censorship*;

p. 224   Cat gear: Ruling, Ottawa, May 14, 1945, LAC RDC, Vol. 5960, File: Japanese;

p. 224   Habbakuk: Library and Archives Canada, Wilfrid Eggleston Papers, MG30-D282, Vol. 26, Atomic Energy Grp. National Research Council, File 20;

p. 225   Balloon bomb mechanism: Memo, John Graham, June 1, 1945, LAC RDC, Vol. 5960, File: Japanese. See also Hugh A. Halliday, "The West Coast Balloon Bomb Attack: Air Force, Part 34," *Legion* magazine, Aug. 22, 2009;

p. 225   Balloon bomb hit power line into Nagasaki plutonium bomb plant: www.axishistory.com/index.php?id=932;

p. 225   Censors cut speculation about percentage of balloon bombs that made it to North America: Memorandum, John Graham, Nov. 13, 1943, LAD RDC, Vol. 5960, File: Japanese;

p. 226   Censors told of U.S. news blackout: Memorandum, John Graham, Jan. 5, 1945, LAC RDC, Vol. 5960, File: Japanese;

p. 266   *Leader-Post* kills balloon story: Memorandum, John Graham, Jan. 13, 1945, LAC RDC, Vol. 5960, File: Japanese;

p. 226   Papers vague about locations: Memorandum, John Graham, June 7, 1945, LAC RDC, Vol. 5960, File: Japanese;

p. 226   George Murray warned: Memorandum, John Graham, Jan. 30, 1945, LAC RDC, Vol. 5960, File: Japanese;

p. 227   Censor explains to *Vancouver Sun* the reason for blackout: Memorandum, John Graham, April 3, 1945, LAC RDC, Vol. 5960, File: Japanese;

p. 227   Tim Tyler's Luck controversy: Memorandum, John Graham, April 23, 1945, LAC RDC, Vol. 5960, File: Japanese;

p. 228   Winchell broadcasts balloon bomb story: Memorandum, R.W. Baldwin, April 23, 1945, LAC RDC, Vol. 5960, File: Japanese;

p. 229   Confusion about lifting of embargo: Memorandum, John Graham, May 5, 1945, LAC RDC, Vol. 5960, File: Japanese, and Memorandum, John Graham, May 7, 1945, LAC RDC, Vol. 5960, File: Japanese;

p. 229   Canadians follow U.S. lead in lifting of embargo: Memorandum, Bert Perry, May 22, 1945, LAC RDC, Vol. 5960, File: Japanese;

p. 230   *Toronto Star* breaks embargo: Memorandum, R.W. Baldwin, May 31, 1945, LAC RDC, Vol. 5960, File: Japanese;

p. 231   Japanese officer says censorship killed balloon bomb campaign: Brig. W.H. Wilbur, "Japan's Last Secret Weapon: Balloons," in *Secrets and Stories of the War*, 464;

p. 231   Censors briefed on Manhattan Project: It is difficult to know to what extent the censors understood the Manhattan Project. Purcell claims his sources at censorship knew at least eight months before the attack on Hiroshima that atomic research might culminate with the creation of a bomb of spectacular power. Like any other bright, curious people tantalized and intrigued by snippets of information, the censors passed information among themselves. As late as July 1945, Graham in B.C. was forwarding clippings from U.S. publications such as *Newsweek*, hinting about big news on atomic research. See his memorandums in LAC RDC, Vol. 5967, File: General-1;

p. 231   Social Credit convention told of atomic bomb: Memorandum, Bert Perry, April 15, 1944, LAC RDC, Vol. 5965, File: General-5;

p. 232   McGill professor hints at atomic bomb possibility: Memorandum, Bert Perry, Nov. 16, 1944, LAC RDC, Vol. 5957, File: General-1;

p. 232   Media warned about covering Eldorado shareholders dispute: John Graham, April 30, 1944, LAC RDC, Vol. 5967, File: General-1;

p. 233   Purcell, media tipped off to Manhattan Project: Purcell thesis, and Memorandum, Bert Perry, July 10, 1944, LAC RDC, Vol. 5967, File: General-1;

p. 233   Censors tried to block coverage of Chalk River reactor: Memorandum, R.W. Baldwin, Aug. 10, 1944, LAC RDC, Vol. 5956, File 1-B-6, Miscellaneous, and Memorandum, Bert Perry, Sept. 14, 1944, LAC RDC, Vol. 5959, File 1-D-3, Air Force Equipment.

Chapter 11: Censorship and the Zombies

p. 234   *Globe* had been pushing for deployment of the draftees since the beginning of 1944: *Globe and Mail* editorial, Jan. 15, 1944;

p. 235   Most of the major details of the Terrace mutiny can be found in Daniel German, "Press Censorship and the Terrace Mutiny: A Case Study in Second World War Information Management," *Journal of Canadian Studies/Revue d'études canadiennes*, Vol. 31, No. 4 (Winter 1996/97), 124–142;

p. 235   Generals' attitude to political oversight and their support in the media: Richard J. Walker, "The Revolt of the Canadian Generals, 1944: The Case for the Prosecution," in Coombs, ed., *The Insubordinate and the Non-Compliant: Case Studies of Canadian Mutiny and Disobedience, 1920 to the Present*, 57–63;

p. 235   Kiska campaign: For the political and military context of this campaign, see Perras, *Stepping Stones to Nowhere: The Aleutian Islands, Alaska, and American Military Strategy, 1867–1945*;

p. 236   Casualty rates, Normandy: Beevor, *D-Day: The Battle for Normandy*, 522. Beevor analyzes the replacement-troops training issue and its military repercussions throughout the book;

p. 237   Censors kill story of 250 soldiers going AWOL in 1943: Ruling, John Graham, Vancouver, July 15, 1943, LAC RDC, Vol. 5956, File 1-B-1, Miscellaneous Military;

p. 237   Calgary fight: Ruling, John Graham, Vancouver, July 19, 1944, LAC RDC, Vol. 5956, File 1-B-1, Miscellaneous Military. The riots are analyzed in Dean Oliver's "'My Darlin' Clementine': Wooing Zombies for $6.50 a Night. General Service–NRMA Relations in Wartime Calgary," *Canadian Military History*, Vol. 7, No. 3, Summer 1998, 46–55;

p. 237   Cowichan *Leader* story on beating: Memorandum, John Graham, Aug. 16, 1944, LAC RDC, Vol. 5956, File 1-B-1, Miscellaneous Military, and Drew's speech: Granatstein, *Canada's War*, 340. See also chap. 6 and 9;

p. 237   Conn Smythe's campaign: Copp, *Cinderella Army: The Canadians in Northwest Europe*, 178–179;

p. 239   Cabinet meeting drama: Mackenzie King Diary, Oct. 19, 25, and 26, 1944, and Granatstein, *Canada's War*, 346, 359, and 369;

p. 242   B.C. reporters start reporting Zombie anger: *Vancouver News-Herald*, Nov. 20, 1944, 1;

p. 243   Censors, government believed fighting might break out in the army: *Final Report of the Directorate of Censorship*;

p. 244   Censors begin dealing with draftee disturbances: Memorandum,
John Graham, Nov. 24, 1944, LAC RDC, Vol. 5954, File 1-B-1,
Troop Embarkations;

p. 244   Bray complains, censors censor second-day stories from mutiny
regions: Memorandum, John Graham, Nov. 25, 1944, LAC RDC,
Vol. 5954, File 1-B-1, Troop Embarkations;

p. 244   General staff asks for news crackdown: Memorandum, John
Graham, Nov. 25, 1944, LAC RDC, Vol. 5954, File 1-B-1, Troop
Embarkations;

p. 244   Memo posted in press gallery, Graham believes disturbance is
political, not military issue: Memorandum, John Graham, Nov.
27, 1944, LAC RDC, Vol. 5984, File 41-G (Draftees);

p. 245   King's broadcast statement was made in the House of Commons
and can be found at *Hansard*, Nov. 27, 1944, 6614–6618;

p. 245   Ottawa censors and military prepare for stories: Memorandum,
R.W. Baldwin, Nov. 28, 1944, LAC RDC, Vol. 5954, File 1-B-1,
Troop Embarkations;

p. 245   Public attitudes to mutiny: In a memorandum to cabinet dated
Dec. 11, 1944, Wartime Information Board General Manager A.D.
Denton wrote, "There are further reports of hostilities among
English-speaking people against Quebec, and of resentment
against the 'Ontario conscriptionists' among French-Canadians.
The crisis has been followed by a number of comments from
both areas, deploring the outbursts of extremists, and regretting
the lack of an educational system which makes such fundamental
divergences impossible. Newspapers were again criticized for
their inflammatory tactics and for sensationalism in the treatment of minor disturbances." Library and Archives Canada, RG
36-31, Boards, Offices and Committees (Records of the Wartime
Information Board), File: W-34-10. Many Canadians also believed
the sensationalist reporting of the conscription issue and the
disturbances at military camps made Canada look bad, especially
to observers in the United States, and gave "aid and comfort to
the enemy." Library and Archives Canada, RG 36-31, Boards,
Offices and Committees (Records of the Wartime Information
Board), File W-34-10. Dec. 4 memorandum;

p. 249   Fear of mass resignation of senior officers: For a detailed look at this aspect of the crisis, see Richard J. Walker, "The Revolt of the Canadian Generals, 1944: The Case for the Prosecution," in Coombs, ed., *The Insubordinate and the Non-Compliant: Case Studies of Canadian Mutiny and Disobedience, 1920 to the Present*;

p. 247   Purcell refuses Hyde request: Memorandum, John Graham, Vancouver, Nov. 28, 1944, LAC RDC, Vol. 5954, File 1-B-1, Troop Embarkations;

p. 248   Eggleston and Frigon called into cabinet meeting: Mackenzie King Diary, Nov. 29, 1944;

p. 248   Eggleston tells Graham about cabinet meeting: Memorandum, John Graham, Nov. 29, 1944, LAC RDC, Vol. 5954, File 1-B-1, Troop Embarkations;

p. 248   Eggleston fought in meeting to keep voluntary system: *Final Report of the Directorate of Censorship*;

p. 248   East Block meeting of King, ministers: Mackenzie King Diary, Nov. 30, 1944;

p. 248   Air force threat rumour: J.L. Granatstein and J.M. Hitsman, *A Trust Betrayed*, 232;

p. 249   Pearkes and Root: John Graham, Nov. 29, 1944, LAC RDC, Vol. 5954, File 1-B-1, Troop Embarkations;

p. 249   Bertram visits newsrooms: B. Bertram, "An Appeal for Calm," Nov. 30, 1944, LAC RDC, Vol. 5956, File 1-B-6, Miscellaneous;

p. 249   Laurendeau article: Memorandum, B. Bertram, Montreal, Nov. 30, 1944, LAC RDC, Vol. 5956, File 1-B-6, Miscellaneous;

p. 250   New West Coast "bomb-shell": Ruling, John Graham, Dec. 1, 1944, LAC RDC, Vol. 5956, File 1-B-6, Miscellaneous;

p. 251   Baldwin blames military: Memorandum, R.W. Baldwin, Dec. 5, 1944, LAC RDC, Vol. 5956, File 1-B-6, Miscellaneous;

p. 251   More Quebec problems: Memorandum, B. Bertram, Dec. 16, 1944, LAC RDC, Vol. 5967, File 1-general;

p. 252   Zombies go AWOL in London: Ruling, Bruce Perry, Dec. 29, 1944, LAC RDC, Vol. 5956, File: Miscellaneous, and Memorandum, R.W. Baldwin, Jan. 1945, LAC RDC, Vol. 5956, File: Miscellaneous;

p. 252   King's description of the meeting is from a letter in LAC, MG2-382, Wilfrid Eggleston Papers, in "National Research in

Canada: The NCC 1916–1966." For a good description of King's post-1944 decline, see Eayrs, *In Defence of Canada, Vol. III: Peacemaking and Deterrence*, Introduction.

p. 253   *London Free Press* complains: *Final Report of the Directorate of Censorship*;

p. 253   Baldwin tries to calm Bird: Bird to Baldwin, Jan. 27, 1945, and Baldwin to Bird, Jan. 29, 1945, LAC RDC, Vol. 5956, File: Miscellaneous;

BIBLIOGRAPHY

A/ PRIMARY SOURCES:

I. Library and Archives Canada

Government Records
Canadian Broadcasting Corporation
Directorate of Censorship
External Affairs
National Defence
National Film Board
Privy Council Office
Wartime Information Board
Secretary of State

Personal Papers
Biggar, O.M.
Eggleston, Wilfrid
Fraser, Blair
King, William Lyon Mackenzie
Lapointe, Ernest
Pearson, Lester B.
Shoyama, Thomas
Stursberg, Peter

II. National Defence Historical Section
Censorship Records (Military Intelligence)

III. Carleton University Archives
Wilfrid Kesterton papers

Interviews/Personal Correspondence
Fulgence Charpentier
Sen. Joyce Fairbairn
Prof. G. Stewart Adam, Carleton University
Prof. Joseph Scanlon, Carleton University

B/ SECONDARY SOURCES:

Books

Adachi, Ken. *The Enemy That Never Was*. Toronto: McClelland & Stewart, 1976.

Anglin, Douglas. *The Free French Invasion: The St. Pierre and Miquelon Affaire of 1941*. Toronto: University of Toronto Press, 1996.

Beauregard, Claude. *Guerre et censure au Canada, 1939–1945: L'expérience canadienne durant la Seconde Guerre mondiale*. Sillery: Septentrion, 1998.

Beeby, Dean. *Cargo of Lies: The True Story of a Nazi Double Agent in Canada*. Toronto: University of Toronto Press, 1996.

Beevor, Antony. *D-Day: The Battle for Normandy*. London: Penguin, 2009.

Betcherman, Lita-Rose. *The Swastika and the Maple Leaf: Fascist Movements in Canada in the Thirties*. Toronto: Fitzhenry & Whiteside, 1975.

Bishop, Chris. *Kriegsmarine U-Boats 1939–1945*. London: Amber Books, 2006.

Bowman, Charles. *Ottawa Editor*. Sidney, British Columbia: Gray's Publishing, 1966.

Brennan, Patrick. *Reporting the Nation's Business: Press–Government Relations in the Liberal Years, 1935–1957*. Toronto: University of Toronto Press, 1994.

Broadfoot, Barry. *Years of Sorrow, Years of Shame: The Story of the Japanese Canadians in World War II*. Markham, Ontario: Paperjacks, 1979.

Bryden, John. *Best Kept Secret: Canadian Secret Intelligence in the Second World War*. Toronto: Lester Publishing, 1993.

Buckley, Brian. *Canada's Early Nuclear Policy: Fate, Chance and Character*. Montreal & Kingston: McGill–Queen's University Press, 2000.

Chalmers, Floyd S. *A Gentleman of the Press: The Story of John Bayne Maclean and the Publishing Empire He Founded*. Toronto: Doubleday, 1969.

Coates, Kenneth, ed. *The Alaska Highway: Papers of the 40th Anniversary Symposium*. Vancouver: University of British Columbia Press, 1985.

Cook, Ramsay. *The Politics of John W. Dafoe and the Free Press*. Toronto: University of Toronto Press, 1963.

Cook, Tim. *Clio's Warriors: Canadian Historians and the Writing of the World Wars*. Vancouver: University of British Columbia Press, 2006.

Coombs, Howard G., ed. *The Insubordinate and the Non-Compliant: Case Studies of Canadian Mutiny and Disobedience, 1920 to the Present*. Toronto: Dundurn Press/Defence Academy Press, 2007.

Copp, Terry. *Cinderella Army: The Canadians in Northwest Europe*. Toronto: University of Toronto Press, 2006.

Crone, Kennedy. *The Press Gallery (Ottawa), 1937–38*. Montreal: Beaver Hall Press, 1936.

Dancocks, Daniel. *In Enemy Hands—Canadian Prisoners of War 1939–1945*. Toronto: McClelland and Stewart, 1990.

Dickson, Paul Douglas. *A Thoroughly Canadian General: A Biography of General H.D.G. Crerar*. Toronto: University of Toronto Press, 2007.

Douglas, W.A.B., Roger Sarty, and Michael Whitby, with Robert H. Caldwell, William Johnston, and William G.P. Rawling. *A Blue Water Navy: The Official Operational History of the Royal Canadian Navy in the Second World War, 1943–1945*, Volume Two, Part 1. St. Catharines, Ontario: Vanwell Publishing, 2007.

——. *No Higher Purpose*: *The Official Operational History of the Royal Canadian Navy in the Second World War, 1939–1943*, Volume Two, Part 2. St. Catharines, Ontario: Vanwell Publishing, 2002.

Eayrs, James. *In Defence of Canada, Volume II: Appeasement and Rearmament.* Toronto: University of Toronto Press, 1965.

Eggleston, Wilfrid. *The Queen's Choice: A History of Canada's Capital.* Ottawa: National Capital Commission, 1961.

——. *While I Still Remember.* Toronto: Ryerson Press, 1965.

Fisher, Louis. *Nazi Saboteurs on Trial.* Lawrence, Kansas: University of Kansas Press, 2005.

Gibson, Frederick W., and Barbara Robertson, eds. *Ottawa at War: The Grant Dexter Memoranda, 1939–1945.* Winnipeg: The Manitoba Record Society, 1994.

Godin, Pierre. *La Lutte pour l'information: Histoire de la presse écrite au Québec.* Montreal: Les Idées du Jour, 1981.

Granatstein, J.L. *Conscription in the Second World War, 1939–1945.* Toronto: Ryerson Press, 1969.

——. *A Man of Influence: Norman Robertson and Canadian Statecraft.* Toronto: University of Toronto Press, 1981.

——. *Canada's War: The Politics of the Mackenzie King Government, 1939–1945.* Toronto: University of Toronto Press, 1990 edition.

——. *Ottawa Men: The Civil Service Mandarins, 1935–1957.* Toronto: University of Toronto Press, 1998.

——. *Canada's Army: Waging War and Keeping the Peace.* Toronto: University of Toronto Press, 2002.

——. and H.M. Hitsman. *Broken Promises: A History of Conscription in Canada.* Toronto: University of Toronto Press, 1977.

Greenfield, Nathan M. *The Battle of the St. Lawrence: The Second World War in Canada.* Toronto: HarperCollins, 2004.

Greenhous, Brereton. *"C" Force to Hong Kong: A Canadian Catastrophe, 1941–1945.* Toronto: Dundurn Press/Canadian War Museum, 1997.

Hadley, Michael L. *U-Boats Against Canada: German Submarines in Canadian Waters.* Montreal & Kingston: McGill–Queen's University Press, 1985.

Harkness, Ross. *J.E. Atkinson of the Star.* Toronto: University of Toronto Press, 1965.

Henderson, T. Stephen, Angus L. Macdonald. *A Provincial Liberal.* University of Toronto Press, 2009.

Hesketh, Bob, ed. *Three Northern Wartime Projects: Alaska Highway, Northwest Staging Route, Canol*. Edmonton: Canadian Circumpolar Institute and Edmonton and District Historical Society, 1996.

Hilliker, John. *Canada's Department of External Affairs, Vol. I: The Early Years, 1909–1946*. Montreal & Kingston: McGill–Queen's University Press, 1990.

Hillmer, Norman, et al., eds. *On Guard for Thee: War, Ethnicity, and the Canadian State, 1939–1945*. Ottawa: Canadian Committee for the History of the Second World War, 1988.

Hutchison, Bruce. *The Far Side of the Street*. Toronto: Macmillan, 1976.

Kealey, Gregory S., and Reg Whitaker, eds. RCMP *Security Bulletins: The War Series, 1939–1941 (Vol. 1), 1942–1945 (Vol. 2)*. St. John's: Committee on Canadian Labour History, 1989.

Keshen, Jeffrey. *Propaganda and Censorship during Canada's Great War*. Edmonton: University of Alberta, 1996.

———. *Saints, Soldiers and Sinners: Canada's Second World War*. Vancouver: University of British Columbia Press, 2004.

Kimber, Stephen. *Sailors, Slackers and Blind Pigs: Halifax at War*. Toronto: Doubleday Canada, 2003.

La Violette, Forrest E. *The Canadian Japanese and World War II*. Toronto: University of Toronto Press, 1948.

Leslie Mantle, Craig, ed. *The Apathetic and the Defiant: Case Studies of Canadian Mutiny and Disobedience, 1812–1919*. Kingston: Dundurn Press, 2007.

Levine, Allen. *Scrum Wars: The Prime Ministers and the Media*. Toronto: Dundurn, 1993.

Lippmann, Walter. *Public Opinion*. New York: Harcourt Brace and Company, 1922.

Malone, Col. Dick (Richard). *Missing from the Record*. Toronto: Collins, 1946.

———. *A Portrait of War, 1939–1943*. Toronto: Collins, 1983.

March, William. *Red Line: The* Chronicle-Herald *and the* Mail-Star, *1875–1954*. Halifax: Acadiensis Press, 1986.

Masterman, J.C. *The Double Cross System in the War of 1939 to 1945*. New Haven: Yale University Press, 1972.

Milner, Marc. *Canada's Navy: The First Century*. Toronto: University of Toronto Press, 1999.

———. *Battle of the Atlantic*. St. Catharines, Ontario: Vanwell Publishing, 2003.

———. *North Atlantic Run: The Royal Canadian Navy and the Battle for the Convoys*. St. Catharines, Ontario: Vanwell Publishing, 2006.

Mordal, Jacques. *Dieppe: The Dawn of Decision*. Toronto: Ryerson Press, 1962.

Morton, Desmond. *A Military History of Canada*. Edmonton: Hurtig, 1984.

Mount, Graham. *Canada's Enemies: Spies in the Peaceable Kingdom*. Toronto: Dundurn Press, 1993.

Munro, Ross. *Gauntlet to Overlord: The Story of the Canadian Army*. Toronto: Macmillan, 1945.

Nemni, Max, and Monique Nemni (translated by William Johnson). *Young Trudeau, 1919–1944*. Toronto: McClelland & Stewart, 2006.

Nicholls, M.E. *The Story of CP*. Toronto: Ryerson Press, 1948.

Nolan, Brian. *King's War: Mackenzie King and the Politics of War, 1939–1945*. Toronto: Random House, 1988.

O'Donnell, Pierce. *In Time of War: Hitler's Terrorist Attack on America*. New York: The New Press, 2005.

Parrish, Thomas. *The Submarine: A History*. New York: Viking/Penguin, 2004.

Perras, Galen Roger. *Stepping Stones to Nowhere: The Aleutian Islands, Alaska, and American Military Strategy, 1867–1945*. Vancouver: University of British Columbia Press, 2003.

Pope, Maurice A. *Soldiers and Politicians* (memoirs). Toronto: University of Toronto Press, 1962.

Powley, A.E. *Broadcast from the Front: Canadian Radio Overseas in the Second World War*. Toronto: Hakkert, 1975.

Roazen, Paul. *Canada's King: An Essay in Political Psychology*. Oakville, Ontario: Mosaic Press, 1998.

Smith, Colin. *England's Last War Against France: Fighting Vichy, 1940–1942*. London: Weidenfeld & Nicolson, 2009.

Sotiron, Minko. *An Annotated Bibliography of Works on Daily Newspapers in Canada, 1914–1983*. Montreal: Self-published, 1987.

Stacey, C.P. *Arms, Men and Governments: The War Policies of Canada, 1939–1945*. Ottawa: Minister of National Defence, 1970.

Stacey, Charles. *A Very Double Life: The Private World of Mackenzie King*. Toronto: Macmillan, 1976.

Stursberg, Peter. *The Sound of War*. Toronto: University of Toronto Press, 1993.

Taras, David. *The Newsmakers: The Media's Influence on Canadian Politics*. Toronto: Nelson Canada, 1990.

Trudeau, Pierre. *Memoirs*. Toronto: McClelland & Stewart, 1993.

Vincent, Carl. *No Reason Why: The Canadian Hong Kong Tragedy: An Examination*. Stittsville, Ontario: Canada's Wings, 1981.

Wiegman, Carl. *Trees to News: A Chronicle of the Ontario Paper Company's Origin and Development*. Toronto: McClelland & Stewart, 1953.

Williams, David Ricardo. *Duff: A Life in the Law*. Vancouver: University of British Columbia Press/Osgoode Society, 1994.

Articles

Atkey, Ronald. "Reconciling Freedom and National Security." *University of Toronto Law Review*, Vol. 41 (1991): 38–59.

German, Daniel. "Press Censorship and the Terrace Mutiny: A Case Study in Second World War Information Management." *Journal of Canadian studies/Revue d'études canadiennes*. Vol. 31, No. 4 (Winter 1996/97): 124–142.

Hallahan, Kirk. "Mackenzie King: Rockefeller's 'Other' Public Relations Counselor in Colorado." *Public Relations Review*, Vol. 29 (2003): 401–414.

Kerr, George D. "Skirting the Minefield: Press Censorship, Politics and French Canada, 1940." *Canadian Journal of Communication*, Vol. 8, No. 2 (1982): 46–64.

Keyserlink, Robert H. "'Agents within the Gates': The Search for Nazi Subversives in Canada." *Canadian Historical Review*, Vol. 46, No. 2 (1985): 221–240.

Oliver, Dean. "'My Darlin' Clementine'? Wooing Zombies for $6.50 a Night. General Service–NRMA Relations in Wartime Calgary." *Canadian Military History*, Vol. 7, No. 3 (Summer 1998): 46–55.

Robinson, Daniel. "Planning for the 'most serious contingency': Alien Internment, Arbitrary Detention and the Canadian State." *Journal of Canadian Studies*, Vol. 28, No. 2 (1993): 5–20.

Vance, Jonathan F. "Men in Manacles: The Shackling of Prisoners in World War II, 1942–1943." *Journal of Military History*, Vol. 59, No. 3 (1995): 483–504.

Vipond, Mary. "Canadian Nationalism and the Plight of Canadian Magazines in the 1920s." *Canadian Historical Review*, Vol. 57, No. 1 (March 1977): 43–63.

Ward, W. Peter. "British Columbia and the Japanese Evacuation." *Canadian Historical Review*, Vol. 47, No. 3 (Sept. 1976): 289–308.

Whitaker, Reg. "Official Repression of Communism during World War II." *Labour*, Vol. 17 (1986): 135–166.

Young, William R. "Academics and Social Scientists versus the Press: The Policies of the Bureau of Public Information and the Wartime Information Board, 1939–1945." *Papers of the Canadian Historical Association* (1978): 219–239.

Unpublished Theses

Balizer, Timothy John. "The Information Front: The Canadian Army, Public Relations, and War News during the Second World War." Ph.D.: University of Victoria, 2008.

Purcell, Gil. "Wartime Press Censorship in Canada." M.A.: University of Toronto, 1946.

Young, William R. "Making the Truth Graphic: The Canadian Government's Home Front Information Structure and Program during World War II." Ph.D.: University of British Columbia, 1978.

INDEX